Family Psychodynamics in Organizational Contexts

This fascinating book shows how an understanding of the psychodynamics of the extended family, from parental relations to sibling rivalries, can provide insight into many of the key issues faced by organizations today.

Covering topics such as change management, creativity, autonomous groups, leadership and democracy, it shows how deep-rooted family dynamics unconsciously frame the way we relate to each other in the workplace, and how they can have a profound influence on the broader trajectory of organizations.

This book features:

- Examples on how to use the extended family as a framework for understanding organizational behaviour.
- A look beyond parental relationships to discuss sibling relationships as well.
- Examples to illustrate key topics of practical relevance to consultants and managers.

Family Psychodynamics in Organizational Contexts is an important read for students and scholars of organizational psychology, organizational studies and psychodynamics, as well as consultants and coaches working in organizational contexts.

Steen Visholm is a Professor in the Department of People and Technology, Center for Organizational Psychology, Roskilde University, Denmark.

Family Psychodynamics in Organizational Contexts

The Hidden Forces that Shape the Workplace

Steen Visholm

Routledge
Taylor & Francis Group

LONDON AND NEW YORK

First published 2021
by Routledge
2 Park Square, Milton Park, Abingdon, Oxon OX14 4RN

and by Routledge
605 Third Avenue, New York, NY 10158

Routledge is an imprint of the Taylor & Francis Group, an informa business

British Library Cataloguing-in-Publication Data
A catalogue record for this book is available from the British Library

Library of Congress Cataloging-in-Publication Data
Names: Visholm, Steen, author.
Title: Family psychodynamics in organizational contexts : the hidden forces that shape the workplace / Steen Visholm.
Description: Milton Park, Abingdon, Oxon ; New York, NY : Routledge, 2021. | Includes bibliographical references and index.
Identifiers: LCCN 2020056612 (print) | LCCN 2020056613 (ebook) | ISBN 9780367819453 (paperback) | ISBN 9780367759674 (hardback) | ISBN 9781003164913 (ebook)
Subjects: LCSH: Organizational behavior. | Psychology, Industrial. | Families--Psychological aspects.
Classification: LCC HM791 .V57 2021 (print) | LCC HM791 (ebook) | DDC 302.3/5--dc23
LC record available at https://lccn.loc.gov/2020056612
LC ebook record available at https://lccn.loc.gov/2020056613

ISBN: 978-0-367-81945-3 (pbk)
ISBN: 978-0-367-75967-4 (hbk)
ISBN: 978-1-003-16491-3 (ebk)

Typeset in Times New Roman
by Taylor & Francis Books

Dedicated to Michelle, Thomas and Asta

Contents

Illustrations

Figures

Table

Preface

The original Danish edition of this book, which came out in 2013, was almost 10 years in the making. The thoughts unfolded here were inspired by Juliet Mitchell's book *Siblings: Sex and violence* (2003) and a concurrent consultancy process with self-managing teams.

Above all, the book aims to demonstrate the benefits of applying a family dynamic perspective in organizational psychology. As Mitchell pointed out, psychoanalysis has traditionally overlooked the significance of sibling relationships in the family. By incorporating sibling relationships in the classic triangle involving mum, dad and little Oedipus, the vertical dynamic (parent-child) is supplemented with horizontal ones (child-child and dad-mum). This highlights the drama of generational change that is also part of the Oedipus complex: which sibling is going to be 'promoted' and take over 'the family farm'. The understanding outlined here does not claim to be exclusive and exhaustive; rather it is put forth as a perspective that may help explain certain otherwise incomprehensible and puzzling organizational phenomena that involve very complex emotions.

The book is based on thinking and practices derived from the Tavistock tradition and systems psychodynamics and, to some extent, group analysis (Visholm, 1993; Heinskou & Visholm, 2004, 2011). However, the book also challenges the concepts of groups and systems that characterize these traditions.

The differences between a family, a joint-stock company, a public administration, a democratic association, a dictatorship, a crowd/mass movement and a project team are so significant that it is not meaningful simply to consider the inherent psychology across these contexts as 'group phenomena'. Systems theory is indispensable, as it allows us to study both differences and similarities between systems and their mutual exchanges, but we need a more specific approach to capture the psychological dynamics at play in the different types of systems. My proposal for a differentiation includes six different systems categories: family/organization, democracy, market, tyranny, mass and panic. There are key psychological differences between systems where the leaders are elected (authorization from the bottom up), such as democracies and mass movements; systems where the leaders are appointed (authorization from the top down), such as families, organizations and tyrannies; and systems such as markets and states of panic, where there is no hierarchy. And there are key psychological differences in our emotional reactions to leaders depending on whether they are top executives (idealized parental figures) or middle managers (devalued promoted siblings). Group psychology may be regarded as a rebellion against the family and the authoritarian father, but a pure sibling psychology ignores the factors of gender and generations and thus the life-and-death drama they give rise to.

During the writing process I discussed some of the ideas presented in the book with my colleagues at OPU and MPO:[1] Kristoffer Lande Andersen, Kirsti Andersson, Ulla Beck, Thomas Birkholm, Jytte Bonde, Birgitte Bonnerup, Annemette Hasselager, Torben Heinskou, Inger-Margrethe Holm, Poula Jakobsen, Bent Jørgensen, Peter Koefoed, Åse Lading, Hanne Larsson, Zanne Lorenzen, Thea Mikkelsen, Lars Robl, Dorte Sandager, Klaus Stagis and Lotte Svalgaard. I also presented parts of the book at ISPSO's Annual Meeting in Baltimore, Maryland, in 2005 and in Stockholm in 2007 and at the OPUS[2] conference in London in 2006. In spring 2006 I had the opportunity to discuss key points with Clare Huffington, Sarah Miller and David Armstrong of the Tavistock Consultancy Service, a discussion that continued for some time, particularly with Huffington and Miller. I thank everyone for contributing critique, ideas and inspiration. Special thanks go to Associate Professor, MA (psych.) Susanne Lunn of the University of Copenhagen, who was kind enough to provide a critical reading of the manuscript, and to Poula Jakobsen and Helene Krasnik, with whom I have a longstanding collaboration and continuous exchanges on topics related to family dynamics.

Warm thanks to clients over the years and participants at OPU and MPO, whose life stories and current challenges have taught me so much. And thanks for continuous and invaluable inspiration from family members over the years: Torben, Birthe, Grethe, Søs, Vibeke, Kristian, Anne, Nina, Jytte, Folmer, Erik, Henning, Erling, Vagn, Birgit, Lis, Jørgen, Jørgen, Nanna, Trille, Lotte, Merete, Birgitte, Kristian, Pia, Frida, Anton, Sigrid, Tina and Claus and his brothers.

Steen Visholm
Copenhagen, May 2013

References

Earlier versions of Chapters 4, 6 and 11 were published in Visholm (2006a), and the main points were presented at the 2006 OPUS conference in London.

An earlier version of Chapter 5 was published in Visholm (2005b, 2005c, 2005d, 2011c) and the main points were presented at ISPSO's 2005 Annual Meeting in Baltimore, MD.

An earlier version of Chapter 7 was presented at ISPSO's Annual Meeting in Stockholm in 2007.

Earlier versions of Chapter 10 were published in Visholm (2011a, 2012), and its main points were included in my inaugural lecture on 27 December 2012 at Roskilde University.

Notes

1 OPU: Organisationspsykologisk Uddannelse (Educational Programme in Organizational Psychology) at the Institut for Gruppeanalyse (Institute for Group Analysis) in Copenhagen. MPO: Master of the Psychology of Organisations, Roskilde University.
2 ISPSO: International Society for the Study of Organizations. OPUS: Organisation for Promoting Understanding of Society.

Chapter 1

Introduction

Connections between family and organization

This book deals with open and hidden family dynamics in organizations – a topic in organizational psychology. Through theory and examples, the book demonstrates how an understanding informed by family dynamics can often explain phenomena in organizations that may at first glance seem strange or meaningless and which are a drain on the organization's time and energy.

The family is a system of individuals in relationships that have been established through sexual reproduction. This relational system contains a number of positions: mother, father, daughter, sister, brother, maternal grandmother, paternal grandmother, great-grandfather, cousin, second cousin, great-uncle, aunt and so forth. A person may simultaneously occupy several positions in the systems: a father is also a son; he may be a maternal grandfather and so forth. Inheritance laws describe this in specific detail.

Like other social systems, the family has one primary task. The family's primary task, according to Shapiro (1988), is to facilitate age-appropriate development for all the members. Families also have an inherent timeline: falling in love, moving in together, pregnancy, first child, second child, subsequent children, juvenile crisis often simultaneous with parents mid-life crisis, generational change, children leaving home and starting the cycle over again as the parents figure out what to do until the grandchildren show up. Shifts in the family members' roles are driven by this timeline. The open family dynamics play out in organizations where an actual family is in charge of management or otherwise plays a significant role.

The organization's hidden family dynamics work via transferences, an important concept in psychoanalysis. Life events that we find ourselves unable to deal with, for one reason or another, are repressed, meaning that our memory of the event is severed from the language it might be told in. However, the repressed material returns. Unconsciously, we seek to repeat the repressed scene in real-life situations that are somehow reminiscent of the original scene. A supervisor addresses us in a particular tone of voice, a repressed memory of a stern father is activated, and the supervisor is perceived the same way we perceived our father. The repressed memory of the father is transferred onto the supervisor. The supervisor has no idea why the employee is so upset. The employee's behaviour makes no sense in the current situation. Only by tracing the current scene back to the original situation can we hope to make sense of the behaviour.

There is nothing new about viewing life in the organization through the lens of family dynamics. The new contribution of the current effort lies in applying an expanded understanding of family dynamics on organizations. The transference of parental figures onto leaders and managers has been described many times. The Oedipus complex, with its father-mother-son triangle, is a widely used model. In the early 2000s, however, a growing number of psychoanalytic books appeared that addressed sibling relationships (Mitchell, 2003; Coles, 2003, Lewin & Sharp, 2009).

In 2004, I was able to draw on some of this literature in connection with a consultancy project on self-managing teams in industry (Visholm, 2005c, 2005d 2006a, 2011c). I found the added nuance and the broadening of the psychoanalytic lens that comes from expanding a triangle into a more complex figure profoundly inspiring.

On a more general level, this book is situated within the paradigm of systems psychodynamics (Gould et al., 2001; Heinskou & Visholm, 2004, 2011; Bonnerup & Hasselager, 2008; Beck, 2009; Lading & Jørgensen, 2010). Systems psychodynamics combines the psychoanalytic approach with open systems theory. Not everyone working within this paradigm views family dynamics as central. This book argues that family dynamics offer a rewarding perspective.

In this introductory chapter I seek to explain why family dynamics can provide a fruitful and necessary contribution to group and organizational psychology.

I Connections between family and organization

Ever since the emergence of the modern notion of civil society in the late 18th century, family and work have been regarded as separate and virtually opposite phenomena. However, this dichotomy blurs a number of similarities and connections between families and workplace organizations, and a closer study would improve our understanding of both.

During many previous historical periods – not least during the Middle Ages, when people lived in so-called traditional societies – family and organization were one and the same. Work and family life unfolded within a single 'sociotope'. Within the framework defined by squires and other high-ranking figures, the father was the head of both the family and the enterprise, whether the latter was a farm or a smithy. The eldest son and his wife would presumably take over when the parents retired. The parents decided who would take over and when, whom the children could marry, what sort of training they would get and what trade they would take on if they were not destined to take over the family enterprise.

The generational change and the issue of inheritance were hugely important for both generations, as illustrated in myths, fairy tales, art and literature. Generational change and inheritance also define the situation that constitutes the climax of many of these stories: the proposal and the wedding, which mark the start of a new generation. The phrase 'and they lived happily ever after' is a way of concluding the story that should probably be read less an idyllic vision and more as an indication that 'what happened next is another story'.

In modern welfare society, state and market have interjected themselves in between the generations, to some extent replacing their mutual interdependence, in part, with freedom and, in part, with a new dependence on the state and the market. The parents no longer decide who marries whom or what sort of training the young person gets. As individual citizens, we decide who we want to date, have sex with and raise a family with – to the extent our desires match our intended partner's desires. In the same way we decide what training to pursue – to the extent that we meet the given criteria and pass the requisite tests and exams. Thus, our reliance on local and family ties has been replaced with 'societalization'. In modern society, the date of our birth is more significant than the family we are born into. We develop shared experiences with same-age peers, enter the labour market alongside them – into a feverishly inflated bubble economy or into a recession – or are perhaps unfortunate enough to be sent to fight a war, where young men of a certain age span are decimated at the front (Manheim, 1993). Today, there is little talk of generational change in most families, although certain patterns can be observed with regard to who gets or claims the honour of hosting the extended family for Christmas. Today, the generational concept is mostly used to characterize a segment of youth of a certain decade with shared tastes in music and fashion, political outlook and so forth: the flappers of the 1920s, the hippies of the 1960s, Generation X and so forth.

Men and women are now equal, in principle. Both men and women can enter the job market and decide over themselves and their property – unless they enter into other contractual arrangements. Thus, women no longer depend on men for economic support, and more and more men are able to hold their own when it comes to cooking, cleaning, washing the dishes, doing laundry and raising a child.

Sexuality, which had been severely suppressed since the witch trials of the late Middle Ages, was increasingly liberated during the 20th century: contraception was legalized, as was abortion, with certain restrictions, which unshackled the sensuous qualities of sexuality from its reproductive ties. Sexual minorities, in particular homosexuals and sadomasochists, were increasingly accepted and were no longer regarded (exclusively) as deviants. Giddens aptly describes the radical separation of sexuality and reproduction in today's society:

> Sexuality came into being as part of a progressive differentiation of sex from the exigencies of reproduction. With the further elaboration of reproductive technologies, that differentiation has today become complete. Now that conception can be artificially produced, rather than only artificially prevented, sexuality is at last fully autonomous. Reproduction can occur in the absence of sexual activity; this is a final 'liberation' for sexuality, which thence can become wholly a quality of individuals and their transactions with one another.
>
> (Giddens, 1992, p. 27)

Giddens (1992) introduces the concepts of 'plastic sexuality' and 'the pure relationship' which he posits as characteristics of late modern relations. Plastic sexuality is a malleable sexuality that can be shaped to match the 'reflexive project of the self' without regard for reproduction (Giddens, 1991, p. 202). The pure relationship should be understood as a relationship of love and sexuality that is entered into for its own sake and is continued only as long as it still works in these two regards (Giddens, 1992, s. 58). In late modern society, individuals shape their own life story, structuring it into a narrative that is continually developed via reflection. The art, as Ulrich Beck (1986/1992) has observed, is to make the life story form a coherent narrative with the narrator as the one making the decisions – even if many of these decisions were in fact already made by other people and factors:

> Even where the word 'decisions' is too grandiose, because neither consciousness nor alternatives are present, the individual will have to 'pay for' the consequences of decisions not taken.
>
> (Beck, 1986/1992, p. 135)

However, Giddens and the current sociological-political mainstream understanding he represents tend to overstate the extent of individualization. Giddens ignores the fact that parents and children remain connected, regardless whether the child was conceived with or without sex and love. To a high degree, who and what the child is depends on the parents' combined DNA. The reproductive link between parents and child is a biological fact. Giddens, however, verges on painting a picture of the late modern individual as a person devoid of age, gender and development or, perhaps, rather as someone who is forever 33 years of age, modifies their sexuality slightly, occasionally replaces their partner, pieces together their own personal religion, rolls their own sushi and ultimately weaves it all together into a compelling narrative.

However, in relation to both sex and reproduction, there continues to exist a mutual dependence between the sexes. To have a child, one must come to terms with one's dependence on another person's reproductive resources and thus suffer the indignity of not being complete on one's own. A heterosexual person further has to tolerate his or her dependence on love from the other sex.

The majority of people still dream about establishing a family, with a husband, a wife and a certain number of children, who should be cute, funny, intelligent and beautiful and grow up to have good or accomplished lives, or both, and perhaps spare some time for the parents when they reach old age and need help and support. All in all, the family plays a bigger role in late modern society than sociology would suggest. Its citizens are not gendered- and ageless individuals who spend their waking hours reflecting on their 'selves'. They are children and adults, husbands and wives, fathers and mothers, sons and daughters, sisters and brothers, grandparents and grand-children, who are born, grow, reproduce and die.

Although work and leisure, family and working relationships, children and adults, men and women, sex and reproduction, education and work have been separated since the traditional societies fell apart, they are not so separate that they do not also connect in a multitude of ways.

The main link between family and work is that the former is the motivation for the latter. We spend most of our income on family expenses – rent, food, clothing, school, a car, holidays, insurance and so forth – and these material goods also serve as the visible markers of success (or the lack thereof) in work.

The positions we manage to attain in the workplace also contribute to our value as love objects. Rock singers and photo models have the widest choice of suitors, but statistics reveal that certain traditional attitudes still persist, as high-earning women are less likely to be in a steady relationship than men with a similar status, and low-income men are less likely to have a partner than low-income women. Many jobs have strong gender connotations; in Danish, for example, the word 'nurse' is explicitly gendered, while plumbers and tunnel workers have an unmistakable masculine air about them. These gendered job perceptions are gradually dissolving, however.

Further, to borrow a term from Hirschhorn (2003), the family acts as an evaluation team in both an internal and an external sense. Family birthdays and other occasions where the family members can exchange news and experiences serve as arenas for flaunting one's latest achievements and per-haps for one's siblings to make sure the family is updated on one's latest fail-ures and setbacks. Experiences from psychotherapy and role analysis seem to suggest that preferences in the choice of life partner, education and career are shaped by inner and outer dialogues, not least within the family. The superego is thus peopled with other figures besides the parents (Freud, 1923/1961a); siblings will make their opinions known when the internal evaluation team assesses the individual member's actions (Koefoed & Visholm, 2011).

Finally, apart from the hospital maternity ward, the family is the first organization we encounter. Hence, it comes to serve as a prototype or basic model for our experiences in and of organizations – our 'organization in the mind' (Armstrong, 2005). The family thus becomes the primary source of transferences in organizations.

This lets us identify the following fairly firm connections between family and working life: 1) the family is the motivation of work (our pay goes to provide for the family), 2) work helps determine our value as love objects, 3) the family serves as an internal and an external evaluation team and 4) the family is the first organization we come into contact with.

II The family in group and organization literature

Despite the connections between family and working life, both open and hidden family phenomena are absent from traditional group and organization literature.

Adrian Furnham's *The psychology of behaviour at work: The individual in the organization* (2005) contains two family references. One (p. 16) is a delimitation: although a family can be said to be an organization and thus may be seen as an open system, Furnham reserves work psychology to work organizations. The second reference is about job preferences, where Furnham points to an author who believes family background might play a role (p. 120).

Motivational psychology similarly does not attribute any significance to open and hidden family dynamics. Maslow breaks the overall project of finding a partner, having children and becoming the master or mistress of one's own household into fragments, interpreted and ranked according to the hierarchy of physical needs for safety, belonging, esteem and development. Helle Hein's 2009 book *Motivation*, which otherwise serves an excellent introduction to its topic, also does not address family dynamics.

Group psychology tends to position itself as a progressive alternative to both the isolated individual and the family authority, and phenomena such as gender, age and generation are rarely addressed. Group psychology is thus inclined to view the group as primary, but it seems fair to ask whether most groups include fathers, mothers, sisters and brothers.

Brotheridge & Lee (2006) have sought to identify empirical literature that draws on the family as a metaphor for the organization. They organize their findings into four categories: 1) papers that use blended families as a metaphor for post-merger organizations, 2) papers that view the birth of an organization through the lens of multi-generational families, 3) papers where the participants in qualitative studies use the family metaphor to describe their organization and 4) case studies where methods from family therapy or family consultation are used to improve workplace functioning.

In Bion's central *Experiences in groups and other papers*, the family dynamic is toned down but not excluded (Bion, 1961, pp. 187–189). Miller and Rice (1967) did not use family dynamics in their classical group relations model. In the group relations tradition, many agree with Bion's distinction between the two perspectives of Oedipus and Sphinx (1961). The Oedipus perspective is informed by the relationship between analyst and analysand, describing the individual's specific vantage points in relation to the other group members. The Sphinx perspective pertains to the group's ability to gain knowledge and to mobilize the individual members in this process, representing the environmental context and the system (Lawrence, 2006).

In the group relations literature there appears to be a tug of war between 'group' and 'family', as we saw during the 1960s, when family was 'out' and group was 'in'. Echoes of this view seem to persist to this day, as some scholars appear to side with the sibling perspective (group, democracy and so forth) against the parent-child relationship (family, authority and so forth), a point that Britton touches on in a discussion with Mitchell (see Chapter 3).

It is a characteristic aspect of the group relations tradition that it seems to be impossible to write a paper in this tradition without referring to Bion's *Experiences in groups and other papers* (1961). The key significance of this book, as I discuss in more detail later, is that Bion is the first to articulate that groups, like individuals, can change state, so that they are sometimes in a task mode and sometimes in a state of regression. Bion proposes just three states of regression for groups: dependence, fight-flight and pairing. Other authors have later sought to add new basic-assumption groups: in 1985, Turquet proposed 'oneness' as the fourth basic assumption, while Hopper in 1997 spoke of 'incohesion: aggregation/ massification'. Finally, Lawrence, Bain and Gould (1996) proposed 'me-ness' as a fifth basic assumption, recognizing Turquet's proposal as the fourth basic assumption (Heinskou, 2004). However, Eric Miller, who co-founded the Tavistock tradition together with Rice, insisted on one of his last publications that there are three, and only three, basic-assumption groups, and that these are biologically defined: dependence, fight-flight and pairing (Miller, 1998).

In a paper presented at the Belgirate Conference in 2009, inspired by a backbreaking generational change in Group Relations Australia, Susan Long and Bridget Nossal proposed getting rid of 'the family template', because it stood in the way of a more creative and open mindset (Long & Nossal, 2012). In a later paper, presented at ISPSO's AM 2010 in Elsinore, Denmark (Nossal, 2010), however, Nossal had thought better of it and instead proposed positioning the family template as a basic-assumption group alongside the others.

My own proposal would be that the three basic assumptions should be considered as being contained within the family dynamic, with dependence being associated with the early mother-child relationship, fight-flight being associated with the aggression of the anal phase and the rivalry of the oedipal dimensions, and pairing relating to forming a family. With this approach, family figures emerge the same way transference does, superimposing themselves on the organizational reality. Family figures activate powerful emotions, which often only make sense if we see them as springing from a family dynamic. Family figures are general patterns related to individual family experiences and their repression.

The group relations tradition combines psychoanalysis and open systems theory (Miller, 1993), and within psychoanalysis, the preferred approach is Melanie Klein's psychoanalysis, which revolves around the mother and child, while Freud, who assigns key significance to the role of paternal authority, is also frequently quoted. In a paper from 1980, Hirschhorn and Gilmore discuss the possibilities of using concepts from family therapy in consultancy. In 1991, Ed Shapiro and Wesley Carr (1991) wrote the interesting book *Lost in familiar places: Creating new connections between the individual and society*, where they combine psychoanalysis and systems theory and take their analysis from individual to family, from group to organization and, from here, to society and religion.

III Current reasons to put family on the agenda

Since the economic crisis of the 1980s, emotions, personality, commitment, learning and similar issues have become important dimensions of organizational life (Hirschhorn, 1997; Visholm, 2004b; Koefoed & Visholm, 2011). Although the Weberian organization assigned emotions and personality to the privacy of the home and the political domain, ever since the crisis of the 1980s, companies have been calling for commitment, creativity, learning, self-management and so forth. In modern society, emotions are placed alongside family and femininity as the polar opposites of reason, work and manliness. However, this rigid polarization is being challenged by the growing legitimization of emotions in the workplace. Further, in what appears to be an overlooked fact, once the door is opened to psychology, emotions that conveniently contribute positively to the bottom line are not the only ones that come to the surface. If we want creativity, envy comes along as part of the bargain. If we want commitment, we are also going to see a higher level of conflict and so forth. When we let emotions and personalities into our working life, transferences and projections come in as well and make their presence felt.

Since the Second World War, authority relations in general have been changing, shifting authority from the role to the person. While people used to be more inclined to follow the directions of formal authority figures, those who seek to exercise authority in a role today need to invest more of their personality into the role in order to be sufficiently effective (Hirschhorn, 1997; Meyrowitz, 1986; Visholm, 2004b).

The disparities between managers and employees, men and women, children and adults have been reduced (Meyrowitz, 1986). Today, the idealization of authority relies more on personal qualities than on rank or job title alone.

The division of labour between men and women has also changed and continues to change. Today there are, in principle, no remaining gender-segregated domains. Men and women work side by side and compete both at work and in the family. Many new constellations arise during this process. Female doctors would probably be justified in complaining that female nurses are much more service-minded towards male doctors. As workplaces become a mixed-gender setting they also increasingly become an arena for pairing. It will be interesting to see the impact of the mixing of genders on productivity.

In both *The managed heart* from 1983 and *The time bind* from 1997, Arlie Hochschild addresses the relationships between work and family life.

In *The managed heart* she examines the stress people experience when their work requires them to show feelings they do not have or, worse, to experience feelings they do not have. In *The time bind* she looks at how management concepts are sneaking into family life, while family phenomena are beginning to make their way into our organizations. This trend is facilitated by information technology, which enables highly flexible and fluid boundaries between work and home or leisure.

In another study (Brotheridge & Lee, 2006), 204 of 289 employees in a Canadian public-sector organization rated statements about their workplace in questionnaires about family functioning and working environment. The questionnaire on family functioning was adapted to match the workplace context; for example, a statement such as 'Our family is good at solving problems together' was changed to 'Our group is good at solving problems together'. The study found that the respondents perceived a high degree of congruity between families and organizations.

However, the Brotheridge and Lee paper also identified that both the study and the informants refer to a particular family concept. In this context, family implies closeness, permission to show feelings, network as opposed to hierarchy and arriving at solutions through dialogue rather than relying rigidly on rules. Moreover, there is a connection between 'family' and 'female'. Indeed, the paper concludes with a quote by Atchison cautioning against over-extending the family metaphor in the current economy:

> The concept of family is collective. It encourages loyalty from the employee and protection by and from the employer. The push towards ridding the organization of low performers and downsizing in general are [*sic*] antithetical to the idea of family. Families turning out or leaving behind children are illustrations of the most extreme negative circumstances in literature and history.
>
> (Atchison in Brotheridge & Lee, 2006, p. 158)

This underscores that the concept of family or family dynamics in this book is not a normative one. Since the emergence of the modern bourgeois society during the 18th century, the family has been positioned as the polar opposite of the hard, cold working life – as the place where one could simply be a human being and so forth – but that perception does not reflect reality in today's workplaces or families. The rhetorical use of the 'family' term in certain companies, where the manager or the owner proclaims that 'here, we are all one big family' deserves to elicit a shudder and enhanced vigilance. Indeed, the many family-owned and family-run organizations are not uniformly idyllic. The L'Oréal scandal is widely known, and Petriglieri and Stein (2012) wrote about the raging conflicts at Gucci. Families are arenas of life and death, love and hate, nurture and abuse, hope and fear – as illustrated in history, literature, art, fairy tales and myths.

IV The structure of the book

In the following, the sibling perspective is first presented in the context of the Oedipus complex. As mentioned earlier, this leads to the development of a more complex family model that draws a distinction between horizontal (at the top: father and/or mother, at the bottom: siblings) and vertical axes (son and/or daughter, father and or mother). The key concept of *promoted siblings* is introduced. Chapter 3 examines art, religion and mythology, where family dynamic is shown to play a key role. Chapter 4 discusses Lewin's widely quoted concept of democracy and compares it to Winnicott's concept of democracy, where elected representatives in democracies are regarded as temporary parents. Chapter 5 presents a psychodynamic understanding of self-managing teams. Chapter 6 presents an expanded version of systems psychodynamics and criticized the tradition's group concept for being far too abstract to capture the most important social dynamics. Instead, a typology based on six distinctly different system types is proposed: organizations and families, democracies, tyrannies, crowds and mass movements, states of panic and markets. Chapter 7 explicitly brings gender into the family dynamic and describes and analyses dynamics based on gender differences. Chapter 8 presents role analysis, an element in investigative and developmental approaches in organizational psychology that, in the Danish version presented here, draws on an expanded version of the Oedipus complex that includes siblings. Chapters 9 and 10 present and analyse family dynamic approaches to mergers and innovation in organizations. Chapter 11 rounds off the book by applying a societal and global perspective on the altered social systems in our globalized network society.

Chapter 2

The Oedipus complex – now with siblings

Lines of argument

The one component of psychoanalytic theory that Freud was most proud of having discovered and formulated was, without a doubt, his theory of the Oedipus complex. This chapter proposes some expansions on the concept, some aspects being in line with recent psychoanalytic literature on sibling relationships and others offering novel contributions. The chapter will not offer a comprehensive presentation and assessment of Mitchell's or Coles' sibling projects but instead draws on sound ideas and observations from both (Coles, 2003; Mitchell, 2003) and from the literature that followed up on these contributions work (Coles, 2011; Lewin & Sharp, 2009).

The Oedipus complex consists of two parents and a child (Figure 2.1). From the son's point of view, the father possesses the desired object: the mother. Hence, the son identifies with his father and wishes to claim his position. The resulting feelings are jealousy-hate and idealization in recognition of the father's superior power and status as an ideal or 'role model'. The son's hate leads to a passive fear of punishment and retribution, and his idealization leads to a desire for the father's approval (Freud, 1923/1961; Andkjær Olsen, 1988). The same is true of the daughter, with the necessary modifications and specifications.

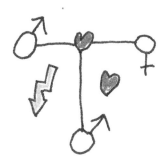

Figure 2.1 The classical Oedipus complex.

In this chapter, we first expand the complex by adding siblings and then, in extension of Mitchell (2003), introduce a distinction between the vertical dimension (parents–children) and the horizontal (children–children).

I Siblings

As mentioned, psychoanalysis has in recent years come under criticism for overlooking or even suppressing the significance of sibling relationships for the individual's personal development (Coles, 2003, 2006; Mitchell, 2003). One of the instances when Freud actually addresses the role of siblings is in his 1921 thesis *Group psychology and the analysis of the ego*, where he expands the perspective from the oedipal triangle to a family with several children. A 'group', according to Freud, may be defined as 'a number of individuals who have substituted one and the same object for their ego ideal and have consequently identified themselves with one another in their ego' (Freud, 1921/1955b, p. 80).

The description of the group thus includes both the relation to the leader (or the leading idea) and the relations to the other members of the group. In the group, both these relations carry a positive emotional charge.

Freud explains the identification between the group members as a reaction formation: a defence mechanism towards the mutual hate that is the siblings' basic attitude towards one another:

> Then for a long time nothing in the nature of herd instinct or group feeling is to be observed in children. Something like it grows up first of all, in a nursery containing many children (…). The elder child would certainly like to put its successor jealously aside, to keep it away from the parents, and to rob it of all its privileges; but in face of the fact that this child (like all that come later) is loved by the parents in just the same way, and in consequence of the

Figure 2.2 Freud's model of group psychology.

impossibility of maintaining its hostile attitude without damaging itself, it is forced into identifying itself with the other children. So there grows up in the troop of children a communal or group feeling, which is then further developed at school. The first demand made by this reaction-formation is for justice, for equal treatment for all. (…) If one cannot be the favourite oneself, at all events nobody else shall be the favourite. (…) What appears later on in society in the shape of *Gemeingeist, esprit de corps,* "group spirit", etc., does not belie its derivation from what was originally envy. No one must want to put himself forward, every one must be the same and have the same. Social justice means that we deny ourselves many things so that others may have to do without them as well (…). This demand for equality is the root of social conscience and the sense of duty.

(Freud, 1921/1955b, pp. 86–88)

Mitchell (2003) explicitly introduces the notion of sibling trauma: a perceived existential threat from a new sister or brother. The first child perceives him/herself as *the* child and feels exclusive and secure in this position. The child imagines there can only be one child in a family. Similarly for newborns, who initially have exclusive possession of the mother but later discover that she has to be shared with others, and that as the youngest, the infant is at the bottom of the sibling hierarchy. It is crucial to work through the sibling trauma:

> The sibling organizes narcissism into self-esteem through accepted loss – through a mourning process for the grandiose self, the 'death' of His Majesty the Baby. This is the necessary acceptance that one is ordinary, which does not mean one is not unique – just as all those other brothers and sisters are also ordinary and unique.

(Mitchell, 2003, p. 205)

In some cases, however, the sibling trauma persists:

> The shock of the sibling trauma will also be repeated and have to be reworked through in any future event that displaces and dislodges a person from who and where they thought they were. If the first or subsequent shocks are too great, then the trauma is introjected and forms a core of violence within the person.

(Ibid.)

Every time a person perceives a threat to important positions in social networks (job loss, transfers and so forth) or family networks (going away to boarding school, going through a divorce and so forth) the sibling trauma is activated and has to be reworked through.

II Rivalry and alliances

Combining sibling relationships with the classic Oedipus complex produces a situation where the daughters have a common interest in ousting the mother; next, however, it still remains to be determined who will take her place and take exclusive possession of the father (Figure 2.3). The boys, similarly, have a common interest in ousting the father, but after the deed is done, they find themselves in mutual competition about which of them will have exclusive possession of the mother.

The combination of the Oedipus complex and the contributions on family dynamics from group psychology thus produces a more complicated family dynamic. In extension of Mitchell's (2003, p. 11) work, we can label the child's relation to the parents in the Oedipus complex a vertical dimension, while sibling relations can be labelled a horizontal dimension. The extended family thus contains two simultaneous desire/conflict axes: child–adult and child–child. Mitchell attributes the horizontal axis a certain degree of autonomy, a notion that Angela Joyce challenges (2011). Joyce regards the vertical axis as more important. To grasp the full family dynamic it is necessary to introduce a third desire/conflict axis, the adult–adult axis, because the parents' mutual relationship is so important for their relations with the children and for the children's mutual relations.

The key tension between oedipal desires and sibling relations stems from their striving and yearning to be the parents' favourite child versus striving to thwart this effort or its discovery, as that would activate sibling hate and envy and jeopardize the cohesion of the sibling group. Coles describes this very aptly, based on a client he was seeing:

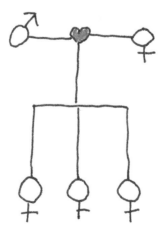

Figure 2.3 The Oedipus complex with the addition of siblings.

On the one hand, she wanted to have all the attention and the limelight. She wanted her parents' assurance that they preferred her to her siblings and that they thought her the most beautiful and intelligent. However, the moment that she felt close to achieving some recognition for herself, she knew that it would put her relationship with her siblings into jeopardy. She knew she needed them. She did not know how to straddle the conflict between the wish to be the preferred child and the wish to be part of the sibling clan.

(Coles, 2003, p. 15)

It is worth noting that parents do not always agree, and that the children also operate with the possibility of pitting the parents against one another, convincing the kinder parent to make the more restrictive parent loosen up and so forth. The *Old Testament* story of Esau, who sold his birth right to his younger brother, Jacob, for a bowl of lentil stew, offers a variation on this theme.

From a dynamic perspective, the Oedipus complex is a story about generational change in the family.

III Generational change

In traditional communities, generational change played a crucial role. On the one hand, the parents clearly had an interest in seeing one of the children, and the child's spouse, pick up where they left off, whether they were passing on a kingdom, an estate, a smithy or a farm. Over the course of life, the relative power balance between child and parents gradually shifts, and if the parents live long enough, they begin to depend on their children. It is difficult to pick the right moment to hand over the reins to the eldest son and his wife and go into retirement, retreating to smaller, humbler quarters. Waiting too long may make the young couple resentful over having to wait so long and thus less inclined to treat the retirees with kindness; on the other hand, moving too soon means spending years at the mercy of the son and daughter-in-law (Shorter, 1979).

In traditional communities, there was something important at stake. The parents had the final say over the children's choice of spouse, training and occupation. Economic criteria, such as finding a good breadwinner for the daughter and enabling the son to expand the family property, played a key role when the parents set out to find partners for their children. Because the family farm was typically passed on to the eldest son, finding good partners and occupations for the other children was an important task for the parents.

This system thus contains vital conflict dimensions, which explains the persistent intensity of the complex feelings between siblings and between children and parents, the latter possessing what the children desire: initially the mother or father themselves, and later the means of subsistence. Generally, Freud believed that inter-generational tension was the driver of cultural development:

> At the same time as these plainly incestuous phantasies are overcome and repudiated, one of the most significant, but also one of the most painful, psychical achievements of the pubertal period is completed: detachment from parental authority, a process that alone makes possible the opposition, which is so important for the progress of civilization, between the new generation and the old.
>
> (Freud, 1905/1953, p. 227)

In Ole Andkjær Olsen's interpretation, the young man does not commit patricide but satisfies his revanchism by outperforming his father and this usurping his position (Andkjær Olsen, 1988, p. 391).

To this, we should add sibling competition and rivalry, both with regard to taking over 'the family farm' and with regard to advantageous positioning in terms of marriage, training and occupation.

> Each succeeding generation has to face the fact that a *primus inter pares* will have to be chosen to inherit the mantle of power from the parental generation and restore the world to its normal state of inequality
>
> (Wilke, 1998, p. 269)

Thus, the Oedipus complex with the addition of siblings not only pertains to the child's fantasies of the father and mother but also to how the children can position themselves in love and work in competition with both parents and siblings.

In light of this, I have suggested elsewhere (Visholm, 2005a, 2005b, 2006, 2007; Huffington & Miller, 2008) that we add another tier to the family hierarchy, namely that of the promoted sibling: the brother or sister who is temporarily assigned to lead the other siblings, acting as a temporary parent without being one, and who will perhaps later be the preferred child to take over the family farm.

IV The parentally promoted sibling

With the promoted sibling we now have a three-tiered family hierarchy with father and mother at the top, the promoted sibling in the middle and the remaining sibling group at the bottom.

When the parents authorize a member of the sibling group to take on a leadership role or act as temporary parent, for example if the parents are going away for the weekend, that will trigger jealousy and envy among the other children (Figure 2.4). They might hope that having a sister or a brother take on the parents' role means that they will have freer reins, now that 'one of our own' is in charge. However, if the brother or sister takes their role seriously, the others feel doubly betrayed: by the parents, who abandoned them, and by the sibling, who let down the group and sided with the enemy. The

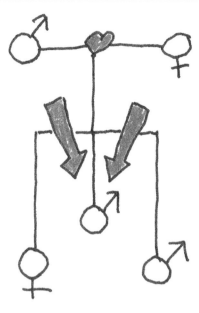

Figure 2.4 The parentally promoted sibling.

promoted brother or sister adds another degree of separation from the parents, to whom the promoted sibling now has privileged access, while the others only have indirect access via the promoted sister or brother. The unpromoted siblings yearn for the real parents to return and feel intense hate towards the substitute. The jealousy and envy are usually expressed as contempt for the promoted sibling, who has sided with the enemy, and for no real benefit, at that. In fact, the promoted sibling is no better off than the others. He or she is simply ethically dubious, susceptive to flattery and willing to sell out for peanuts. By contrast, the siblings who were not promoted are good, 'decent' individuals, with strong morals and a sense of unity.

The promoted sibling has not gained access to the coveted object but remains outside the door to the master bedroom. The promotion does not come with any entitlement or possibility of actually becoming the parent, having one's own children, being creative, but perhaps with a hope of having moved one step closer.

While the parents are the objects of intense idealization by the children, who see them as virtually occupying a world of their own, siblings and promoted siblings belong to the same world order. To the young child, the parents seem like the wisest, most beautiful and most reliable people in the world. During adolescence, however, they discover that the parents are probably quite ordinary people. They feel cheated when they realize that the parents do not live up to the image they formed of them in early childhood. Winnicott (1997) argues that this disappointment leads, to some degree, to a lonely and depressive state where the young person does not feel that he/she can trust anyone and finds it necessary to rebuild his or her perception of the world from scratch. The idealized parental transference, however, seems to resurface later in life in relation to top executives and similar elevated figures (Gabriel & Hirschhorn, 1999).

Thus, we need to distinguish between parental and sibling transferences, and we should expect transference relations to go both ways. If the unpromoted siblings have a transference of contempt to the promoted sibling and an idealizing transference to the parents, the promoted sibling will develop fearfulness in his or her transference to the siblings, matching the hate and the envy he or she would feel if somebody else had been promoted. From their own childhoods, the parents will be familiar with the combinations of hate and love that promoted and unpromoted children feel.

V The demoted parent

Joseph Berke has pointed out that parents may often act like siblings, and similarly, siblings may act as if one or both parents were siblings. From a family therapy perspective, a family where the members are not working on the primary task of facilitating age-appropriate development for all the family members would be seen as a dysfunctional family. If the parents abdicate and regress, and the children take charge, as is often the case in families with substance abuse issues, where the children take care of the family while the parents focus on their dependency, the family is indeed dysfunctional. However, there are milder cases.

> Parents often treat their children, and children their parents, as siblings or compatriots sharing the same stream of love or hate. This may be especially evident during times of marital conflict. Then parents expect their children to take sides in their convoluted feuds. Similar abuse can occur during pregnancy or after childbirth. Many men have commented that they wanted to welcome their newborn child, but found the task too difficult because they simultaneously saw the baby as an intruder, like a younger brother or sister. The arrival broke up the exclusive union the father thought he had with the mother (...). Likewise, a mother suffered a prolonged depression after the birth of her son because he reminded her of a hated brother.
>
> (Berke, 2012, p. 32)

After childbirth, the father may thus feel demoted to a child-like status and may even feel that he has been pushed to the back of the queue when it comes to receiving the mother's or wife's love.

Ariane Mnouchkine's film *Molière* (1978) opens with a rather amusing scene where Molière's beloved mother is seated in a good chair in a large living room.

At her feet, the youngest child in the family sits, content, as she strokes his head. Then the second-youngest child enters and pointedly remarks that there are more important things to do than sitting here, only to occupy the place at the mother's feet when the first child gets up and leaves. The system continues until Molière senior has pushed the eldest son out of the way and taken his place (Figure 2.5).

In cooling marriages, the mother may similarly feel marginalized if the father only shows an interest in the children and never looks her way.

When the parents' midlife crises coincide with the child's puberty or youth crisis, one of the parents may sometimes try to be young with the young, adopting their fashion style and taste in music, and position the other parent as a dusty old fossil. In this situation, it is helpful if the parents can make peace with their actual age and act as adult parents towards the adolescents (Visholm, 2005a, 2010; Winnicott, 2005).

VI The organizational molecule (Jaques)

The three-tier family hierarchy – the parents, the promoted sibling and the other siblings – corresponds to Elliot Jaques's concept of the organizational molecule:

> This [three-level managerial] linkage constitutes an organizational molecule whose characteristics are of great importance: they may be stated in their most general form thus: the manager is accountable to the manager-once-removed for his own work and for the work of his subordinate, and he manages his subordinate within terms of reference set by the manage-once-removed.
>
> (Jaques, 1976, p. 65)

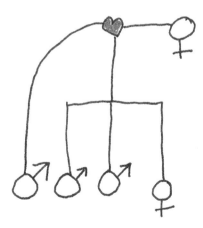

Figure 2.5 Family with demoted father.

In Jaques's view, the middle manager is the interesting element of the organizational molecule, as the middle manager is accountable to his superior for both his own and his subordinates' work. When Jaques speaks of a molecule, his implication is that the same dynamic processes apply on every level of the hierarchy, and that a multi-level hierarchy consists of many organizational molecules. The middle manager and the promoted sibling thus share certain key features in hierarchical relational systems.

VII The sibling-promoted sibling

Jaques distinguishes between two types of organizations: bureaucracies and associations. In the former, the authority flows from the top down; in the latter, by contrast, it moves from the bottom up. In associations and other democratic systems, each level elects its own leaders; in organizations, leaders are appointed and authorized by managers who are one or two levels up (Figure 2.6). Most contemporary organizations rely on combinations of these two directions of authorization.

While Freud (1921/1955b) tends to see the group leader as a father figure, Chasseguet-Smirgel (1964/1970) does not share this view; instead, she sees the leader of the group as an agent of a regressive movement aimed at achieving the blissful state of symbiosis with the mother without needing to go through the trouble of learning anything, let alone acknowledging gender and gen-erational gaps. By contrast, the father represents the demands of real life: the

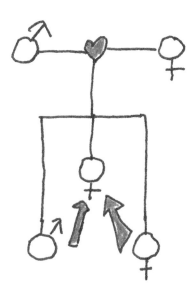

Figure 2.6 A sibling-promoted sibling.

need to be an adult and achieve mastery in order to succeed in work and love. The group leader is thus not a parental figure but a figure that challenges the parental level of the hierarchy: a sibling-promoted sibling. The group feeling anticipates the blissful states promised by the leader: no unpleasant and demanding distinctions; instead, fusion and emotional intensity.

The group leader is thus a different figure than the son or daughter who is chosen to lead the family and run the farm. The group leader is a rebel or a perverse fantasist, while the parentally promoted sibling is authorized and approved by the parents as a child who has learned what he or she was supposed to learn and is capable of handling the responsibility he or she has been entrusted with. It is thus important to distinguish between a top-down promoted sibling and a bottom-up promoted sibling.

VIII The law of the father and the law of the mother

Mitchell has further proposed that just as psychoanalysis overlooked or underestimated sibling relationships, it also overlooked the law of the mother. Traditionally, the law of the father is associated with the prohibition of regression, that is, with the reality principle, while the mother represents alluring regression and satisfaction and is not attributed a law of her own. While Freud's group psychology emphasizes that all children must be loved equally by their parents, Mitchell views this as a reflection of Freud's patriarchal bias. By contrast, Mitchell argues that children must be equal in their difference from each other for their mother before they are equal in their sameness to each other for their father. Exercising the law of the mother thus means containing the siblings' mutual hate of each other, helping each child find his or her own identity and making sure there is room for everyone:

> By differentiating between her children, the mother and her law allow for the concept of seriality to be internalized – John has to know he has lost the possibility of being Jane. One is a child in the same position as one's siblings in regard to one's parents, as one's peers in regard to one's teacher or boss, but one is also different: there is room for two, three, four or more. (…) Hate for the sibling enables the first step: I hate you, you are not me, is the precondition of seriality. The mother restricts this hate – enjoins its non-enactment.
>
> (Mitchell, 2003, p. 52)

Mitchell claims that all spontaneous play is about seriality; she is mistaken in this point ('playing house' and 'playing doctor' are just two examples of non-serial play), but seriality is clearly a factor in much child play, with musical chairs as one obvious example. We may debate her concept of the law of the mother and question whether the mother necessarily holds a monopoly on difference, while the father is restricted to monopolizing general principles, just as we may debate whether fathers are necessarily always strict and fair while mothers are permissive and unfair.

In any case, however, the comparison of the two mindsets can help clarify an important issue in both leadership and parenting: how to be fair and just while acknowledging differences.[1]

IX Democracy

In Winnicott's concept of democracy (1986), which we will revisit later, elected democratic representatives are referred to as 'temporary parents'. This seems to be aligned with the thinking behind the notion of promoted siblings. However, democracy may be seen as a three-tier hierarchy, where the parents are replaced by the constitution. The actual parents are out of the picture, but in order to regulate the cooperation between siblings/peers and to prevent or reduce destructive rivalry, it is necessary to install a substitute for the parents (Figure 2.7).

The constitution may be regarded as the combined laws of the father and the mother. The law of the father represents equality before the law, while the law of the mother represents the right or the freedom to be different within the framework of the law. In psychodynamic terms, siblings choose to promote someone from their midst to represent them for a limited period within the regulations imposed by the constitution. This makes the constitution an important instance to make sure the hate of the sibling is sublimated and translated into just and legal leadership.

Figure 2.7 Democracy – promoted siblings/temporary parents.

X The other group

Just as Freud and psychoanalysis may be criticized for overlooking the significance of sibling relationships in the family, Freud's group psychology may be criticized for lacking a horizontal dimension: the relation to the other group or the double crowd – to borrow Elias Canetti's (1960/1981) term. Freud has many observations of and comments on ambivalent feelings between groups, for example 'the narcissism of minor differences' (Freud, 1929/1961b). However, he does not integrate this into his theory but tends to treat them as a slightly peculiar detail. In *Civilization and its discontents* from 1929, in a discussion of aggression between groups with considerable similarities (the English and the Scots, the Spanish and the Portuguese), he writes:

> We can now see that it is a convenient and relatively harmless satisfaction of the inclination to aggression, by means of which, cohesion between the members of the community is made easier (...). Neither was it an unaccountable chance that the dream of a Germanic world-dominion called for anti-semitism as its complement.
>
> (Freud, 1929/1961b, p. 59)

Freud suggests that the dream of world domination is only complete once another group is mobilized to be the carriers of evil and the object of hate (Figure 2.8). As a modern reader will know, there was nothing particularly harmless about the Germanic 'satisfaction of the inclination to aggression'.

Figure 2.8 The other group.

The key point here is that the hate of siblings is not dissolved when the members of the crowd identify with the idealization of the leader. The hate is repressed and projected on another group and thus acts as a precondition for the warm feelings within one's own group. Thus, there is reason to assume that the emotional intensity of in-group or out-group phenomena draws on transference feelings from early and powerful hate-love dynamics between siblings.

The other group is not necessarily positioned as evil; it may also represent attractive knowledge and culture, charming love objects, better opportunities in life and motivations for emigration, grand tours and journeys of discovery. We may hate our own group for being provincial, having lousy food and unpredictable weather and, conversely, idealize other groups for the sound of their language and for their cuisine, music, sunshine, tax rates and so forth.

XI The other family

The family dynamic parallel to the other group is the other family. According to Chasseguet-Smirgel's (1964/1970) interpretation of the Oedipus complex, the child has to come to terms with the gender and generation differences. The latter implies that children should, ideally, emerge from the Oedipus complex with an understanding that they need to grow up and learn before they can 'take the father's role and possess his mother' (p. 61), as she writes, with a Freudian slip. Chasseguet-Smirgel tends to overlook that the successful outcome of the Oedipus complex is, of course, not an act of incest with the mother but instead, as Freud puts it, the liberation of one's libido from the opposite-sex parent and its transferral to 'an outside sexual object' (Freud, 1916–17/1963, p. 418). These external sexual objects are the children of other fathers and mothers 'out there in society'. This motif is clearly represented in classic fairy tales, for example, Hans Christian Andersen's *Clumsy Hans*, where the king, who has an unwed daughter on his hands, invites suitors from other families to appear before the princess. The successful suitor stands to gain not only the princess's hand in marriage but also half the kingdom. Usually, in these cases, the youngest of the three sons is the victor. These types of fairy tales address two family dynamics: on the one hand, the princess's, which is whether she is mature enough to see through the superficial flimflam and pick the right suitor; on the other hand, the suitors', 'the three sons', whose sibling dynamic revolves around the two older sons' well-behaved adaptation versus the youngest boy's creative autonomy. In this context, it is sufficient to note that part of the family dynamic is – another family (Figure 2.9).

The Oedipus complex is generally assumed to play out around the age of three to five years and to be reactivated during puberty. Mario Erdheim argues that the latter is not mere repetition, but that the task changes from the first working through of the Oedipus complex to the second. The task in

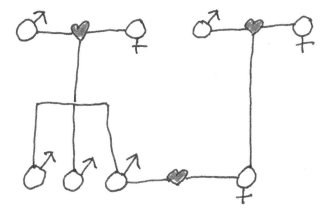

Figure 2.9 The other family.

connection with the first Oedipus complex at the age of three to five years is to adapt to the family reality: acknowledging the difference between adults and children and between male and female. The dissolution of the Oedipus complex sends the child into the latency phase, during which the sexual energy is discharged into learning. The task in connection with the second Oedipus complex is to open up towards the surrounding society and to connect with the surrounding culture, not least potential love objects and employers or collaboration partners (Erdheim, 1988).

XII Paths of authorization in organizations

To offer a more complete family dynamic model – an Oedipus complex that includes all the important entities in connection with the generational change – we have now added the following to the oedipal triangle: 1) siblings, 2) the promoted sibling in two variants: promoted from the top down or from the bottom up, 3) the other family or group – in part as a necessary resource for pairing and in part as an object for the projection of sibling hate and, finally, 4) the law of the mother. Thus, we are beginning to see the contours of a model of organizational psychology, where we can distinguish between social systems where the authorization moves from the top down: families and organizations; and systems where it moves from the bottom up: democracy and crowds (Figure 2.10).

In fact, most organizations contain both directions of authorization. The entire public sector, from nursery schools to the military, are fundamentally subject to the leadership of the parliamentary democracy, which elects a Parliament, which in turn appoints a head of government, who is formally authorized by the monarch and who then appoints the government ministers. Via delegated authority, these ministers in turn hire civil servants who

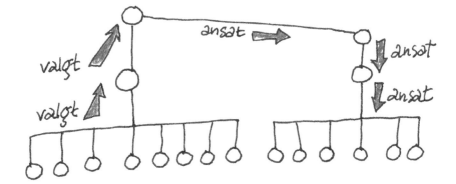

Figure 2.10 Authorization from the bottom up and from the top down (elected (*valgat*) vs. appointed (*ansat*)).

ultimately hire all the public-sector employees. First, there is a movement in the form of a democratic election, next a series of recruitment procedures, where the best applicant is selected. Limited companies are structured in a similar fashion, as each shareholder casts a number of votes, determined by the number of shares they hold in the company, to elect a board, which in turn appoints a CEO, who then hires people to perform the necessary tasks. In trade unions and other democratic organizations the political system is democratic in nature, but as soon as the work exceeds what the chairperson can handle in their spare time, the organization hires personnel that are not democratically elected but tasked with executing the democratic decisions.

Note

1 'The law, in its majestic equality, forbids the rich as well as the poor to sleep under bridges, to beg in the streets, and to steal bread' Anatole France.

Chapter 3

Digression: myths, fairy tales and metaphors

Parental power – the cost of solidarity

By adding the sibling dimension to the Oedipus complex we have established a family dynamic field, which now has three conflict axes and three axes of love/desire in and between the generations. As mentioned in Chapter 1, there may be a tendency to associate family with warmth, nurture, love and protection against a cold and materialistic world. That is, however, a view that is highly ideological and romanticizing with only a tenuous relation to real life.

A family contains many affects, including both love and hate. In 2002–2010, 513 murders were committed in Denmark. Of these, 220 (42%) were took place within the family, including children killed by their parents (34), parents killed by their children (19), persons killed by their cohabiting partner (62), persons killed by their former cohabiting partner (26), other family relations (29) and friends and lovers (50) (https://politi.dk: *Politiets Årstabel 2010*).

This chapter examines myths, literature and metaphors to identify examples of family dynamics that are active in our culture. First, it describes intergenerational tension, then sibling relations and finally a study of the question of why freedom seems to be associated more with sibling relations than with parenthood. References to Greek mythology and history draw mainly on Hjortsøe (2008), Rasmussen (2005) and Dommermuth-Gudrich (2004). Bible quotes are from *Holy Bible: New international version* (2011), with British spelling.

I Intergenerational hate and love

The theme of killing one's only or firstborn son seems to occupy a central role in Judaeo-Christian mythology, as Abraham's sacrifice of Isaac – prevented at the last minute – appears to be retold in the story of Christ's crucifixion and resurrection. In his thought-provoking essay 'The modern project and the feminisation of men' (2002) Larry Hirschhorn looks to the Old Testament for meaning.

According to David Bakan, a central reference in Hirschhorn's essay, the book of Genesis in the Old Testament, contains two layers, the first covered by the second but still peeping through here and there. The first layer shows that the book of Genesis describes the transition from matriarchy to patriarchy. Chasseguet-Smirgel (1976) makes a similar observation. She views Genesis as a story intended to flatter men and console them in their envy of the mother's role in the reproductive process. In a sense, Genesis – where a male god shapes a man, Adam, out of clay, breathes life into him and then goes on to create a woman, Eve, from one of Adam's ribs to relieve his loneliness – is a fairly accurate 'reverse' version of the biological reproductive process.

Paradoxically, the patriarchy is step one in what Hirschhorn calls the feminization of man. During the period covered by the stories in the Old Testament, men discover their role in conception and reproduction and begin to feel responsible for children and family. They stop killing their sons, become aware of the boundaries of the family and begin to take on a more protective role. The story of Abraham and Isaac seems to be repeated in the story of Christ, who follows his father's (God's) will and allows himself to be crucified while exclaiming 'It is finished' and 'My God, my God, why have you forsaken me?' With this, Jesus expresses both that his crucifixion is happening according to an agreement with God, his father, and that he sometimes feels forsaken. The conclusion to the story, of course, is that Jesus is resurrected from the dead, later ascends to heaven where he is seated at the right hand of power, to judge the living and dead. Unlike Isaac and many other sons, he is not going to have a wife and children; he will not have his own business, and like his father he will have eternal life.

The generational conflict is not the reserve of the Judaeo-Christian tradition. It also occupies a central place in Greek mythology. The Oedipus myth is often told as a story of a young man who, unwittingly, kills his father and marries his mother. In a sense, this is the Old Testament stories of fathers (nearly) killing their sons inverted, transformed into a story of a son who kills his father. It is more complicated than that, however. Long before Oedipus kills his father, both his parents have tried to kill him, and he is left in the wilderness to be devoured by wild beasts. Later, when Oedipus actually does kill his father, he does so in self-defence because the father and his men feel that Oedipus got in the way of their carriage.

The story begins with a prophecy: the oracle at Delphi told King Laius of Thebes that if he and his queen, Jocasta, have a son, the son will kill him and marry his widow. When Jocasta does give birth to a son, she and Laius decide to leave him in the wilderness so that the wild beasts may kill him. They pierce his heels, which later becomes his name: Oedipus comes from the Greek *Oidipus*, from Greek *oidein*, swelling, and *pous*, foot: Swollen-foot, cf. oedema. However, the shepherd they charged with leaving Oedipus in the wilderness takes mercy on the infant and passes him on to another shepherd. Eventually the boy is adopted by the king and queen of Corinth, Polybus and Merope, who are childless. At the royal palace, Oedipus grows up strong and wise, learning everything a prince needs to know. One evening at a feast, he hears that he is adopted, and he leaves the court. At a crossroads he has a confrontation with a distinguished gentleman in a carriage. The guards try to move Oedipus off the road by beating him with sticks, but Oedipus gets angry and kills everyone, except the carriage driver. Unwittingly he thus slays his father. Oedipus travels on and meets a sphinx that has long been plaguing Thebes. Meeting a sphinx involves a life-and-death challenge. Either one guesses the sphinx's riddle, and the sphinx perishes, or one fails and dies. The sphinx's riddle to Oedipus was as follows: 'What walks on four feet in the morning, two in the afternoon and three at night?' Oedipus solves the riddle. The sphinx perishes and the plagues on Thebes come to an end. Oedipus gets a hero's welcome and is rewarded with the dowager Queen Jocasta's hand in marriage and the crown. Unwittingly, he thus marries his own mother. The two have a happy marriage and have four children: the sons Polynices and Eteocles and the daughters Antigone and Ismene. Unbeknownst to both Oedipus and Jocasta, the children are also Oedipus's half-sisters and brothers. When the children are grown, new plagues strike Thebes. King Oedipus consults the oracle at Delphi and is told he has to find King Laius's murderer to end the plagues. Oedipus launches an investigation that unearths the full scope of the tragedy. Jocasta commits suicide by hanging, and Oedipus blinds himself.

Child sacrifice and parenticide

Coles presents a fascinating review and reinterpretation of the Oedipus myth in her book *The uninvited guest from the unremembered past* (2011). On the one hand, she points out that Oedipus must have been both blind and dim-witted not to realize he had killed his father and married his mother. This makes the myth a story of self-deception, of turning a blind eye to the truth. She argues that the story of Oedipus, rather than describing a universal desire to kill one's father and marry one's mother, is about a fantasy in adopted children who have learned the truth about their origins and thus the fact that their biological parents had rejected them. Coles argues that lies and suppression of the truth about family relations and origins can generate serious psychopathology, which is passed on from generation to generation. In fact, she explains how the roots of pathology can be sought even earlier in the Oedipus story:

Oedipus comes from the House of Cadmus. Cadmus, Oedipus's great-grandfather, was the founder of Thebes. Two generations later, Labdacus, Cadmus's grandson, Oedipus's grandfather, becomes king of Thebes. He dies when Oedipus's father, Laius, is just one year old. Together with his mother, Laius is cast out from the royal court by his uncle. Laius wanders the world and one day arrives as a guest at King Pelops' court, where he seduces and abducts the king's son Chrysippus. Angered that Laius so dishonours the rules of guest friendship, the gods punish him by prophesying that if Laius ever fathers a boy, the son will grow up to kill him. Laius returns to Thebes and marries his cousin Jocasta. Instead of telling Jocasta of the gods' threat, he instead avoids having sex with her, but one day Jocasta gets him drunk and seduces him in his sleep. Nine months later, Oedipus is born. Two days after giving birth, Jocasta is persuaded by Laius to abandon Oedipus to wild beasts.

Another Greek myth has certain parallels to the story of Abraham and Isaac:

> King Agamemnon and Queen Clytemnestra have three children: Iphigenia, Electra and Orestes. Agamemnon's brother, Menelaus, is married to the beautiful Helen, whom Prince Paris of Troy later abducts and brings with him to Troy. Together with all the other kings in Greece, Agamemnon has sworn to protect the marriage between Menelaus and Helen, and under Agamemnon's command all their armies are to gather in the port city of Aulis, but due to a lack of wind Agamemnon's fleet cannot set out for Troy. Artemis, the goddess of the hunt, whom Agamemnon had previously offended by killing one of her sacred deer, lets Agamemnon know that if he wants wind in his sails he will have to sacrifice his daughter Iphigenia. The cunning King Odysseus comes up with a plan to lure Iphigenia to Aulis: a messenger is to tell Iphigenia and her mother that the brave and handsome Achilles wishes to marry her. The young woman and her mother immediately travel to Aulis, but Iphigenia soon discovers that the proposal is a ruse. However, after considering the dilemma she decides to lay down her life for Greece. At the last moment, Artemis replaces Iphigenia with a deer. Artemis brings Iphigenia to her temple at Tauris, where she is appointed to be the priestess preparing strangers for sacrifice.
>
> Ten years later, when Agamemnon returns victorious from Troy, he is murdered by his wife, Clytemnestra, and her lover: Aegisthus. It is unclear whether Clytemnestra's motive is to avenge the sacrifice of Iphigenia, whom the mother may believe is dead, whether she simply wants to be with her lover, whether she is still angry that Agamemnon killed her first husband and forced her to marry him or whether she is angry that Agamemnon is bringing his mistress, Cassandra, with him as he returns from the war. In any case, there seems to be no shortage of motives. Electra and Orestes decide to avenge their father's death and kill their mother, Clytemnestra. After this act – which in Aischylos's play leads to extensive discussion about whether it is just to avenge one's father or unjust to kill one's mother – the two are hunted by the Erinyes and end up at Tauris. Here, Iphigenia recognizes her brother and sister at the last moment before they are to be sacrificed. The three siblings escape Tauris together.

It may seem odd that Jung in *The Theory of Psychoanalysis* (1913) suggests that the story of Electra may be seen as a representation of the female version of the Oedipus complex. For one thing, Electra has her brother carry out the murder, an objection that might be brushed aside, but moreover, the slaying does not bring her a love relation with her father and only serves the purpose of vengeance or justice.

Agamemnon and Clytemnestra's family drama contains the motif of a god who pressures a father to sacrifice his child only to spare the child at the last moment, a parallel to the story of God, Abraham and Isaac and also to the story of God who has Christ both crucified and resurrected. Strictly speaking, the Oedipus model also fits this template, if we substitute the oracle at Delphi for the god demanding that a father or the parents kill a child and see the shepherd who spares the child's life as the god who rescues the child.

On the face of it, Christian mythology shows that the believers, the most loyal and god-fearing, are allowed to keep their sons. Thus, it makes sense to follow Hirschhorn and read the stories as a description of development from a matriarchy, where the sons need protection from their own fathers, to a patriarchy, where the fathers take responsibility for the family. In Greek mythology, the gods are generally able to pressure the parents because they love their children. Abraham's alternative to sacrifice Isaac is to be a disobedient believer, while Agamemnon's alternative to sacrificing Iphigenia is to be a poor military commander.

It does not seem to take very dire transgression for the gods to choose to pressure fathers into killing their children. Laius violated the rules of guest friendship but did not kill anyone, and Agamemnon had killed one of Artemis's sacred deer. The story of Medea, too, clearly shows how she uses family members in her struggle for love.

Infanticide and jealousy between parents

The story of Medea, a passionate and decisive woman, well versed in witchcraft, whose talents only brought her misery, also belongs in the category of stories of parents who kill their children.

> According to the myth, Medea had fallen in love with the blond Greek Prince Jason, and after he had promised to marry her she helped him get the golden fleece that was in her father's, Aiete's, possession.
>
> When they flee across sea with the golden fleece, Medea's father discovers the theft and pursues them. However, Medea has brought her younger brother along and now dismembers him and tosses the pieces into water, one at a time, to slow down her father's ship (an example of cruelty between siblings of different genders!). She lives happily with Jason in Corinth for a number of years, but then Jason falls in love with King Creon's young daughter and arranges to marry her. Medea pretends to accept the marriage and has her two children deliver gifts to the bride: a coronet and a wedding gown. However, the gifts are magically designed to burst into flames when the bride puts them on. The fire is so intense that both the bride and her father perish in the flames. To complete her vengeance against Jason she then also kills their two children.
>
> (Hjortsøe, 2008)

In this story of Medea, it is her passionate love of Jason that both motivates her very unloving murder of her younger brother and the murder of Jason's young bride, the bride's father and her own and Jason's children. The latter four murders, however, are motivated by love in its miserable form: jealousy. Family members are used simply as pawns in her love intrigues.

Different reasons for hate and love between parents and children

It is not always straightforward to sort out what motivates the gods in their often sadistic and seemingly arbitrary intrigues with and against people and each other. However, there does seem to be evidence of parental love, as the call to sacrifice a child represents the most severe and painful dilemma for the father in these stories. Thus, the reason why children can be used for emotional extortion is that their parents love them. That does not preclude Hirschhorn's thesis, which is that the *Old Testament* can be seen as depicting a process where fathers in return for becoming patriarchs stop killing their children and gradually learn to be responsible heads of family.

However, all children are not equally beloved. There is ample material to show that it is not unheard of to cast children out when one does not have the means to raise them, by abandoning them in the wilderness. In fact the practice still occurs today, for example in China, where girls and disabled children are at risk. Oedipus's pierced feet thus revealed to anyone living in Greece at the time that here was a child who had been cast out by his parents.

Children may be unwanted for many reasons: because there are too many mouths to feed, because they may be evidence of the mother having engaged in illicit sex or because they might challenge the parents when they grow older. Children may also be wanted for many different reasons: because they are an extra pair of hands to share the labour, because having an heir makes life meaningful, because we can turn our dependency on our own parents upside down and seek to demonstrate how parenting is properly done, or simply as a way to act out the humiliations we were subjected to and, finally, because they represent a retirement plan.

Parents may be hated for many different reasons. As one of the 10 commandments tells us to 'Honour your father and your mother', we can assume that this cannot always be taken for granted: because they are in charge and define boundaries; because they are big and competent and all-knowing; because they lecture the child on what the child is feeling and experiencing; because they abuse and neglect the child; because they dictate the child's choice of occupation and partner and the timing of the generational change. And parents may be loved because they take care of the child, feed the child and generally satisfy the child's needs: because they are kind to the child; because many of their instructions turn out to be quite sensible and reasonable.

However, the special dynamic of the parent-child relation is that the roles vary and are inverted over the lifespan. The parents, who were once children themselves, are at the peak of their physical power and strength when they become parents. Their social power may increase while the children are growing up, but by the time the children are adults, the parents have usually begun to feel their age. While children are thus completely dependent on their parents while they are young, the parents become dependent on their children as they grow old. Moreover, the time when the child's emotional relation to the parents is strongest is also the time when the child knows least about life and the world.

II Rivalry and unity among siblings

One of the first stories in the Bible after the story of the original sin and Adam and Eve's expulsion from the Garden of Eden is the story of Cain, who killed his brother, Abel, in anger when God appeared to favour Abel. According to tradition, both men light a fire to offer their sacrifice, but while the smoke from Abel's fire rises straight up to God, Cain's smoke creeps pathetically along the ground. The dynamic in the story is sibling rivalry combined with parental favouritism (with God as the father figure).

The story of Jacob and his moments-older twin brother Esau is yet another example. Jacob and Esau are the sons of Isaac and Rebekah. While she is pregnant, Rebekah receives a message from God: 'Two nations are in your womb, and two peoples from within you will be separated; one people will be stronger than the other, and the older will serve the younger.' As the boys are growing up it becomes clear that the mother loves Jacob more, while the father prefers Esau. One day, Jacob has cooked a stew, and Esau comes in from the open country after a hunt, famished. He pleads with Jacob to give him some of the stew, and Jacob finally gives him a bowl in return for Esau's birth right, his privileged right to inherit as the firstborn. Esau accepts. Later, when Isaac is an old man, Jacob, with Rebekah's help, tricks his father into giving him his blessing and thus makes him the lord of the people – including Esau himself. An interesting additional angle to this story is that the parents seem to be using the children as agents in their own mutual competition.

Another story from the Old Testament is about Jacob, who had 12 sons, two of them, Joseph and Benjamin, with Rachel, who was his favourite wife. Joseph was Jacob's preferred son. To show his love for Joseph, Jacob gave him an ornate robe, a coat of many colours that was as beautiful as it was suited to sparking the envy of the other brothers. They began to plot against Joseph. Their hate only grew stronger when Joseph told them of a series of dreams, which all suggested that he would one day rule over them all, including their parents. In one dream, the sun and moon and 11 stars all bowed down to him. The brothers sold Joseph into slavery in Egypt and told Jacob that Joseph had been slain by wild beasts. Some years later, Joseph had become known for his ability to interpret dreams, and his reputation had even spread to the Pharaoh's court. At the time, the Pharaoh was tormented by nightmares and sent for Joseph. The Pharaoh rewarded Joseph's talent by making him governor over the land, the most powerful man in the realm, second only to the Pharaoh himself. Meanwhile, the Hebrews were struggling with drought and famine, and Jacob had to send his other sons to Egypt to buy corn. Here, Joseph handled their request. When he saw that the brothers were remorseful about their assault on him, he forgave them.

The biblical stories share a common theme of rivalry among same-sex siblings competing for the parent's favour. Fairy tales often have a different pattern of competition and rivalry. Here, the competition is often for a love object, which sometimes involves the ability to charm the object's parents. A king and a queen have a daughter of marriageable age (often a hysterical or otherwise difficult person) and look around for suitors. Another family has three sons. The two elder sons are outrageously useless conformists, while the youngest is a creative and kind-hearted chap with loads of confidence. He knows how to impress the princess and bring out the best in her and wins her hand in marriage and half the kingdom. *Clumsy Hans* is a classic fairy tale built on this template. *Cinderella* is the female version. Cinderella successfully competes by subtle, unseen means and is thus a proper woman, while the two nasty and stupid stepsisters compete in a glaring and unseemly manner.

Shakespeare's tragedy *King Lear* is about a king who wishes to retire and hand over his realm to his three daughters. He divides his land into three parts and determines to give the biggest share to the daughter who loves him most. The two elder sisters loudly proclaim that they love their father more than anything in the world, and he happily laps up their words. Cordelia, the youngest daughter, who is in fact his favourite, is honest and restrained, which displeases him. In his anger he cuts Cordelia off and splits his kingdom between the two elder sisters. The play not only demonstrates sibling rivalry but also the intensity of the destructive forces that are unleashed when parents give up trying to contain sibling hate and forget that love and gratitude cannot be forced; that love and gratitude can only be true if they are freely expressed (Fisher, 2007).

Fairy tales (Sanders, 2004) also seem to feature another important template, that of same-sex siblings competing while siblings of different sexes cooperate. In the story of *The three little pigs* the eldest brother represents delayed gratification, while the two younger pigs just want to play and eat. Ultimately, the wolf eats the two little pigs and then falls down the chimney and straight into big brother's pot, and now the eldest pig can have wolf stuffed with pork for dinner (Bettelheim, 1975). Clumsy Hans and his brothers and Cinderella with her stepsisters also belong to the category of competition between same-sex siblings. By contrast, Hansel and Gretel banded together against their poor and evil parents and later against the evil witch. In Hans Christian Andersen's *The wild swans* the 12 brothers cooperate in order to rescue their younger sister. In Andersen's *The snow queen*, brother and sister Kay and Gerda help each other.

One explanation of this pattern may be that boys and girls traditionally compete for the parents' love, but they do not play by the same rules. A good daughter excels at different things from a good son. Thus, they will often be able to help each other without compromising their own standing in the competition.

However, in the paper 'Orestes and democracy' Hinshelwood and Winship (2006) argue that the relationship between the two siblings Electra and Orestes, whom we encountered above, is the quintessential psychoanalytic model of the relation between brother and sister, while Oedipus similarly incarnates the position of the only child:

> While Oedipus is *the* story of an only child, Orestes and Electra is *the* psychoanalytic template for brother and sister. Orestes and Electra are bonded by their mutual devotion to a joint duty: the avenging of their father's (Agamemnon's) murder by their mother (Clytemnestra).
>
> (Hinshelwood & Winship, 2006, p. 81)

Strictly speaking, Oedipus is an atypical only child, as his own parents attempted to kill him, and he is later adopted by another couple. He also does not remain an only child, as it is later revealed that he is the half-brother of his four children and the father of his four half-siblings. Orestes and Electra also do not appear to be typical siblings, as they join forces to avenge their father by killing their mother. And why are their sisters Iphigenia and Chrysosthemis not included in the endeavour? Hinshelwood and Winship see a rudimentary democratic element in Orestes and Electra's collaboration:

> The dynamic between Orestes and Electra becomes a surrogate, or micro-democratic, unity. It is a space smaller than the horde, but offers a more intimate window into the democratic exchange between siblings.
>
> (Hinshelwood & Winship, 2006, p. 79)

Hinshelwood and Winship equate collaboration with democracy and almost seem to argue that everything good is associated with democracy, while all that is bad is associated with hierarchy, for example in parent-child and leader-employee relations.

Thus, Hinshelwood and Winship should be seen as contributing to the idealization of sibling relations, as expressed in their interpretation of sibling relations as democratic and parent-child relations as authoritarian. Moreover, they miss the point that boys and girls in many regards have different interests, which makes it less problematic for them to help each other.

III The power of parenthood and the cost of unity

The use of the terms 'brother', 'sister', 'brotherhood' and 'sisterhood' in organizations where people are not actually family is highly interesting.

Monks and nuns refer to each other as brothers and sisters. The motto of the French Revolution was 'liberty, equality, fraternity'; this was later taken over by the labour movement and socialists. Secret societies also describe themselves as brotherhoods. Both 'brotherhood' and 'sisterhood' have connotations of solidarity, unity, equality and renunciation.

What may seem slightly puzzling is that what the child most desires – parenthood – has been deselected in favour of the apparent equality of a same-sex sibling group. There is no reproductive sex in a same-sex group. The appearance of equality emerges because the two inequalities of sex and generation are out of the picture, but that leaves the hierarchy of the sibling group untold. Siblings are not equal, after all. Differences of age and competence are jealously guarded.

Indeed, in Freud's myth of the primal horde, it is the brothers who band together to kill the father, who has monopolized the women (Freud, 1913/ 1955a). If they are successful, however, they will become fathers themselves. In this light, brotherhood is a means to fatherhood.

In practice, the French Revolution targeted the royal family, King Louis XVI and Queen Marie Antoinette, and sought to establish a civil democracy founded on universal human rights. Such a royal couple may be seen as parental figures, with the subjects as the couple's children. One might imagine that the revolutionary citizens, in search of a counterimage, saw brotherhood as a suitable substitute. But why relinquish the ambitions of adult sexuality and parenthood? Perhaps Coles' observation of the tension between the desire to be the parent's preferred child versus the desire to be a respected member of the sibling clan (Coles, 2003, p. 15; cf. above, p. x) offers a clue. The desire for parenthood may seem so provocative that it has to be concealed to avoid causing envy. To the unconscious imagination, fighting for liberty, equality and the right to marry and have children (which were not obvious rights for individuals at the time) might seem as an attempt to lay claim to the crown and the kingdom. Parenthood thus becomes a manifestation of power, while brotherhood is seen as representing reciprocity.

As for monks and nuns, their vows include a vow of celibacy. Instead of focusing on the other sex, sexual pleasure and noisy and hungry children, monks and nuns are to be free to devote themselves to praying, reflecting on God and doing good deeds. Later, they may get their reward in heaven. An interpretation of this particular mindset might be that renouncing adult sexuality means refraining from challenging one's owns parents' power, in this case God's, as well as avoiding acquiring a position that might become the object of envy. If we consider gods as projected parental figures, becoming parents is almost like becoming gods. Parenthood has an exclusive character. We may have several brothers and sisters but only one father and one mother. To reject or renounce parenthood is the price to be paid to avoid becoming the target of envy.

In a discussion with Mitchell, the psychoanalyst Britton asks:

> In our prioritising sibling relationships, is there opposition to parenthood, and do people tend to divide as to which their allegiance is going to be (...)?
> (Cohen et al., 2009, p. 82)

With this point, Britton certainly captures a figure at play in the discussion about siblings. It seems that progressives favour the sibling level (= democracy, flat structure, dialogue) over the parental level (= authoritarian dictatorship, hierarchy, top-down orders), while reactionaries hold the opposite view.

This polarization certainly reflects the creative tension between the generations, but strictly speaking, it is a bit of a stretch to posit siblings and parenthood as opposite alternatives. When all is said and done, many parents have siblings, and most siblings become parents. It is perfectly possible to have a society where the citizens are free to marry or find a partner and have children while also democratically electing representatives to Parliament and government.

Clearly, solidarity may entail sacrifices. One may feel the obligation to go on strike in order to change unreasonable conditions, which may have costs in the form of lost earnings or job loss, but we are hardly going to achieve a higher degree of solidarity from giving up sex and reproduction. When the slogan is not 'liberty, equality, parenthood', it is probably because parenthood is seen as the forbidden, unconscious desire to usurp the parents' position, in the sense of ousting a parent and lord it over the other children together with the other parent.

Chapter 4

Promoted siblings and temporary parents

About democracy and psychodynamic in Lewin and Winnicott

> It's coming to America first
> the cradle of the best and the worst
> It's here they got the range
> and the machinery for change
> and it's here they got the spiritual thirst.
> It's here the family is broken
> and it's here the lonely say
> that the heart has got to open
> in a fundamental way:
> Democracy is coming to the USA
> (Leonard Cohen, 1992: Democracy. From the album *The Future*)

The concept of democracy has played an important role in psychology – not least in social psychology. This began during the late 1930s in the United States as a reaction to Nazism and Stalinism; after the war it grew into the group and democracy movement culminating in the 1960s and 1970s and revolutioniz-ing – in both immediate and more enduring ways – education, the thinking on management and organizations, psychiatry and psychotherapy.

Democracy is both an organization form, that is, a method for coordi-nating and leading the activities of a given group, and – in a more fleeting sense – a core value of Western culture, that is, an ideology, a mental state and an as yet vaguely defined atmosphere in a social context. In post-war psychology we see examples of both uses of the word, but it was the latter sense, spearheaded by Kurt Lewin, that became the dominant term. In his 1950 essay 'Some thoughts on the meaning of the word "Democracy"', Winnicott reflects on what conditions have to be met for a society organized as a parliamentary democracy to be workable. Drawing on a family model, he refers to the elected representative as a 'temporary parent' and calls the voters 'children'.

Comparing Lewin and Winnicott, it becomes clear that Lewin looks at democracy in hierarchies, where authority flows from the top down, while Win-nicott deals with actual democracy, where authority moves from the bottom up. Lewin's concept of democracy in his description of the 'democratic leader' has more to do with 'atmosphere' and is, to some extent, designed to ease the mood along the chain of command in top-down systems.

This distinction between democracy as an organization form and atmosphere has not been debated in psychoanalysis or social psychology. The concept of the group has been very generally formulated as applicable to virtually all sorts of organizations. In light of the critique of psychoanalysis pertaining to the absence of sibling relations in the psychoanalytic understanding (Coles, 2003; Mitchell, 2003), as demonstrated above, we may construct a more expansive model of organizational psychology that is able to capture the distinction between organizations with a top-down versus a bottom-up authorization process.

It is no secret that the world has undergone profound changes since Lewin and the Second World War and since the debate about democracy and group was last active, in the 1960s and 1970s. Globalization and information technology have reorganized and continue to reorganize the structure of society, from the global market to family life, and the axes of political conflict have shifted from the east-west polarization of the Cold War to now, when the world situation appears to be more open and unsettled, after strong forces during the presidency of George W. Bush in the United States sought to establish a polarization between the West and Islam. The radicalized modernization process continuously gives rise to various forms of resistance. Together, these changes call for a rethinking of the relationship between democracy and psychology.

This chapter offers a contribution to the development of a psychodynamic theory about the psychology of democracy as well as contribution to a psychologically reflected rethinking of democracy in our current situation. Parts I and II discuss the respective concepts of democracy proposed by Lewin and Winnicott. Part III is a psychologically reflected discussion of the concept of democracy in radicalized modernity.

I Lewin – democracy and democratic atmosphere

Texts from the 1930s, 1940s and 1950s with a social psychology perspective abound with references to 'democracy'. It is a highly charged concept of democracy that is at play in these texts, which regard their own purpose as scientific. Democracy appears as a stronger value than, say, truth or objectivity. Thus, in a classic article about the historical background of social psychology, Gordon Allport writes that the roots of modern social psychology are found in 'distinctive soil of western thought and civilization', that social psychology requires a free research tradition and a 'philosophy and ethics of democracy' (Allport, 1954). In the same text, Allport explains how contemporary social and political tensions inspired the social sciences:

The First World War (...) followed by the spread of communism, by the great depression of the '30's, by the rise of Hitler, the genocide of the Jews, race riots, the Second World War and its consequent anomie, stimulated all branches of social science. A special challenge fell to social psychology. The question was asked: how is it possible to preserve the values of freedom and individual rights under conditions of mounting social strain and regimentation? Can science help provide an answer? This challenging question led to a burst of creative effort that added much to our understanding of the phenomena of leadership, public opinion, rumor, propaganda, prejudice, attitude change, morale, communication, race relations, and conflicts of value.

(Allport, 1954, p. 4)

In his Foreword to the 1948 edition of Lewin's *Resolving social conflicts: Selected papers on group dynamics*, Allport further writes:

The next three chapters expand the theme, with special reference to the problem of democratic re-education. If there are features in a national character that are inimical to the peace of the world, the remedy for the situation lies in altering the political and cultural climate within which the hostile character develops. To make the Germans more democratic, for example, requires an alteration in leadership and in values. For unless the inclusive group structure is altered, individuals cannot basically be changed.

To Lewin the crucial determinant of group atmosphere lies in leadership. A successful resolution of social conflicts requires in nearly all instances the activity of trained, democratic leaders. Nor is such leadership a mere matter of utilizing a few fancy tricks to make people feel good: a democratic leader is not simply a clever persuader. The democratic process is complex, and it is necessary to train both leaders and group members to play their respective roles within it.

(...)

There is a striking kinship between the work of Kurt Lewin and the work of John Dewey. Both agree that democracy must be learned anew in each generation, and that it is a far more difficult form of social structure to attain and to maintain than is autocracy. Both see the intimate dependence of democracy upon social science. Without knowledge of, and obedience to, the laws of human nature in group settings, democracy cannot succeed. And without freedom for research and theory as provided only in a democratic environment social science will surely fail. Dewey, we might say, is the outstanding philosophical exponent of democracy, Lewin its outstanding psychological exponent. More clearly than anyone else has he shown us in concrete, operational terms what it means to be a democratic leader, and to create a democratic group structure.

(Allport, 1948, pp. xi–xii)

A central aspect of this democratic psychology movement is the experimental studies that Lewin, Lippitt and White carried out at Iowa Child Welfare Research Station in 1938–1942. These experiments showed that groups with a democratic atmosphere performed better than groups with an authoritarian and groups with a laissez-faire atmosphere (Figure 4.1). They were efficient, and the children in the groups thrived better. Let us, however, take a closer look at what Lewin meant by 'democracy' in this context. Each group had been assigned a group leader (an adult student), who had received detailed instructions on how to lead the children. Lewin defines the difference between democratic and authoritarian leadership as follows:

1	**Democratic**: All policies a matter of group determination, encouraged and drawn out by the leader.
2	**Authoritarian**: All determination of policy by the strongest person (leader).
3	**Democratic**: Activity perspective given by an explanation of the general steps of the process during discussion at first meeting (clay mould, plaster of Paris, papier-mâché, etc.). Where technical advice was needed, the leader tried to point out two or three alternative procedures from which choice could be made.
4	**Authoritarian**: Techniques and steps of attaining the goal (completed mask) dictated by the authority, one at a time, so that future direction was always uncertain to a large degree.
5	**Democratic**: The members were free to work with whomever they chose and the division of tasks was left up to the group.
6	**Authoritarian**: The authority usually determined autocratically what each member should do and with whom he should work.
7	**Democratic**: The leader attempted to be a group member in spirit and in discussion but not to perform. He gave objective praise and criticism.
8	**Authoritarian**: The dominator criticized and praised individual's activities without giving objective reasons and remained aloof from and active group participation. He was always impersonal rather than outwardly hostile or friendly (a necessary concession in method).

Figure 4.1 The difference between democratic and authoritarian leadership according to Lewin (1939/2000, s. 75–76).

The key question, of course, is what constitutes the particularly democratic aspect of the 'democratic' leadership approach. If we look first at the authority relations, that is, who has authority over what and whom, it is clear that the children do not actually decide who is going to be their leader. They also do not decide what task to work on or what resources are available for the task. They do not decide what group they want to be in or with whom. We do not know much about what sort of contract the leader has with the children. We might guess that the group leader was authorized by the head of the school where the children were recruited, and that this person had the ultimate responsibility, as he or she presumably has an agreement with the children's parents. Within these conditions, the children are now free to make decisions as a group. They can break up the work in different ways, break into smaller groups or do some of the work individually.

The group leader sets himself up as a sort of consultant to the process. The children can ask for advice, and he is then instructed to respond in a particular manner. When the group leader acts as a consultant, we must assume that he has been instructed to withhold certain forms of knowledge, as the format is designed to let the children make experiences on their own. If the children were to run off, we would assume that the group leader would step of out his role as consultant and quickly retrieve the children to keep them from getting hurt in traffic and to ensure that their parents can trust them to be at the club. The leader further acts as a moderator when the children make decisions about their activities, and he acknowledges being in a position of greater knowledge as he provides objective criticism and praise. The leader strives to provide task-focused rather than person-focused leadership. In relation to praise and criticism, the group has to be able to take an objective or task-related perspective to avoid any personal favouritism and minimize fantasies of such favouritism. However, the authority system that the democratic leadership is embedded in is not made explicitly clear to the children. It is also not revealed how the leader handles any serious disagreements in the group, or how any necessary but unpleasant leadership interventions are implemented.

Next, we may look at the participants' relationship with the task at hand. Here, it is key that the participants are introduced to the nature of the primary task and to the steps along the way, as this offers an overview and lets them identify with the task as a whole. In this regard, the authoritarian leadership stands out by monopolizing the holistic overview and thus removes the context that makes the individual tasks meaningful. This places the relationship with the authority figure centre stage and offers no encouragement for the participants to apply their own thinking or imagination. The finished work appears as a result of the leader's mysterious ability to combine a number of meaningless components into a meaningful whole.

However, even with the democratic leadership approach, little is in fact left up to the children. The nice thing about the activity is clearly that the task is well defined and that the participants are able to see the overall point. This also enables them to be critical of the authority figure, since they have access to the relevant information. In extension of this, we may also say that the children are being acknowledged as competent partners. They have competency, and the leader expects something of them. They are capable of making experiences. Any mistakes will have consequences for them. However, the deceptive aspect of the endeavour is that the authority systems is obscured. The focus is on the decisions that lie within the children's scope of autonomy, but what lies beyond remains untold. The 'technical advice' in the democratic leadership approach, where the leader offered two or three alternatives for the children to choose between, may sound like a delegation of responsibility that promotes the children's development, but on the other hand, we may also recognize it as the technique applied in connection with hypnosis: the freedom to choose among three alternatives removes focus from the lack of freedom in the way the choice is defined. If the guide on a fantasy journey says, 'You are now entering a lift. It is up to you whether you want to go up to the second or the fifth floor or down to minus two', the participant may become so focused on choosing among the three permitted floors that he or she forgets to notice that he or she was just ordered into the lift.

Jaques (1976) takes the criticism of the manipulative aspect a step further, distinguishing between associations and bureaucracies. The former are groups of people who organize in pursuit of a common interest – from anglers, shop assistants and office staff, shareholders or motorcycle enthusiasts to citizens in a society. When the pursuit of these interests requires more work than the chairperson and the board are able or willing to put in on a voluntary basis, a bureaucracy is hired to execute the association's decisions. Associations are generally democratic – one person, one vote or one share in a company, one vote – but naturally, this democratic format cannot be implemented in a bureaucracy, which has been put into the world for the purpose executing the association's decisions. In the following I build on Jaques's analysis, although I replace the term 'bureaucracy', which fundamentally means 'the power of the office', with the term 'organization'. Organization thus serves both as a general term for a wide range of organizations, from families to dictatorships, and as a more specific term for organizations that are not associations or democracies, and whose authority flows from the top down: families, the civil service, limited companies and so forth. The context will make clear when 'organization' is used as a general term and when it is used in the more specific sense.

In a comment on Lewin and his colleagues' experiment, Jaques argues that the group leader simply has to let the children decide for themselves, since they are in no way his subordinates. They are either members of an association that has hired the group leader, who is thus subordinate to the members, or they are consumers of a service and thus equal to the group leader. In Jaques's opinion, it is essential to distinguish between associations with democracy and organizations where the leader is responsible for the work of his subordinates. While the leader is in charge, 'In effect, the group is free to take any decision it wishes – so long as the manager is in agreement' (p. 200).

Since the culmination of the group movements in the 1960s and 1970s, it has not been very clear in the public sector that one cannot both participate in a democratic society and insist on democracy in public workplaces. There are many opportunities for influencing one's work, both in terms of working conditions and with regard to creative approaches to the tasks at hand, but the workplace cannot be a democracy.

It would be easy to dismiss 'democratic leadership' as a delusion and an abuse of the concept of democracy, as many did during the late 1960s – and rightly so. The very term 'democratic leadership' ought to raise red flags. However, we are also speaking of a concept whose impact can hardly be overstated. These Lewinian experiments became an important part of the group and democracy movement that, with roots in social psychology, organizational psychology and education, spread throughout the Western world after the Second World War (Visholm, 2002, 2004c, 2006a). From a different perspective, Rose described the movement as follows:

> In the 1930s, from a range of different directions, a new intersubjective entity was born – the group. The group represented a field for thought, argument, and administration that was genuine supraindividual and yet not of the order of the crowd or the mass. The group would exist as an intermediary between the individual and the population, it would inhabit the soulless world of the organization and give it subjective meaning for the employee, it would satisfy the social needs of the atomic and fragmented self isolated with the rise of the division of labor and the decline of community, it would explain ills and could be mobilized for good, it could bring about damage in its totalitarian form and contentment and efficiency in its democratic form. In the medium of the group a new relay was found where administration in the light of psychological expertise could come into alignment with the values of democracy.
>
> (Rose, 1996/1998, p. 136)

Rose tends to see the group and the concept of democracy as a slick medium of integration, a clever way to control the citizens in liberal democracies, which in my opinion is a restricted understanding (Visholm, 2002).

Democratic leadership contains an ungainly mix of progressive elements and deceptive manipulation techniques. A clear task formulation and an acknowledgement of the participants' competency and right to their own perceptions and opinions are progressive, while obscure authority relations and the leader's rehearsed manner of providing advice are aspects of deceptive manipulation.

To the extent that we are acknowledged as being competent and as the holders of opinions and abilities that are worth including, our interest in the workings of the bigger whole begins to awaken, however. It is not difficult to see through the hypocrisy of it all, and the exclamation 'isn't this just a democratic sham' in fact articulates an aggressively investigative stance towards the system. 'We're not content just picking the colour of the loo paper!' and 'We want the world, and we want it now!' as people used to say and shout. The emphasis on task clarity and the competence of the participants in 'democratic leadership' provides a connectedness to reality that enables the participants to evaluate themselves and each other on a realistic basis and to criticize the leader. These inherent contradictions in the concept of 'democratic leadership' can thus be seen as contributing to the antiauthoritarian movements of the 1960s. Now that the dust has settled after the rebellion, however, it is clear that one progressive outcome of the group and democracy movement was an authorization of groups in society that had not previously had a voice. Population groups whose experiences and opinions no one had paid any attention to before now gained a voice or a psyche with related experiences, opinions and attitudes. It was not until after the Second World War that anyone began to take an interest in workers', women's and children's ideas and perceptions. Until then, they had been viewed from a more behaviouristic perspective as individuals who could be made to do or not do certain things by means of rewards and punishment, almost like training circus animals. One of the key initiatives was to ask people what they thought of problems in the organization and in their own life. Prior to the era of progressive education, if a child could not go to sleep, the adults might say 'go to sleep now, or you'll be spanked' or 'if you go to sleep now, you can have a lovely apple when you wake up'. With a progressive educational approach, they might now instead ask, 'How come you can't sleep?' and the child might reply that he could not fall asleep because he did not like having his head in the dark corner of the crib. The adult might then solve the problem by simply turning the child around (cf. Sigsgaard, 2001). That may not be democracy, but it makes good sense all the same.

II Winnicott – democracy and family dynamics

Winnicott wrote in his essay on democracy in 1950, five years after the end of the Second World War, that a society may attain democracy once certain conditions are in place. Moreover, he argued that both societies and individuals have a certain inherent tendency towards or striving for democracy. The key quality is maturity. For a society to build a successful democracy, it has to have a sufficient number of mature members. Among these mature people there would naturally be a 'tendency towards the creation and recreation and maintenance of the democratic machinery' (Winnicott, 1950/1986, p. 243).

Winnicott divides the population into four categories: the mature, the openly anti-social, the indeterminate and the hidden anti-socials, the latter reacting to appearing to be pro-social but in fact react to their inner insecurity by identifying with the authority rather than with society.

Maturity in relation to democracy implies the ability to contain and identify with society as a whole and all its constituent part. Somehow, we have to be able to see matters from the point of view of workers and capitalists, farmers, fishermen and shop-owners, public-sector employees, men and women, children, ethnic minority groups and so forth.

If I read Winnicott correctly, a mature democrat is someone who is capable of balancing their self-interest with the interests of the community and the preservation and development of democracy itself. However, if the number of mature members is too small, democracy is under threat. Hidden anti-socials will be tempted to put the openly anti-social into positions of power, which will result in a polarization of society, because the anti-socials are incapable of containing and integrating conflicts of interest; thus, due to their immaturity, they will have to find a group to persecute instead (p. 244).

What creates mature citizens, according to Winnicott, is 'ordinary good homes' (p. 246). Maturity is the capacity for identification with ever larger groups, and this capacity is nurtured by interaction experiences within the family:

> The parents' attempt to provide a home for their children, in which the children can grow as individuals, and each *gradually add* a capacity to identify with the parents and then with wider groupings, starts at the beginning, when the mother comes to terms with her infant. Here the father is the protecting agent who frees the mother to devote herself to the baby.
>
> (Winnicott, 1950/1986, p. 248)

However, Winnicott also sees democracy as 'a game of parents and children'; a game that is harder than it sounds and which demands mature participants:

> To some extent, in the democratic election mature people elect temporary parents, which means that to some extent the electors remain children. (…) As political leaders, and only as such, they are temporarily parents, and after being deposed at an election they revert to being children. It is as if it is convenient to a game of parents and children because things work out better that way. In other words, because there are advantages in the parent-child relationship, some of this is retained; but, for this to be possible, a sufficient proportion of individuals need to be grown-up enough not to mind playing at being children.
>
> (Winnicott, 1950/1986, p. 254)

Winnicott's image of the democratic organization is siblings who elect people from their midst to act as temporary parents. The point is not, as Hinshelwood & Winship (2006) appear to argue, that democracy infantilizes the participants. Winnicott underscores that this exercise requires mature citizens who are adult enough to be able to hand authority to an equal. Someone who has not sufficiently worked through their sibling jealousy would prefer any alternative to handing authority to a brother or sister.

Winnicott also notes the tendency to install parental figures on top of democracy, a phenomenon that is particularly pronounced in the United Kingdom, where the House of Commons has a superstructure in the form of the House of Lords, which is only superseded by the Crown, which in turn puts its faith in God. This is far from an exclusive British feature, and many heads of state tend to involve God in their deliberations either when they are facing a crisis or if they have a high degree of inner insecurity (cf. Rothstein & Rothstein, 2006; Kahleelee, 2004).

While Winnicott in his 1950 essay thus regarded maturity as something that gradually develops from identifications with, first, the parents, then smaller groups and ultimately all of society, 20 years later – and a few years after the culmination of the youth rebellion – in *Playing and reality* from 1971, he presents a theory on becoming an adult that places a stronger emphasis on the notion of a breach or confrontation. In this book, he discusses generational change:

> If in the fantasy of early growth, there is contained *death*, then at adolescence there is contained *murder*. (...) Growing up means taking the parents' place. *It really does*. In the unconscious fantasy, growing up is inherently an aggressive act. And the child is now no longer child-size.
>
> (Winnicott, 1971/2005, p. 195)

In addition to the feelings of guilt associated with the fantasy of taking the place of one of the parents, the experience of thus also accepting shared responsibility for all the evils of the world makes the maturation process tough, both for the young people themselves and for the people around them. Winnicott underscores that the parents must survive:

> Parents can help only a little; the best they can do is to *survive*, to survive intact, and without changing colour, without relinquishment of any important principle. That is not to say they may not themselves grow.
>
> (Ibid., p. 196)

If, on the other hand, the parents abdicate, the outcome is grim:

> However, it is different when, as a matter of deliberate policy, the adults hand over responsibility; indeed, to do this can be a kind of letting your children down at a critical moment. In terms of the game, or the life-game, you abdicate just as they come to killing you. Is anyone happy? Certainly not the adolescent, who now becomes the establishment. Lost is all the imaginative activity and striving of immaturity. Rebellion no longer makes sense, and the adolescent who wins too early is caught in his own trap, must turn dictator, and must stand up waiting to be killed – to be killed not by a new generation of his own children but by siblings. Naturally, he seeks to control them.
>
> (Ibid., p. 168)

If the parents abdicate, they confirm the oedipal fantasy that makes the process so difficult for the young person: growing up means taking the father's place in relation to the mother or the mother's place in relation to the father. If the parents stand their ground and survive, the children learn that taking the parents' place means assuming an adult role and being prepared to become parents themselves. They are still their parents' children, but now they are adults and participants on equal terms in democratic society.

Winnicott advocates that adults need to take both themselves and the young persons seriously, engage in confrontations and be ready to be challenged by their ideas, neither abdicating nor positioning themselves as the ones who necessarily know best. This confrontation constitutes what Freud (1905/1953) calls cultural development. When the young generation provokes the older generation, throwing everything they have at them, and the older generation throws everything into defending itself, the outcome is qualified innovation and mutual respect.

III Democracy and boundaries

Winnicott also has some thoughts on the role of geography for democracy. He considers natural geographical borders a key condition for a democracy and in fact gives the sea around the United Kingdom part of the credit for the mature British democracy:

> A state that has no natural frontier cannot relax an active adaptation to neighbours. In one sense, fear *simplifies* the emotional situation, for many (...) become able to identify with the state on the basis of a cohesive reaction to an external persecution threat. This simplification is detrimental, however, to the development towards maturity, which is a difficult thing, involving full acknowledgement essential conflict, and the non-employment of any way out or way round.
>
> (1950/1986, pp. 255–256)

On the one hand, Winnicott claims that natural borders are necessary for developing sufficiently relaxed relations with the neighbour countries; on the other, he argues that the identification with the state or the nation that is crucial for democracy should not be based on the fear that comes from seeing the neighbouring countries as threats. The polarization between in-group and out-group does not lead to mature identification with society. Winnicott goes on to argue that no one can progress further in their societal outlook than they have in their personal development:

> For these reasons we regard with suspicion the use of terms like 'world-citizenship'. Perhaps only a few really great and fairly aged men and

women ever get as far in their own development as to be justified in thinking in such wide terms.

(Ibid., p. 256)

Winnicott's claim that our capacity for democracy depends on our psychological maturity is an important notion. It takes maturity to be able to delegate authority to a peer or a sibling, if even for a limited period, a specific task and within a specific territory. It takes maturity to resist the urge to persecute an out-group. And it takes maturity to identify with the larger group or community while still maintaining a balanced regard for one's own personal interests.

But why does Winnicott stop at identification with the nation and reserve world citizenship for the few and wise? And why does he cling to the United Kingdom's natural borders? He does not present any arguments for why he thinks it has to be that way.

When Denmark voted to join the European Economic Community (now the European Union) the Danish priest, right-wing politician and EU critic Søren Krarup wrote the following, a statement he reiterated in 2006:

> The people are the premise of a popular democracy. But what is the premise of the people? Its political independence. In the nation-state the people have a home, within whose walls it is free to shape its own life, and the existence of the home is the condition for the people to settle its affairs by peaceful means at the ballot box. The national border is the wall of the home. There are doors and windows in the wall, so people can look and travel in and out. The border does not cut the people off from its neighbours and the world around it. But it does give the people the freedom to be itself in certainty and peace.
>
> (Krarup, 2006) [translated for this edition by Dorte H. Silver]

Here, Krarup introduces the metaphor of the house, with the nation-state as the people's home. That is consistent with the national family metaphor, where the nation-state is the fatherland, and we speak our mother tongue. In a sense, Krarup's metaphor is also consistent with systems theory, where a system is perceived as something that engages in cross-border (through doors and windows) interactions and exchanges with its environment.

Kai Sørlander (2011) has offered a rational justification for the universal benefits of democracy:

> Democracy is a rational political system. It requires persons to be citizens. Persons are living beings who have a language and who are capable of acting based on knowledge of the consequences and who can therefore be given a responsibility. Thus, persons are also subject to the requirement of ethical consistency and its political consequences. Democracy, with its

condition of political equity, is the governing form that a community of persons together should strive to build because they are each subject to the requirement of ethical consistency.

(Sørlander, 2011, s. 171) [translated for this edition by Dorte H. Silver]

Sørlander (2011) makes a coherent argument – which one can appreciate without, in my opinion, needing to agree with his points about religion and the superiority of Christianity – that democracy is the best form of government from the point of view of the requirement of ethical consistency. However, in relation to the issue of the boundaries of democracy, he seems to revert to the same fixation on the quasi-biological character of the nation that Winnicott and Krarup are stuck in. He describes borders as a largely practical issue:

> In principle, the requirement of ethical consistency applies to every person. Thus, the ethical obligation that underpins the democratic requirement of political equity knows no borders. In practice, however, a democracy has to have borders. It has to apply to the persons who live within a pre-defined territory. There has to be a clear definition of where the borders are and, thus, who is included and who is not – who is in and who is not. That is a condition for responsible and practically feasible democratic decision-making procedures.
>
> (Sørlander, 2011, p. 174) [translated for this edition by Dorte H. Silver]

All things being equal, it is true that a democracy has to know who the members are, who is eligible to vote and who can stand for election, just as there have to be procedures in places to make sure no one casts their vote more than once – and so forth. But we need an explanation as to why these principles are being held up specifically in relation to the nation-state. After all, they also apply to student councils, grassroots organizations and other democratic entities!

Sørlander continues to posit history, language and geography as practical conditions that do not, seemingly, require further explanation:

> The territory of a specific democracy must be historically determined. It must be linked with the spread of the language. And as an underlying aspect, it must be determined by natural geographic borders. However, in today's political reality, it is mainly determined by political agreements between the different states.
>
> (Sørlander, 2011, p. 174) [translated for this edition by Dorte H. Silver]

There is no compelling logic here, and the idyllic representation of national border drawing is notable (geography, language, agreement). Nation-states are not unrelated to geography and language, but the other determinants are far from romantic. Most borders are the results of wars and subsequent peace treaties – and a small minority of referendums.

Sørlander goes on to explain that it is democratic to leave it to people in other countries to create their own democracies – or dictatorships, if that is the way it has to be. We cannot force people to favour democracy. That would be a contradiction in terms. But where does that leave the requirement of ethical consistency? A historical reflection on the boundaries of democracy may offer an indication.

The struggle for democracy has been waged on several fronts. First, it was against internal unelected absolute rulers such as princes, kings and emperors, who were ousted in favour of democratic republics with or without approved royal candidates. Then followed the struggle for a suitable expansion of the group of citizens who were eligible to vote – from the situation in Denmark where only white male independent business owners of a certain age were enfranchised to the current situation, where the suffrage includes all adult men and women over the age of 18 years regardless of ethnic origin, income level or income source. And finally, there was the struggle against external rulers, such as colonial powers.

Few of the people who conquered the New World ever considered that democracy would apply to the conquered lands as well. The spread of Christianity was one thing; democracy was something else entirely. Thus, Britain was able to build the world's largest colonial empire and still consider itself the seat of the world's oldest living democracy. Native Americans didn't have much of a home left for their people after the European immigrants had taken over their land. Political equity thus depends both on the democracy itself and on its inclusion and exclusion criteria.

What criteria could we apply to inclusion and exclusion, besides Sørlander's above-mentioned suggestions of language and the capacity to understand the consequences of actions or the more or less national-romantic territorial delimitations? One sensible criterion might be responsibility and relevance in relation to the areas for which the democracy is to pass and reinforce laws.

Just as Meyrowitz (1986) argued that the electronic media undermine the classic sociological notion of situations (analogous with the systems concept), which is based on boundaries in the form of brick and mortar, doors and windows, Castells (1996/2000) and others have suggested that globalization has, broadly speaking, eliminated any reliable link between many of the forces that operate in nations and the regime governing the individual nation.

Castells and others underscore that not least due to the electronic media, the world has become a network society that the individual nation-states have little ability to control. The transport of raw materials and waste, CO_2 emissions, mass media and our mutual dependence mediated by the global marketplace are all examples of phenomena that operate on a global basis and has no concern for national borders.

Globalization is providing the practical motivation for developing a new understanding of borders, while the requirement of ethical consistency provides the moral imperative. A nation-state that thinks it can control what is happening within its own national borders is in denial about a great many phenomena like the ostrich burying its head in the sand. However, that is not a compelling argument for making the leap to abolishing the nation concept. Krarup is a contributor to the polarization that is casting the EU and the nation as each other's opposites. Applying the same logic, however, one might just as well posit the nation and the family as mutually exclusive alternatives. Although family, mother tongue, God, king and fatherland are key aspects of the conservative ideology, it is not hard to imagine conflicts where one would have to choose between family and nation. Similarly, there can easily be conflicts between the EU and individual nations.

From a systems psychodynamic perspective (Gould, Stapley & Stein, 2001; Visholm, 1993, 2004c) individuals, families, groups, organizations, nations, regions and so forth can all be regarded as systems with boundaries that, on the one hand, distinguish one system from another and imbue it with identity, while, on the other hand, enable the systems to meet and interact.

Children have no problem handling the notion of being part of several embedded systems: 'I live at number 12, Southampton Street, North Harbour, Copenhagen, Denmark, Europe, the World, the Milky Way Galaxy, the Universe.' By contrast, many more or less adult persons find the concept unsettling and think of embedded systems as mutually exclusive alternatives: you are either a Dane or a European and so forth.

From a reasonable perspective, a democracy should strive, ideally, to include everyone living on this planet – making all of us citizens of the world. A global democracy does not rule out the existence of regions, countries, municipalities, families and so forth. On the contrary, it seems sensible to manage things at the level where it makes most sense. Naturally, the United Nations should not decide what you should have for dinner or whether Denmark should have more schools, but having a global strategy for dealing with climate challenges would be a very sensible approach.

One problem for the global democracy is the lack of an out-group that we could occasionally define ourselves in contrast to as a way of bolstering our sense of community.

Chapter 5

The foreman's ghost – sibling rivalry in self-managing teams

Self-managing teams, problem-driven project teams, co-managing teams and similar groups are all based on ideas that sprang from the group and democracy movement that began in the United States during the interwar years and culminated in the Western world during the 1970s. Self-managing teams have aspects of Lewin's 'democratic atmosphere' and 'democratic leadership', as they contain a progressive element in their insistence on the competency of employees and students as well as an element of manipulation. The company that provided the empirical input to this chapter initially introduced a 'self-management' concept. One Thursday at noon, the team members decided they had done enough work for the week and went home. When they reported back in on Monday morning, the 'self-managing' team had been renamed a 'co-managing' team. The term 'self-managing' signals that no one has external authority over the team, which is not the case; it also has connotations to something that 'runs itself', effortlessly – which is also not the case. Group work in education usually has more to do with actual self-management but lacks leadership to protect the participants against their own brutality, which can often turn group work into a traumatic experience.

This chapter describes the hidden family dynamics in self-managing teams based on a study of the Comtech company.[1] The study was commissioned by TekSam, a collaboration between the trade union CO-industri and the private business and employers' organization the Confederation of Danish Industry (DI), which is tasked with inspiring cooperation committees in industry. Tek-Sam's interest in self-managing teams in industry sprang from pilot studies of the working environment in industry[2] which showed that psychological stress due to role ambiguity was a significantly more frequently occurring phenomenon in industry than in other sectors.

We[3] assumed that role ambiguity was a result of new management approaches in industry and decided to conduct an interview study of a typical company in this regard in order to elaborate on the problems that had been identified in the original questionnaire study. The interview material from Comtech thus sheds light on cooperation and problems among various actors within the company.

The chapter's analysis begins with a definition of the lack of clarity and some reflections on what sort of societal and organizational context problems with role ambiguity spring from. After a presentation of Comtech the chapter offers a psychological analysis drawing on concepts from systems psychodynamics (Gould, Stapley & Stein, 2001; Visholm, 1993, 2004a).

I About role clarity and ambiguity

A role is traditionally defined as a set of expectations for a particular position in an organization (a social system, a team, a society and so forth). A role may, for example, be that of a police officer, a leader, an employee, a coordinator, a feedback provider and so forth. There are certain specific requirements associated with the role of a police officer, for example, defining what a police officer should do in certain situations and what he or she should absolutely not do. However, there is also a certain latitude, where the police officer's personality may influence his or her way of performing the role.

Role ambiguity occurs when the expectations or the description of the individual employee's tasks, mandate and responsibilities in the organization are unclear. Although role ambiguity may lead to psychological stress, it should not be seen purely as a negative feature that is to be avoided. Complete role clarity, in principle, rules out any room for personality, freedom, thinking and creativity, because the actions the employee is supposed to take can only be carried out in one specific way, described in painstaking detail. At the other end of the continuum we find roles with no clarity whatsoever, where the person has no idea what to do, whom to report to and so forth. This contrast illustrates that the optimal answer is neither complete clarity nor the complete absence of clarity but an 'adequate' degree of role clarity.

The presence of role ambiguity can be understood from a historical perspective. In the traditional Weberian or Taylorian organization the roles were clear (cf. Hirschhorn, 1997). The individual employee reported to one superior, and the work itself was structured according to the principle of 'one right way'. Feelings, personality and creativity were not considered relevant aspects of working life. However, this clarity came at the cost of a high degree of rigidity in the organization, which hampered the employees' development, creativity and job satisfaction and also meant that many of the employees' resources were untapped.

Since the Second World War, many ideas have been proposed for creating more flexible organizations where the employees can have influence, suggest new approaches and take responsibility for independent areas of production. Concepts such as self-managing teams, workplace democracy, network organizations, flatter structures, toppled pyramids, borderless organizations and so forth have been put into play as alternatives to the traditional clear but inflexible bureaucracy.

The optimism surrounding the new ideas led to a tendency to idealize the new approaches and the notion that this would resolve problems of authority, gaps in terms of skills, education and talent, professional boundaries, conflicts of interest and challenges related to issues of group loyalty versus loyalty to the company.

As these differences, boundaries and conflict dimensions are not immediately visible in organizational structures, many mistakenly assume they do not exist. They do. The difference is that they can no longer be addressed with reference to an organization diagram with clear roles but often have to be handled in the social and psychological processes that unfold in connection with ongoing work activities (Hirschhorn & Gilmore, 1992).

Generally, stressful role ambiguity is the negative experience or downside of flexible work, development-driven work and the flexible organization. It arises due to a general failure to acknowledge that what makes the work interesting and promotes growth and development is that it involves both risks and opportunities: the risks that come with added responsibility in the form of the possibility of making mistakes, misreading situations, having conflicts, being dependent on others and so forth and the opportunity for great achievements, innovation and, not least, the emotional benefits of being part of a well-functioning team in a successful company.

However, the question is whether companies have found a suitable level of role clarity. A suitable level of role clarity promotes creativity, cooperation, efficiency, openness and well-being and reduces suspicion, paranoia, closed doors, gossip and so forth. When role ambiguity reaches a level where it is perceived as stressful, as is the case in many companies, we might consider whether role ambiguity may also serve as a psychological defence mechanism. Sometimes, ambiguity is preferred if the aspects that the clarity would reveal are unpleasant or scary. That is the underlying working hypothesis of this chapter.

Psychological defence mechanisms are unconscious and serve to dampen or avoid anxiety and unpleasant thoughts and feelings (Visholm, 1993, 2004a). They alter our perception of reality, making it less anxiety-provoking but at the cost of impairing our grasp of reality and interfering with our contact with the task and the people around us. A frequent defence is to reduce complex situations that involve whole persons (whole objects) into simplified situation peopled with good and bad persons: projecting all the bad and good aspects on the others and keeping the good aspects for ourselves. Another common defence in groups and organizations is to make the organization resemble (through transference) a family.

II Co-management at Comtech

We visited Comtech in spring 2004, spending some time talking to four employees from production, Martha, Daria, Jenna and Lena, two heads of production, John and Steve and the shop steward, Ellie. In the following, excerpts from our transcribed audio recordings of these conversations are used to illustrate problems related to role ambiguity. We chose examples that shed light on role ambiguity in general. The material has been anonymized and edited for clarity. After processing the material we went back to Comtech and discussed our findings with key persons at the company.

For a number of years, Comtech had been using various self-managing team formats and were now into their sixth year of using the so-called co-management concept. Most of the participants seemed proud of the concept but also acknowledged the many challenges it involved. We saw Comtech as a company that was organizationally fairly advanced and whose difficulties hold useful lessons for other companies.

Comtech had around 180 hourly paid employees, mainly women. They were organized into 20 teams, divided into five shifts. There were two heads of production. In principle, all the employees were equally responsible for the work in the teams, but over time, certain roles had emerged that the employees took on in turns, for shorter or longer periods of time: coordinator, quality supervisor, machine supervisor and feedback provider. The two heads of production assigned tasks to the teams and were to be called in whenever the teams encountered problems they could not handle on their own.

Thus, on the one hand, the co-management concept had a formal structure that described authority relations and the distribution of labour: who was in charge and responsible for what and who performed which functions. On the other hand, there was an informal culture that had a significant impact on the practical realization of the co-management concept.

One thing everyone agreed on was that it was positive not to have any foremen. If an employee acted too managerial, he or she was soon put in their place, for example with a comment like, 'You think you're the foreman or something?'

On the other hand, everyone acknowledged there were weak and strong employees. There seemed to be several different types of 'strong' employees. Some were very engaged in the co-management process, taking on roles as coordinators or quality supervisors and pushing for the team to meet and make decisions together whenever something needed to be determined or dealt with. Some were 'strong' because they were skilled, fast workers, and some were 'strong' because they were influential via their social networks and their personal demeanour and behaviour. The latter did not speak up much during team meetings, but sometimes they would decide that now it was time to increase the pace or that a particular batch or quota of work should be completed before the break – independent of the group's explicit decision-making processes.

In the interview group, the prevailing views were, on the one hand, that there would always be team members who are not very interested in co-management and who do not have the nerve to speak up in the team and, on the other hand, that there were examples of weak employees growing stronger and of members being placed in the role of coordinator or another key function growing with the task.

The two heads of production felt that the employees were well qualified and had such a good understanding of the overall production process that the heads could easily have taken a month off without any negative impact on production. However, they also noted that the employees drew a distinction between the team and the heads of production, as the team saw it as important to handle certain tasks and situations without involving them.

The shop steward seemed to have been handed and accepted the role of providing the caring aspect of management, and much of her work consisted in consoling employees who were upset or helping to resolve conflicts. The shop steward was the first to deal with these problems; when the problem persisted, the head of production was mobilized. The head did not engage in the conflicts but transferred people to another team if the current team was unable to work things out.

The Law of Jante[4] or personal development

It was a demanding task to be an active participant in the co-management concept. The individual members had to overcome their own anxiety or nervousness, find their own authority, dare to speak up in the team and handle the uncertainty about whether the others would be receptive to their comments or ideas or whether they would be dismissed or even ridiculed. Below, two of the interviewees talk about the potential for personal development in the co-management concept:

JENNA: I think that gave her some ballast and made her stand tall. She's the kind of person who feels that when she comes in to work, she's just supposed to do her job.

MARTHA: It definitely shifted her personal boundaries. She had never ever imagined that she might speak up in a group. She was scared stiff: 'I just can't,' and 'No, I couldn't possibly,' and whatever. But she discovered that she actually did have it in her.

If an employee overcame their nervousness and was backed up by the others, he or she would undergo an important development process. From being an anonymous member with no personal presence in the team, she now became someone who could take on a role, speak up and contribute to the group's performance.

In the interview group there was a consensus that there was another reality at play too: the Law of Jante. Daria had taken on the role of 'flier', that is, the coordinator who oversees which teams have too few or too many employees in a given shift and facilitates temporary transfers to ensure an optimal distribution of work. It is difficult not to see this as a managerial role, as it deals with the distribution of labour among the workers. However, as soon as a role had even a semblance of management or leadership, the employees would shrink back and get themselves into major emotional and verbal difficulties.

DARIA: No, that's not it. It's that I'm worried that people might perceive me as someone who thinks I'm above everyone. So that's why I'm not sure how excited I really am about this role. But I am just sort a hub, if you can put it like it that.

INTERVIEWER: The Law of Jante …

DARIA: Yes, exactly, that's what I'm worried about, that the others will suddenly think or believe I'm, like, 'head of' something. And I'm not. I mean, we're all equal here.

INTERVIEWER: Are you?

LENA: Yes, down here, in production. It's the same in the individual teams, I think. Of course there are strong and weak persons. And suddenly, the roles are just distributed differently. (…) I mean, it's like, you fall into a pecking order, like it is in the animal world, but still, officially, we are all equal.

The employees' fear of taking charge is not without reason. If the others see someone acting 'managerial', the push-back is immediate:

LENA: But you'll often get that reaction of, 'Oh, she put on a bloody cap now,' and she thinks she's better than us. Where that's not the intention at all. I only do it to be helpful.

The interview group clearly struggled to discuss differences and similarities among the employees. The participants in the interview group all seemed torn between their tendency to get engaged and make things work and their fear of being seen as managers. The intention is to make everything work smoothly, and it feels wrong when this is perceived as an attempt to take charge. Management at this level is thus only recognized for its malignant or aggressive qualities. The idea that management might involve being helpful is not what comes to mind.

Formal and informal managers

However, it turned out the employees exercised two different and mutually competitive forms of management. There were the employees who were committed to the co-management concept, had overcome their fear of speaking up in the group and invested their own commitment and emotions in getting the task done by adhering to agreements about group decisions and so forth. And then there were persons and subgroups of strong individuals who occasionally took on a managerial role, not by eliciting support for a suggestion at a team meeting but simply by circumventing the team and its meetings.

JENNA: Well, for example, if you stick your neck out, then the strong and the weak are going to gang up, because the strong will turn their back on you, and then the weak members do it too, because they follow the strong, and then you're completely isolated.

MARTHA: Some time ago, I came in one morning and was ready to start work, and then two others just grabbed some things and began to flow-test some items, and they didn't say anything to the rest of us. That made for a really unpleasant atmosphere, because it was like, 'Hey, what just happened?'

MARTHA: Sometimes, someone will just put on the chieftain's cap, you know, and then they'll just muscle through and decide in a smaller, cohesive group that …

Conflicts of interest and role ambiguity

The shop steward was busy resolving conflicts in the teams. The implementation of a new robot sparked a variety of reactions among the staff.

ELLIE: It's leading to terrible friction. And it means that the ones who are not so strong and the ones who are not so fast are bawled out by the others and get really upset. And the others feel they're entitled, because 'This is our task. We have to go 160 [km] per hour, right.'

The previous year, Comtech was compelled to reduce the staff by about 50%. Until then, the company had seen nothing but progress, but now there were additional competitors on the market, and it was necessary to look at cutting costs, outsourcing to other countries and introducing automation. The layoffs were handled fairly smoothly, but the mood had changed, even if things had improved since then, and some of the people who had been laid off had since been rehired.

The conflict between the toilers and the ones who could not keep up with the pace could be seen as one of the reactions to the uncertainty in a more competitive market. The focus was not on co-management and group discussions. Instead, fear and panic began to spread, and the strong employees tried to make themselves noticed at the cost of the weaker ones. John, one of the heads of production, felt that the situation was very tense:

JOHN: … with everything that's been happening over the past year or so, where the staff was actually reduced by half, there is a strong focus on, 'Hey, where do I stand in comparison to my co-workers?' So sometimes, I've had – well, it's actually that stark sometimes – that someone will come up to me and say, 'John, you are aware, right, that that one, she's kind of slow,' meaning, 'That one, she's slower, at least (…) than I am.' They don't say it in so many words, but that's the message, I'm sure. And the comment to the co-worker sitting next to them: 'Ah, well, at least you're making an effort.' Meaning, unlike that person over there.

The difficulty of managing self-managing teams

The employees spoke of a struggle between the formal and the informal managers in the teams. This reflected the general difficulty concerning authority relations in self-managing teams. After a talk in the team, Martha had accepted the task of training Helga to be a feedback provider. When Martha returned after being away for a few days, another team member had begun to train someone else. The team was not supposed to have more than two feedback providers. When Martha got angry and said that they should have talked to her and Helga first, and that it was wrong of them not to complete Helga's training first, the result was a major conflict in the team.

MARTHA: In the end, we had to involve the heads of production. There was a lot of conflict and a lot of discussions, back and forth. In the end, the other girl was allowed to be the feedback provider anyway, and I was transferred out of the team. It wasn't very pleasant to be there afterwards, because they were angry that I was angry that they hadn't checked first to see if what they were doing was okay.

It is difficult not to see management's decision as undermining the co-management concept. Martha stuck to the co-management rules and stood up for the concept but ended up being transferred out. The informal leaders won the conflict. Thus, the head of production confirmed that the authority rested with the informal leadership.

However, the heads of production felt it was difficult to get close enough to the problems to be able to act on them. One of the problems was a privacy barrier:

STEVE: When you come in as the new guy and begin to ask, 'So, how are things here?', they'll all say, 'Why do you ask? We're fine. We'll handle it, okay!' So we decided to make it official and said that internal problems in a team are solved internally. If they can't sort it out, they can come to Steve or me and say, 'We've done all we could.' 'Fine, if you have done all you could and gone through that process, maybe we have to turn to the heavier tools and say, 'Hey, if there's a conflict between these two persons, then we'll just to transfer someone out.'...

The heads of production also found that the employees behaved well while management was present, while various nasty tactics were employed once they left.

JOHN: If I walk into a room, you could say that I'll simply suppress the conflicts that exist. When I leave, I only hear about it second-hand, right?

STEVE: That makes it difficult to come in as a manager, because it's all plain sailing: 'Everything is fine.' You hear about second-hand, third hand, and that's neither here nor there.

The solution that emerged at Comtech was to have the shop steward handle the more empathetic side of conflict management, while the heads of production handled the practical decisions.

STEVE: As John explained, it's not always the most helpful approach for us to come into the team and attempt to put the lid on an issue. As a first step, it's better to have someone else take the point, to get a better handle on the situation, our shop stewards, for example.

Thus, the management form came to resemble a traditional family, where the mother (the shop steward) does her best to make the children (the employees) get along, and when that is not enough, the father (the head of production) has to step in with the 'heavier' tools.

These stories from Comtech demonstrate several examples of role ambiguity:

1   The power struggle between formal and informal management makes what is expected of the employees ambiguous. Should they follow the formal or the informal leadership?
2   The team's privacy barrier in relation to the head of production and the fact that the head of production respects it makes it unclear whether the employees are expected to adhere consistently to the co-management concept. The head of production also discards the team structure and the co-management concept when things get difficult, and he does not feel that he can rely on his knowledge or that he has the necessary knowledge. Thus, the heads of production do not have a clear understanding of their own management role in managing self-managing teams.
3   Similarly, the employees do not have a clear understanding of what is expected of their role as employees in self-managing teams. They are torn between perceiving themselves as employees rather than managers and perceiving themselves as members of self-managing teams who do have management responsibilities. This ambivalence leads to tension in the individual employee, in the teams and in the organization overall.

One commonality of these forms of role ambiguity is the lack of adequate authority. When the system came under pressure, the co-management concept was discarded, and various types of problems affected the decision-making processes as the team decisions were flouted.

III Role ambiguity and self-managing teams

The interview material does not seem to suggest that the role ambiguity stems from any organizational necessity. It is therefore worth examining whether a psychodynamic interpretation may shed light on the phenomenon.

Psychodynamic processes in hierarchies

In a traditional hierarchical system, each member reports to the manager, for example the foreman, who in turn reports to the head of production, who reports to the CEO. In hierarchical systems we can distinguish between vertical and horizontal relations. The employees' mutual relations are horizontal, while the relations within the chain of command are vertical. In traditional hierarchies, the employees' mutual relations are serial. According to the structure, they can only relate to each other through the manager. The employees perceive each other as equals facing the same authority. The manager is authorized to make decisions about the work, and the employees are supposed to comply with these decisions.

The relation between manager and employees is usually polarized. In many cases, a 'collusion' (Sievers, 1994, p. 64) emerges: a sort of unconscious game between two parties regulated by implicit rules that are never articulated explicitly. The parties focus on their differences and polarize their roles while denying or repressing their common ground. The employees have none of the properties that characterize the manager, and the manager has none of the properties that characterize the employees. In this collusion between manager and employees, the manager manages, and the workers work and also, the workers definitely do not manage, and the manager definitely does not work. No one talks about the fact that the manager is typically an employee too and actually does work, just as the managerial acts that the employees engage in are not described as such. The polarization often expands to the extent that the parties mutually attribute each other a number of negative qualities, while they themselves have a monopoly on good ones.

The employees perceive this psychodynamic distribution of roles as enforced infantilization (ibid.). They feel they are being treated as children, monitored and controlled, as if they are not expected to be able to figure out the slightest thing for themselves. This enforced infantilization places the employees in a position of dependency. They yearn for the good manager who cares about them and is able to turn the workplace into a warm, happy place. Since that obviously does not happen, the manager becomes the object of hate and aggression. Owing to the distribution of power between manager and employees, however, these feelings cannot be expressed explicitly or directly. In the traditional hierarchy, the employees thus harbour strong feelings of hate and aggression towards the manager, feelings which they cannot express. This can lead to one of three possible reactions (ibid.): 1) depression, where the anger is turned inwards, back upon the persons themselves, 2) schizoid withdrawal, shutting off contact to one's own feelings and thus to the task, the other employees and management or 3) rebelliousness, where the aggression is directed outward, preferably at a stand-in for the authoritarian management.

These reactions make the manager's role difficult. It is easy for the manager to see the employees as misbehaving children, to fear attacks and loss of control and to feel dependent and at the mercy of the employees that the manager was supposed to lead. To deal with these feelings of powerlessness, the manager begins to degrade and feel contempt for the employees and is tempted to apply increasingly primitive management methods. The result is a negative spiral, where the manager and the employees gradually encourage each other to resemble their worst images of each other.

To counterbalance these aggressive and hateful relations, the managers and the employees establish seemingly warm and good relations at their respective horizontal levels. While the manager may appear to be false and sadistic, the employees may seem to each other as decent, warm and reliable: 'Here on floor, at least, we're all decent people and we have each other's backs.' Similarly, the manager and his colleague have a great time trading amusing anecdotes about how foolish the employees are, and how competent they themselves are and would be if only the employees were not so unbelievably infantile.

The system thus contains no whole persons – there are only 'the good' and 'the bad'. This polarization rests on such a simplified perception of reality that it blocks people's ability to learn and form new experiences and arrests their personal development. Instead of learning, the participants seek confirmation of their preconceived notions (cf. Olsén & Clausen, 2000). Sievers (1994) assuming that this parent-child pattern dominates traditional working life in Western cultures.

In principle, hierarchies can have an unlimited number of layers. The smallest meaningful unit for analysis – the organizational molecule – according to Jaques (1976) consists of three layers: top, bottom and middle management. In this context, the middle manager can neither be positioned as child or parent. The middle manager was originally a member of the sibling group who attained a special position within the family, was handed and accepted a parental role without being a parent, because the parents have to go away for some time or have left for good (Figure 5.1).

According to Mitchell (2003), siblings inherently feel murderous hate towards one another, even if the parents have told big brother or big sister all sorts of feel-good stories about how wonderful and exciting it will be to have a new little playmate. Having a younger brother or sister initially feels like a threat to the older child's very existence. The child cannot imagine that there is room for two and therefore fears that the new arrival will take his or her place in the family. It is thus an important task for the parents to make sure

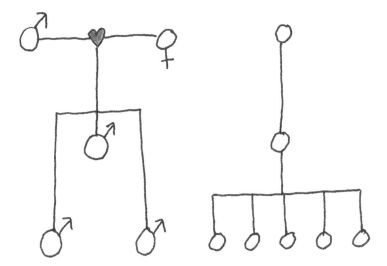

Figure 5.1 Isomorphia: family hierarchy and the organizational molecule.

all the children feel that they have a place in the family. Normally, siblings also develop strong feelings of love, but hate and fear still exist.

When a member of the sibling group takes on a parental role – for example, if the children are going to be home alone while the parents go away – the others experience feelings of jealousy and envy. Initially, they might hope that having a sister or a brother in the role of a parent means now one of their own will be in charge, and the restrictions imposed by the parents will be lifted. However, if the brother or sister seriously embraces the role as parent, the other siblings will feel doubly betrayed – by the parents who abandoned them and by their 'turncoat' sister or brother. The promoted brother or sister increases their distance to the parents to whom the promoted sibling now has privileged access, while the others only have indirect access via the promoted sibling. The other children yearn for the return of the real parents and vehemently hate the substitute.

The psychological image (the transference) of the middle manager is thus that of a traitor who has sucked up to management, betrayed his or her own people for a measly bribe, feels superior to others, thinks he or she excels in skills and talent but in fact only stands out from the group due to his or her weak character, which is open to bribery and flattery. That appears to be the employees' mental image of the typical foreman (Figure 5.2).

However, the bad qualities of the middle manager allow the employees to idealize top management. Since the employees do not necessarily encounter this level in practice, there is room for fantasies, which makes it an excellent place to position the good, caring mother or the strong, decisive and just father.

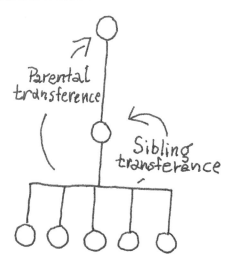

Figure 5.2 Parental and sibling transferences.

Psychodynamic processes in self-managing teams

This leads to some psychologically highly interesting changes in the mutual transferences when the organization changes from a traditional hierarchy to self-managing or co-managing teams (Figure 5.3).

Self-management involves eliminating the level of the foreman and delegating the foreman's authority to the team, which now, as a group, refers to a manager one level above the foreman. While it used to be the manager's job to make the employees work together to get the task done, it is now up to the employees themselves to manage the team. The foreman has suddenly disappeared from the systems, and with the foreman, the 'bad' qualities appear to have vanished too. Now, all that remains in the organization is warm feelings and cooperation, efficiency and job satisfaction (Figure 5.4).

However, it is soon revealed that the foreman's bad qualities were a projection. The bad qualities were not his alone, and suddenly they pop up within the self-managing team, and there it is: the foreman's ghost (Figure 5.5). With the foreman's exit, the collusion between manager and employees collapses. The suppressed and projected qualities return. The employees' idealized self-images fall apart, and they are suddenly confronted with each other's presence as real and whole persons. The focus turns to their mutual differences. If a team member is working too fast or too slow, is too lax or too careful, does not communicate well, is mean, unpleasant and so forth it becomes the team members' common concern. While feelings of anger and aggression were once directed at the manager, they are now turned inward in the team, turning the previously close-knit team into an arena of conflicts and complex emotions.

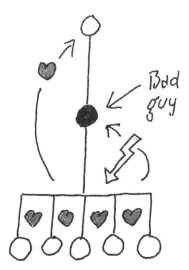

Figure 5.3 The foreman appears to be the bad guy.

Figure 5.4 The utopia of the self-managing team.

To get the task done, the group members' work needs to be coordinated, and there are continuously decisions to be made. In other words, leadership is a necessary component of any collaboration. To make a decision is to choose one alternative over other ones. Any decision negates certain options and thus

Figure 5.5 The return of the foreman's ghost.

contains an aspect of aggression. If we avoid making decisions, thus failing to mobilize the necessary aggressiveness, if we cannot bear to give up one option in favour of another, we will get nothing done and be left frustrated.

When it is necessary to exercise leadership in the group, including making decisions, the person who takes a leadership initiative, however, moves into the foreman role, which is, as we saw, the most hated position in the system. Thus, anyone who takes a leadership initiative will immediately be seen as a foreman, a role that few people, understandably, would want to have. Each of the employees in the self-managing team will thus be torn between the need to achieve something meaningful, get the task done and be seen as competent versus the fear of being cast in the role of foreman and thus become the target of a hate whose intensity is only too familiar. This situation represents a sibling rivalry, where the participants are actually more willing to accept failure, in terms of the task, than they are to hand authority to any single person. The result is an authority vacuum.

The vaguer the organizational structure is – with vague roles, vague leadership and so forth – the more leadership is left to the informal system (cf. Jessen & Hvenegaard, 2001). While formal leadership is visible and clear, informal leadership is more or less invisible. We can challenge formal leadership, hold it accountable, contact it and so forth, while informal leadership generally denies even being leadership and tends to disappear the harder we look for it. When a person takes on a formal leadership role, he or she becomes visible, and with visibility comes vulnerability. The person is open to attack, accountability, seduction and so forth. Informal leadership is less exposed.

At the level of the head of production, on the one hand, there is an awareness that the traditional 'foreman style' (leadership via control) is not tenable in a modern organization (Hirschhorn & Gilmore, 1992). On the other hand, it is difficult to imagine that it is possible to avoid the foreman role and, thus, the aggressive projections associated with it, if one takes on an active and engaged leadership role. To avoid the need to establish close relations with the employees, the heads of production appear to think that since the teams are, after all, self-managing, well, they can be left to their own device. 'Democracy' is used as an excuse to avoid embracing authority. At Comtech, there further seemed to be a notion that the women in production would sometimes act 'crazy', as only women can – a state or behaviour men cannot possibly hope to understand, and which will only get worse if they try to interfere. The heads of production were convinced that they would need to use unreasonably authoritarian methods of coercion and punishment to have any impact – something they were, quite understandably, loath to do.

Even the heads of production were thus worried about ending up in a position where they were seen and treated as promoted siblings. They defended themselves by acknowledging the privacy boundary between leadership and employees and distancing themselves. In effect, they thus contributed to the authority vacuum, as fear drove the employees to bullying, destructive power rivalry and a demoralized struggle for survival.

Generally, vague roles thus act as a common defence mechanism against the foreman figure and its undertones of family dynamics, a promoted sibling. No one dares move into this lonely position and expose themselves to the hate and the contempt it attracts.

IV Leadership via containing

Of course, a company is not, in fact, a family. When family dynamics play out in companies, they do so because we tend to repeat and transfer earlier life experiences to current situations, rendering the unknown and overwhelming familiar and manageable by making it resemble something we are familiar with. The more pressure an organization and its members are under, and the vaguer the workings of the authority relations are, the more tempting it is for people to let go of their sense of reality and to forget the distinction between families and organizations.

That said, there are similarities between families and organizations. Both may be seen as organizations that exist to do a task. In the family, the primary task is to create the right conditions to ensure the age-appropriate development of all its members. In this task, the parents have a leadership role in the family. As part of this role, the parents have to be able to contain the children's anxiety and difficult emotions (Bion, 1962/1984a, 1967/1993). According to Hirschhorn and Gilmore

(1992), it is this leadership principle (leadership via containing) that is called for in postmodern organizations.

The concept of containing was originally developed by Bion, based on the mother-child relationship. When a young child trips or falls on a knee, the parent will typically pick up the child and speak with an emotional engagement that demonstrates that the parent is aware of the child's pain. By expressing understanding for the child's fear and pain, the parent makes sense of the painful experience, and by holding the child, the parent demonstrates that the problem is not so overwhelming that the parent cannot maintain his or her leadership role and remain in control of the situation. Containing thus involves making sense of anxiety-filled experiences and keeping these experiences in realistic proportions. If the parent is unable to contain the child's difficult emotions, the child's anxiety risks spinning out of control.

The signs of demoralization and disorganization in groups that we saw in connection with the layoffs and the increased competition at Comtech clearly reflected a failure to contain the anxiety stemming from the increased competition. When we are unable to talk about what scares us – to contain our anxiety by putting it into words in a conversation – it appears more threatening and demonic and is manifested in mindless, aggressive attacks on others. It takes courage for a leader to make a frightening reality visible to the employees, but the frightening reality is already there; it will only get more terrifying if we think we can make it go away by refusing to talk about it.

The stressful and unconstructive struggle between the informal leaders and the workers taking part in leadership through their involvement in the co-management scheme may have to do with a group of female workers being envious of the young employees' skills and opportunities. By choosing to transfer an employee, management shows that it is incapable of containing the feelings of aggression, that envy is too toxic a feeling to be contained and that flight is the only option when one is dealing with aggressive women. That produces even more anxiety in the system, and any hope that the warring parties might be reconciled around the work task is abandoned.

The strong degree of ambivalence towards leadership among the employees stems from management failing to put sufficient authority behind the co-management concept. When there is a lack of authority in the system, there may be a sudden outburst of destructive sibling jealousy and rivalry.

Paradoxically, self-managing teams and similar structures that involve the employees thus seem to require more leadership and more authority than traditional hierarchical structures. However, what is required is a new type of leadership, not leadership through control and carefully meted-out reward and punishment but leadership via containing.

Notes

1 The company has been anonymized.
2 Using the medium-length questionnaire on psychological working environment from the Denmark's National Institute of Occupational Health, Arbejdsmiljøinstituttet, 2004.
3 Peter Dragsbæk, CO-industri; Niels Sejrsen, DI; the author.
4 The Law of Jante (Danish: *Janteloven*) is a literary element that has been assumed by some to explain the egalitarian nature of Nordic countries. It characterizes not conforming, doing things out of the ordinary, or being personally ambitious as unworthy and inappropriate. The attitudes were first formulated in the form of the ten rules of the Jante Law by the Dano-Norwegian author Aksel Sandemose in his satirical novel *A Fugitive Crosses His Tracks* (*En flyktning krysser sitt spor,* 1933) (Wikipedia).

Chapter 6

Systems psychodynamics and subsystems

Family or organization, tyranny, democracy, crowd, market and panic

Central to group relations thinking, group analysis, psychodynamics and group psychology overall are two key assumptions that, in my opinion, are, if not entirely wrong then too inaccurate to be considered right. The first assumption is that the 'group' or 'system' is a representation of 'the social' sphere and can be seen as a sort of biopsy of society. If you have seven or eight people sitting in a circle, society's main dynamics are presumed to be represented in the group. The second assumption is that any organization is a type of group where, regardless of the type of organization – from an ice cream shop to a shipping company, from a government ministry to a nursing home, from a political party to a trade union, from an angling club to a motorcycle club – the same set of group dynamics plays out. These two assumptions reflect a progressive trend during the 20th century that highlighted the social sphere as superior and the opposite to the individual.

However, these two assumptions operate on much too abstract a level to apply to the important dynamics in play across different social systems. It is not insignificant whether the authority flows from the top down, as it does in families, organizations and tyrannies, or from the bottom up, as it does in democracies, associations and mass movements. It is not insignificant whether the system contains a hierarchy, as organizations, families, democracies, mass movements and tyrannies do, or whether the hierarchy is absent, as it is in a market or during a panic. It is also not insignificant what different mental states and psychological processes are at play in the various systems.

This chapter presents six different types of systems: 1) family or organization, 2) tyranny, 3) democracy, 4) crowd or mass movement, 5) market and 6) panic. Each has its own dynamic, and when it is under pressure it may regress to the dynamics at play in some of the other systems. Although there are commonalities and parallel processes in and among the different systems, a family, for example, that begins to function as a democracy is just as dysfunctional as a democracy that begins to function as a family. Integrating the six different systems in a general psychodynamic systems theory we can examine the interactions and parallel processes among the different systems.

The differentiation of the six systems is derived from a combination of the two dimensions. The first dimension is authorization. Here, a distinction is drawn between where authority is delegated from above, where authority is delegated from the bottom up and without a hierarchy. Are we dealing with a system where authorization flows from the top down, such as families, organizations and tyrannies, or are we dealing with authorization from the bottom up, such as associations and democracies? Or are we dealing with a system without a hierarchy, such as markets and panic situations?

The second dimension is about mental states in systems. This applies, above all, to Bion's distinction between work groups and basic-assumption groups (Bion, 1961). A group can either be in a work group state and approach its task in a rational manner, or it can regress to a basic-assumption group (dependence, fight-flight or pairing). This Bionic distinction can be further elaborated by adding Klein's two positions (Klein, 1946, 1952/1975a), the paranoid-schizoid position and the depressive position. We will also consider Halton's notion of evolutionary creativity (Halton, 2004).

In the paranoid-schizoid position, aspects are viewed as unambiguously good or bad, and feelings are strong. In the depressive position, the thinking is realistic and nuanced, and feelings are complex. Volkan's work (1997, 2004, 2006) on psychological processes in large groups with a history (nations, ethnic groups, religious communities and so forth) contributes to our understanding of mental processes in systems, including his very accurate descriptions of the primitive thinking that emerges when two polarize in relation to each other.

Thus, tyrannies, totalitarian organizations and societies, mass movements and people in a state of panic are characterized as basic-assumption groups fixated in the paranoid-schizoid position. Families, organizations, associations and democracies and markets, when they operate in a work group mode, are in a depressive position. In other words, when families, organizations, democracies and markets function normally, their members are capable of mentalizing (cf. Jørgensen, 2006; Heinskou & Krasnik, 2008; Beck & Heinskou, 2011), while the mentalizing capacity is lost in tyrannies, mass movements and states of panic.

The following first reviews systems psychodynamic thinking as the framework used to categorize the six different social systems. Next, Bion's, Klein's and Volkan's contributions to our understanding of mental states in social are discussed. Finally, the six are presented one by one (Table 6.1).

I Systems psychodynamics

According to open theory (von Bertalanffy, 1968), any open system is existentially dependent on its exchange with the environment through the system's boundaries. In 1963, Kenneth Rice (1963/2001), one of the founders of the Tavistock tradition, made a first attempt at applying open system theory to the study of people and organizations.

Table 6.1 A systems psychodynamics model – six subsystems.

The six subsystems	Basic-assumption group Paranoid-schizoid position	Work group Depressive position Mentalizing
Authorization from the top down	Tyranny and totalitarianism	Family and organization
Authorization from the bottom up	Mass movement	Democracy and associations
No hierarchy	Panic	Market

Systems psychodynamics first of all lets us describe the various systems or contexts an individual is involved in (family, work, friends, football club and so forth), which in turn lets us compare the and map their mutual connections. Second, it enables us to define a context for studying the interaction between conscious and unconscious motives and between regressive and rational behaviours.

In systems psychodynamics (Visholm, 1993, 2004a; Gould, Stapley & Stein, 2001) a social system (and a social situation) is defined by 1) the system's primary task, the purpose of the activity, 2) the boundaries in time and space within which the system's activity unfolds and 3) the persons involved in the activity. Further, a distinction is drawn between a rational and a psychodynamic field within the system. The rational field includes the processes that are motivated by the primary task and which are carried out rationally with a view to completing the task. The rational field also includes a set of formal roles which facilitate the distribution of tasks that make up the system's primary purpose (for example school director, teacher, student, mother, father, son, daughter; consultant, chief nurse, nurse, orderly, psychologist, occupational therapist, physiotherapist, social worker and so forth). These roles are defined in accordance with the primary task, the employment contract and the continuous negotiations and agreements about the specifics of the job or position. In parallel with the rational activity, various informal, unconscious and psychodynamic processes unfold. Human thus also give rise to informal psychodynamic roles that the participants place themselves and each other into, via projective identification processes. These may include, for example, the informal leader, the creative person, the victimized person, the person who is good to talk to, the mediator, the outspoken person, the irreverent person and so forth. These roles spring from both the group's dynamics and the individual participants' personalities.

The rational and the psychodynamic fields interact. If the primary task is hampered, for example by a lack of resources because a large number of employees call in sick, and the demands remain unchanged, the resulting pressure may push the system to regress and resort to defence mechanisms. The reverse also occurs, when a person is so difficult to deal with, due to his or her personality, that this hampers the effort to complete the primary task. The effect is obviously more pronounced if it is one of the leaders who has personality issues (Kernberg, 1998). For example, if the leader is obsessive and paranoid, the focus on control measures and formal procedures can make the organizational flow so rigid that development grinds to a halt. In this case, the psychodynamic factors impact the rational field.

In the psychodynamic field, we further need to distinguish between processes unfolding between the individual and the group and processes unfolding in the group as a whole. The processes between the individual and the group concern what is playing out among the members of the group, the various roles they are given and take on and the conflicts and alliances this gives rise to. Processes in the group as a whole concern the common ground among the members of group, their shared basic assumptions (Bion, 1961), which are less visible to the group members precisely because they are shared.

The concept of the primary task is applied in a basic sense and in a dynamic sense. Defining the primary task of a given system establishes a yardstick or a criterion (or a set of criteria) to be used for evaluating how well the system is functioning. The basic definition of a system's primary task classifies it among other and contributes to the system's identity, seen from the system's own vantage point as well as from the outside. The dynamic primary task is defined as the activity that a given system, at a given time, has to make its top priority if it wants to survive. In many regards, the definition of the primary task is a political process, which means that it may be the result of compromise. Sometimes, the primary tasks of certain may contain subtle internal contradictions. For example, what is the primary task for a human being, a teenager, a family, a group of friends, a school, a prison, a burger joint, a birthday party or a psychiatric hospital? And who decides what is the primary task for whom? However, the fact that it is generally a difficult and complex process to determine the primary task for a given system does not make it any less necessary, as it is impossible to assess and evaluate a system without having a relevant criterion or yardstick.

The exchanges between a given system and its environment (input and output) takes place via the system's boundaries. The boundaries serve both to separate the system from its environment and to connect them. The relationship between the primary task and the boundaries defines the system in relation to other and, thus, define the system's identity. If the boundaries are too permeable the system risks being invaded, dissolving and losing sight of its primary task. If, on the other hand, they are too rigid, the system becomes isolated, loses its identity and, again, dissolves. Leadership or management of the system thus overwhelmingly involves managing the movements passing through the system's boundaries, including regulating input and output, the system's inner workings in relation to these movements and the environmental opportunities and cues the system needs to react to. The system's leadership thus needs to sort through and interpret the information that exists both internally within the system and in the environment and, based on this, determine what initiatives are needed.

When we consider an individual as a system from a psychodynamic perspective, the ego constitutes the system's leadership. The ego operates in the borderland between the outer and the inner world or, in classic Freudian terms, between the id and the superego in the inner world on the one hand and the external reality on the other hand. The ego is responsible for translating inner impulses and needs into action, with due consideration for the current reality, and for initiating appropriate reactions to outside cues.

In larger systems (family, school, workplace and so forth) the boundaries describe the system's geographic localization(s), the amount of time available to the system, the specific distribution of tasks within the system, who is responsible for what, who is authorized to handle what tasks and, finally, who belongs and does not belong in the system.

II Mental states in social systems

Group psychology emerged around the same time as psychoanalysis, and experimental social psychology emerged around the turn of the 20th century. Le Bon's book *The crowd* from 1895 is considered one of the first forays into group psychology. Freud discusses Le Bon's work in his seminal paper from 1921 'Group psychology and the analysis of the ego', but the two scholars agree that the crowd has a primitivizing impact on the individual. This notion, which is only fully unfolded by Bion, also seems to be borne out by experimental social psychology. Early experimental social psychology, which was contemporary with psychoanalysis and group psychology, focused primarily on determining whether individuals perform best on their own or in groups.

Post-war social psychology instead looked at the issue of intergroup tension. The stronger the intergroup polarization, the more the members of both groups are reduced to partial objects, which are characterized as either entirely good or entirely bad. Sherif and Sherif (1969) staged their famous summer camp experiment to demonstrate that personality was insignificant while the objective intergroup situation was the main factor determining the development of intergroup relations. The conclusion to Sherif and Sherif's studies was that if the objective situation between two groups was one of competition for scarce resources, the groups would develop mutual hostility, resort to negative stereotyping, neglect differences between group members and develop positive stereotypes about their own group. If the researchers instead established an objective situation where the groups had to work together to achieve a common goal, a more positive and coop- erative behaviour emerged. Further, they found evidence that individuals in groups differentiate and take on different roles when they are not facing a competing group. When the group's focus shifts from intragroup processes to intergroup processes, the group members adapt to common norms and emphasize commonalities and similarities. These findings have since been borne out by Tajfel's (1982) and Turner's (1982) research, which even seems to demonstrate that in-group or out-group mechanisms may also operate when they are not indicated by the objective situation (Visholm, 2004c).

Klein's positions

Seen from a Kleinian point of view the psychology in these intergroup processes, where group members are seen as either entirely good or entirely bad, from an individual psychological perspective can be seen as primitive defence mechanisms belonging to the paranoid-schizoid position. Klein (1946) views the baby in the paranoid-schizoid position as a being who experiences the world in terms of partial objects that are either entirely good or entirely bad. The mother is not considered as a whole, complex and compound object with both frustrating and gratifying qualities; instead she is split into a good breast and a bad breast. The slightly older child, in the depressive position, realizes that the frustrating mother and the gratifying mother are one and the same person, a whole object. Reality in its compound complexity is acknowledged, and the partial objects are integrated. The child develops feelings of guilt over the hate and the anger he or she previously directed at the bad breast, which turned out to be part of the whole, real mother, and mourns the loss of the illusory, entirely good object. The fear that the mother might be dead or dying initiates creative repairs aimed at recreating a whole, lively mother. Depressive anxiety is associated with the fear that the mother is dying, while the manic defence denies aggression and injury. Throughout life, we alternate between the paranoid-schizoid and the depressive position. Bion (1963; Grinberg et al., 1993) argues that creative thinking relies on this back-and-forth process between splitting (paranoid-schizoid position) and integration (depressive position).

From a Kleinian psychoanalytic perspective, the constructions that are put into play in the crowd situations that Le Bon and Freud observed and in the intergroup situations that experimental social psychology staged thus mark a regressive movement from the depressive to the paranoid-schizoid position.

Klein's distinction between the paranoid-schizoid and the depressive positions and Bion's notion that development and creativity spring from the interaction of these two positions is thus compatible with other observations of processes in social systems. The paranoid-schizoid position represents simplified conceptions of reality and powerful emotions, while the depressive position represents acknowledgement of the complexity of reality and thus mixed feelings and difficult decision-making.[1]

Bion's work group and basic-assumption groups

To expand this discussion further, we may include Bion's group theory. As mentioned earlier, Bion wants to move past the assumption in traditional group and crowd psychology that the individual is rational, while the group or crowd is inherently primitive and regressive. Bion thus disagrees with Le Bon's (1895/2016, p. 69) statement:

> The masses have never thirsted after truth. They turn aside from evidence that is not to their taste, preferring to deify error, if error seduce[s] them. Whoever can supply them with illusions is easily their master; whoever attempts to destroy their illusions is always their victim.

While Freud supports Le Bon's statement, Bion instead defines the work group as follows:

> Every group, however casual, meets to 'do' something; in this activity, according to the capacities of the individuals, they cooperate. (...) Since the activity is geared to a task, it is related to reality, its methods are rational, and, therefore, in however embryonic a form, scientific. Its characteristics are similar to those attributed by Freud (1911) to the ego. This facet of mental activity in a group I have called the Work Group.
> (Bion, 1961/1993, p. 143)

Bion distinguishes between the work group, which pursues its task by rational means (corresponding to the depressive position), and three basic-assumption groups, which have regressed in relation to the task and act as if something other than the task is the task (corresponding to the paranoid-schizoid position). In the dependence group, the group is convinced there is a leader who can provide the group with safety and security. The leader is supposed to do the work, while the members are passive and demanding, as incapable of doing anything on their own as they are of doing anything together. In the fight-flight group the basic assumption is that the group should unquestioningly follow the leader in fighting or fleeing from an external enemy. Differences between members, independent thinking and reflection are perceived as treason; members either bow to the leader or are seen as siding with the enemy. The pairing group labours under the illusion that all problems will be resolved once the group has produced a creative couple to conceive a child, who will eventually rise up to address the problems, a Messiah.

Volkan's large-group psychology

The Turkish-Cypriot psychiatrist and psychoanalyst Vamik Volkan, who in addition to practising psychoanalysis is also involved in active conflict resolution in global hotspots, has made important contributions to our understanding of mental states in organizations (Volkan, 1997, 2004, 2006; Visholm, 2007).

One of the limitations of group psychology – and of much of social psychology – is its ahistorical character and the abstract human beings that it deals with. Much group psychology is designed to uncover universal regularities in the relationship between individual and group and in intergroup relations. The less history and the fewer relations the participants bring with them into the laboratories, the more universal the findings are assumed to be.

That mindset may seem applicable in some regards, but it naturally fails to capture the role of history and relationships in group processes. By studying certain real-life processes in very large groups and the presence of these processes in individuals from an analyst's vantage point, Volkan has deduced a number of common characteristics that demonstrate the significance of relationships and a common history. The real-life large groups that Volkan studied are nations, ethnic groups and religious communities, groups with up to several million members.

While Freud's group psychology focused exclusively on the leader and the crowd or group, Volkan considers just one aspect of the dynamic of large groups. In the tradition initiated by the founder of group psychology, Le Bon, Freud similarly tended to see groups and crowds as purely regressive phenomena, while Volkan agrees with Bion's point that groups, like individuals, can be rational and anchored in reality as well as being regressive and primitive.

A core concept for Volkan is 'the chosen trauma'. For example, the chosen trauma that is so crucial for understanding the tragedies in Bosnia in 1992 and in Kosovo in 1999, according to Volkan, is the Serbian defeat in the Battle of Kosovo in 1389. Even though the leaders on both sides – the Ottoman Sultan Murad I and the Serbian Prince Lazar – were killed, and even though Serbia remained an independent nation for 80 years after the defeat, the Battle of Kosovo has become the chosen trauma that marks the end of a period of Serbian dominance and the beginning of a period when Serbia gradually was swallowed up by the Ottoman Empire.

During certain periods, the figure of Prince Lazar was used to unite the Serbs through a common feeling of being victims and martyrs to the Muslim rulers; at other times, Prince Lazar became the symbol of the Serbian desire to avenge humiliation and loss by reclaiming Kosovo. Although the province was reclaimed from the Ottoman Turks in the late 19th century, Lazar's ghost had not yet been laid to rest. When Communism collapsed, Slobodan Milošević and Radovan Karadžić breathed new life into both the Prince and the Battle of Kosovo, reactivating the six-centuries-old 'memory' of humiliation and the accompanying thirst for revenge.

Milošević gained access to Lazar's remains and had his people carry these remains from village to village, giving political speeches and conducting funeral rites, as if Prince Lazar's death had occurred yesterday. On 28 June 1989, on the 600th anniversary of the Battle of Kosovo, Milošević – with the aid of a helicopter – descended from on high to the historical battlefield. Here he gave a fiery speech establishing powerful associations between Jesus, Lazar and himself and vowed that Islam would never again oppress the Serbs. The reactivated chosen trauma caused the Serbs' sense of time to collapse. Now they knew and felt that the time had come for them to avenge and redress the defeat in the Battle of Kosovo in 1389.

These absurd scenes and the extreme acts of violence that followed rested on three conditions: a chosen trauma that had been kept alive for centuries; a current political situation characterized by uncertainty and frustration; and a leadership with a sense for mobilizing this particular large group.

Like individuals, large groups develop and possess an identity, Volkan argues, in part referring to Erik H. Erikson's work (1959). In contrast to concepts such as personality and character, which view the individual from outside, the concept of identity applies to the individual's subjective self-perception. Identity is the individual's working model for him/herself. Identity is an enduring feeling of being oneself while also sharing essential character aspects with others. A person's identity integrates past, present and future into a coherent continuum of remembered, felt and anticipated existence. An individual with an established core identity thus has a realistic body image, an inner sense of physical coherence, subjective clarity on his or her own gender, a well-internalized conscience and an inner solidarity with his or her group and its ideals. Losing one's core identity is intolerable; it is psychological death.

Volkan is interested in the aspect of the individual's core identity that concerns the 'we' in the 'I'. Like the rest of the core identity, the 'we' is established early in life but also continues to develop into adulthood. In a sense, the 'we' is just as ingrained as the 'I' but it also has connections to events that are considerably older than the individual.

Volkan uses the metaphor of a large tent extending from a central pole to illustrate the notion of large-group identity. Under the canvas, there are individuals in different kinds of clothing marking both their individuality and the group and family connection. The central pole is the leader that currently keeps the large-group identity intact. The canvas is woven with seven threads. Various images and stories that tie qualities and events together with the group and elevate the group at the cost of 'the other group' are important threads.

Of particular significance is the group's chosen glories and traumas. While it is easy to understand the pleasure of identifying with the group's glories, the significance of chosen traumas is more problematic. To escape feelings of shame, humiliation and the lack of courage to resist and to mourn – emotions and self-images that are associated with unprocessed traumas – adults can survive by relating to the child as a victim, a perpetrator or both and place these images of their injured self-images in their offspring. The parents thus unconsciously saddle their children with a 'repairing' task that is really their own but which they failed to accomplish: alleviating shame and humiliation, turning passive endurance into action, taming feelings of aggression and mourning the losses associated with the trauma. The injured self-image and the repairing task are passed on. When these inner object relations are mixed up with more or less nuanced narratives about the group's history as a 'we', the result is emotionally charged unconscious fantasies that may be activated at a group level.

Volkan's reparation concept differs from Klein's. It is not about repairing the injuries one inflicted on the object; instead, it is about repairing oneself to overcome injuries and losses imposed by others. The mature approach is to work through the grief and thus attain liberation, but sometimes the traumas can be so anxiety-provoking that the sufferer is afraid to confront his or her own memories. Hence, the traumas remain unprocessed and wordless, are passed on to the next generation and exist as inhibited vitality and a wordless urge to redress the humiliation by seeking revenge.

The new political phenomenon of heads of state apologizing to large groups that their own large group transgressed against generations ago seems to suggest that these apologies, in acknowledging the existence of wrong-doing and atrocities, can contribute to relief and reconciliation both for the person making the apology and for the recipient.

When large groups come under pressure, for example due to war, terrorist attacks or dictatorship, they tend to regress. Leaders who have a good sense of these processes will be able to bring the group together and mobilize it emotionally by reactivating the chosen traumas. The regression consists mainly in organizing the group's thinking into a sharp splitting: them = bad AND us = good; EITHER 'with us' OR 'against us' and so forth. The next step in the regression process is to mobilize the feelings of hurt and vengeance in all their intensity and, finally, by weakening the group's capacity for reality-testing, to bring about what Volkan calls a time collapse. Historical offences are felt as if they happened yesterday. In a contrasting example, the Norwegian Prime Minister Stoltenberg's response to Anders Breivik's terrorist attack in the summer of 2011 had the effect of resisting the regressive pressure and guiding the national grieving process in a forward direction.

Volkan lists a number of characteristics of regressed large groups, and even if the symbols and narratives that are used in this process to some extent are specific to the particular large group's history and culture, the specific features seem to fade, the deeper the regression goes and the more intensely violent it becomes:

1) Group members lose their individuality. 2) The group rallies blindly around the leader. 3) The group becomes divided into 'good' segments – those who obediently follow the leader – and 'bad' – those perceived to oppose the leader. 4) The group creates a sharp 'us' and 'them' division between itself and 'enemy' (usually neighbouring) groups. 5) The group's shared morality or belief system becomes increasingly absolutist and punitive toward those perceived to be in conflict with it. 6) The group uses extensive 'taking in' (*introjection*) and 'putting out' (*projection*) mechanisms and may experience accompanying mood swings, from shared depressive feelings to collective paranoid expectations. 7) The group feels 'entitled' to do anything to maintain its shared identity. 8) Group members experience increased magical thinking and reality-blurring. 9) The group experiences new cultural phenomena or adopts modified versions of traditional societal customs that are intended to protect the group identity. 10) The groups

chosen traumas and glories are reactivated, resulting in a time collapse. 11) The leadership creates a break in the historical continuity of the group and fills the gap with elements such as: 'new' nationalism, ethnic sentiments, religious fundamentalism or ideology, accompanying 'new' morality, and sometimes a 'new' history of the group purged of unwanted elements. 12) Group begin to experience some of the group's shared symbols as protosymbols. 13) Shared images depict and dehumanize enemy groups with symbols or protosymbols associated with progressively more subhuman traits: demons, insects, germs, human waste. 14) The group experiences geographical or legal boundaries as a 'second skin'. 15) The group focuses on minor differences between itself and enemy groups. 16) The leadership ruins basic trust within the family and creates a new type of family hierarchy and morality that interferes with roles within the family (especially women's roles), with normal childhood development, and with the adolescent passage. 17) Group members become overly concerned with the notion of 'blood' and an associated homogeneous or purified existence. 18) The group engages in behaviours symbolizing purification. 19) Group taste has difficulty differentiating what is beautiful from what is ugly. 20) The group turns its physical environment into a grey-brown, amorphous (symbolically faecal) structure (Volkan, 2004, pp. 60–61).

Regressive large groups are extremely dangerous, and the attacks against members of another large group that the regressed large group perceives as the enemy have a high risk of activating chosen traumas within this other group.

Leadership candidates who have internalized injured selves and reparation tasks will be keen to mobilize the group by activating the chosen trauma. It is thus crucial to create leadership that neither underestimates the potential risks of the situation nor gives in to the regression pressure.

When large groups progress or reverse the regression and move towards a normal work group state, the following signs of normalization may be observed:

1) Preserving individuality and the capacity for compromise without damaging one's integrity; 2) Raising new generations of children with intact basic trust and maintaining existing family structures; 3) Halting the devaluation of women; 4) Re-establishing family and clan ties and forming steady sub-groups (...); 5) Valuing freedom of speech; 6) Just functioning of existing civic institutions (...); 7) Maintaining the ability to question what is moral and beautiful; 8) Separating fantasy from reality and past from present; 9) Wondering about human aspects of the enemy groups and caring about the enemy's physical reality; and 10) Not dividing the world into idealized 'us' and evil 'them'.

(Volkan, 2004, pp. 86–87)

III Draft of an organization psychological model

The following reviews the six subsystems, all of which are recognized as in the systems psychodynamic model. However – and this is my claim – the key psychodynamic characteristics only appear here, at the more concrete level of each of the six subsystems: family or organization, tyranny, democracy, crowd or mass movement, market and panic.

As the subsystems are presented here, they are just models, and as such, are only simplified representations of real-life systems. Most organizations, for example, combine features from democracy and organization. A trade union is a democracy that hires people to manage a bureaucracy. A limited company is a group of owners who employ a team of managers, who establish an organization to pursue the company's task. Mass movements may have a democratic leadership. An organization may be owned by a family and so forth.

Under certain types of pressure, families and organizations may regress into tyranny, mass movement, democracy, panic and, for that matter, markets. Democracies may regress into families, tyrannies, panic and markets, and they may be taken over by a mass movement. A tyranny may be overthrown by a mass movement or by panic and be transformed into a democracy. Mass movements may overcome tyrannies as well as democracies.

First subsystem: family or organization

As mentioned above, families and organizations were originally one and the same, and even though modernity has, generally, separated family and working life, families and organizations have many dynamic aspects in common.

The family is a system that exists to generate wealth for and develop its members and reproduce itself through work and gendered reproduction. The family is a (particular form of) work group, which is anchored in reality and which measures its success on the number and well-being of its members and on the quality and security of its wealth in both the short and long terms. Learning processes thus continuously unfold in the family: on the one hand, children are learning to become adults and to assume the role of parents, and the parents are learning to be parents; on the other hand, work and its immediate evaluation gives rise to its own learning processes, creativity and innovation.

In the family there are two forms of creativity: 1) a competition-oriented form that is about earning recognition from or defeating the Oedipal rivals and which is linked to generational change, and 2) an evolutionary form (Halton, 2004) that is motivated by gratitude, the desire to pass on the goodness one has received. The inner role model of this latter form is the creative couple who mysteriously conceive babies and achieve other amazing feats (Meltzer & Harris Williams, 1988, p. 83).

The family is thus based on the acknowledgement of the gender and generation gap, which also often involves the acknowledgement of someone from the group of siblings being promoted to take over the family system and pair up with someone from another family system, while the others will have to leave the system and pair up with others from other (cf. Wilke). The generational change is associated with the 'murder' of the parents and their survival (Winnicott, 2005), a confrontation that is resolved through the acknowledgement that this is not about taking the parents' place in a literal sense (murdering the father and having children with the mother or murdering the mother and having children with the father) but instead about finding, creating and taking on a parental role with a 'foreign object'. The family thus not only has to acknowledge the limitations of gender and generational differences (men are not women; women are not men; children are not adults; and adults are not children) but also the limitation that makes the family dependent on society: the need to pair up with someone outside the family. In addition to the creative aspect of the DNA combinations of gendered reproduction, the latter requirement also contains the creativity potential that comes from combining culture and experiences from different family systems.

Given the family's reality orientation, its mental state is anchored in the depressive position, which does not prevent regressions to the paranoid-schizoid position, the creative alternation with the paranoid-schizoid position (Ps <-> D) or states of evolutionary creativity. When families regress, it may, for example, involve one or both parents withdrawing from the parental role and the children feeling the need to step up and take over.

Organizations have features in common with families that set them apart from democracies and associations, and they have features in common with democracies that set them apart from families.

The difference between families and organizational hierarchies is that organizational leaders are also, like democratically elected leaders, 'temporary parents'; even though they are appointed from the top down, they have no right to inherit. Like employees, they can be dismissed, demoted and promoted. Organizations also resemble democracies with regard to succession. They are what is known in the group analytic tradition as 'slow-open groups'. Young people who reach voting age enter democracy at one end, while the old and citizens who die before their time leave the system from the other. Inside the system, in principle, the gender and age differences are constants. The same applies to organizations, where people are recruited, promoted, dismissed and retire while the organization persists.

Unlike democracies, associations and hierarchical organizations, individuals and families have a time cycle and a distribution of roles that are tied to biological circumstances. An individual begins at conception, while a family begins when the parents fall in love. The inequality between parents and children establishes an authority relationship, where the parents care for, teach and make decisions for their immature children, who gradually develop and grow up, while the parents grow old. Family relations are not temporary.

There is no way to change the sequence in the group of siblings or to alter who is father, mother, child. Siblings may be temporarily promoted, and the promotion may be revoked when the parents return home, but the traditional generational change cannot be revoked. The modern generational change takes place when grown-up children move away from home, marry and become parents themselves. Death is thus a relevant factor for individuals and families. The individual dies at some point, and the individual family dies when the parents die or divorce. Death becomes bearable if the individual identifies not with him/herself or the family but with the extended family, a 'clan' or 'kin' and the notion of being part of a self-reproducing immortal system.

However, a common feature of the family and the organizational hierarchy is that authority flows from the top down, and that the course of time puts generational change on the agenda. In more traditional psychoanalytic organizational psychology, transference processes in organizations are discussed within the context of the parent-child paradigm (Gabriel & Hirschhorn, 1999) and rarely in terms of the generational change. The concept of the promoted sibling makes it possible to add nuance to this hierarchical dynamic.

A characteristic aspect of these child-parent transference figures is the persistent idealization, whether they are viewed as malign or benign variants. Transferences to middle managers follows a different pattern where envy and contempt are key ingredients. The promoted sibling (middle manager) has been handed the role of parent without actually being a parent and without gaining access to the desired object. He or she is seen as a traitor who sold out for a ridiculously small reward. He or she does not stand out from the other employees due to his or her talent, skill, good personality traits or leadership abilities, only due to his or her flawed character, openness to bribes and receptiveness to flattery. Moreover, he or she in fact stands in the way of the other siblings' (employees') access to the parents (top management). The promoted siblings generate envy, which is expressed as contempt and devaluation. This projection of bad aspects on the promoted sibling leaves only good, warm feelings and a sense of solidarity among the unpromoted siblings (cf. Visholm, 2005a, 2005b, 2005c).

This transference mode seems to characterize many companies in the Western world (Sievers, 1994), where the polarization between leaders and employees often takes the form of collusion (see Chapter 4, Section III), and the atmosphere in the company has features in common with a tyranny. If top management is malignant, the middle manager, as a link in a system of splitting, may be positioned as the hero and attract idealized qualities. However, the thinking here is that the middle manager is a rebel or a protector who, unbeknownst to top management, is really on the employees' side, which is why this transference is about a sibling who is promoted from the bottom up. The rarely found ideal is an organization without splitting, where the pursuit of the common primary task integrates tensions between employees, between leaders and between leaders and employees.

Companies with self- or co-managing groups – with their twofold purpose of avoiding the cost of middle management, and thus getting rid of the 'bad' aspects of the organization, and of making the most of the employees' potential in a way that promotes their personal development – often face major problems. With the middle manager gone, the system of projective identifications in the company changes. The group members suddenly stop being good partial objects, and the bad object – the foreman's ghost – haunts them in the form of conflicts. To resolve these conflicts, someone has to take leadership, but as soon as someone tries to put their oar in, she is rejected with the comment, 'You think you're the foreman, or something?' After that, no one dares take leadership, the conflicts grow, efficiency drops off, the group members grow frustrated, and tensions increase. Management avoids the problem by referring the group to the democratic concept or quickly finds a scapegoat they can transfer out of the group. When the parents rescind the authorization of a particular sibling, the group is faced with an authority vacuum, which may end up being filled with destructive rivalry (Visholm, 2005a, 2005b, 2005c).

Second subsystem: tyranny, totalitarianism

Tyranny may be seen as a failed generational change, where the promoted sibling has killed the parents, failed at being creative in an evolutionary sense and instead devotes his or her energy to either defending him/herself against the other siblings or uniting them to do battle against another group (cf. Winnicott, 1950/1986). The tyrant is married more to a regressive fantasy, such as the planet or the nation, than to a partner who can engage in reproduction. Dictators rarely make appearances as part of a couple. Their omnipotence is aimed at bigger goals than reality can offer, for example world domination in the thousand-year realm.

Tyranny may be established because the parents abdicate, leaving an opening for one of the siblings to step forward, or because the promoted sibling betrays the implicit trust associated with the promotion and either murders the parents or sends them into early retirement. In light of this, the unpromoted siblings cannot possibly acknowledge the promoted sibling, who rules without authorization, and they either join forces to overthrow the tyrant and establish a democracy or are brought together by the tyrant to take on an outside enemy, who is then construed as the legitimation of tyranny.

Tyranny and totalitarianism are fixated in the paranoid-schizoid position. In the paranoid-schizoid position the child moves between two separate mental states; in either state, the child has no awareness of the other state. In one state, the child plays with the fantasy of having created his or her own world, including the mother herself. The fusion between the child and the mother is such that they live and die together. As the mother actually keeps the child content and safe, she supports the illusion of the child's omnipotent creativity until the child is more mature. When the mother is absent, however, a very different mental state takes over, one where the child experiences helplessness, disintegration and fear of being destroyed. The child thus does not perceive the mother as a whole object but instead either as the partial object of 'the good breast', cherished as the protector and provider, or the partial object of 'the bad breast', hated and cursed as an anxiety-generating monster. The lack of contact with reality also implies a denial of suffering and loss, and human decency does not make it onto the agenda (Halton, 2004, p. 108).

Totalitarianism circumvents these varying mental states by projecting the bad and helpless qualities on another group which can then be persecuted, rendered helpless and destroyed. Without this other group, fear of persecution and helplessness threatens to destroy the omnipotence and world domination. Those in power and their own group are the good, omnipotent partial object, the other group is the bad object. The leaders not only offer an explanation for people's problems and difficulties but also promise a straight path to a future free of uncertainty, danger and social anxiety. By projecting all the bad aspects on the other group, the first group rids itself of its guilt and depressive anxiety.

> Thinking becomes simplified into good and bad, black and white, categories. In this way political leaders avert depressive anxieties and guilt.
>
> (Lawrence, 2005, p. 61)

The totalitarian mental state thus does not operate with whole people who are capable of making mistakes and learning from them. In this state, one is unable to see one's own mistakes, quickly rationalizing them as the enemy's fault or positioning the person who points it out as siding with the enemy. Curiosity, thirst for knowledge and desire to learn do not thrive in a totalitarian culture, where the leaders are omnipotent and would therefore have to acknowledge a gap in their omniscience in order to open a door to discovering or learning anything new. Totalitarian are not reality oriented. Instead of a reality-oriented task, an omnipotent regressive utopia is established: a thousand-year realm, world domination. The universe of differences is reduced to a single difference, the difference between good and bad. Gender differences, generational differences and the differences that turn cross-boundary exchanges into creativity only lead to destructive envy.

Gordon Lawrence, an influential senior researcher and consultant within the Tavistock tradition, also sees a tendency towards a totalitarian mentality in the organizations, not least during the heady years before financial crisis. In organizations,

> fears and anxieties about the unpredictable and chaotic environment could become so high in organizations that all the role incumbents, or the majority at least, colluded in excluding any thought that acknowledged

uncertainty or fateful surprises. Such role holders could only make them-selves available for thought and thinking which supports certainty. In such conditions the majority sanctions a form of leadership which is hubristic.

(Lawrence, 1999, p. 46)

This type of organization demands leaders who can put forward unassailable truths, make clear decisions and translate these decisions into efficient actions. The fantasy of these actions is that they will be able to save the organization from uncertainty.

> Preferably these decisions have to be simple, downsizing or re-engineering. Arrogance in the face of death is called for in such leadership by, in fantasy, taking the place of the gods, that is, hubris.
>
> (Ibid.)

Cynicism is a core aspect of totalitarian thinking. A common concept in totalitarian organizations is the notion of 'the game', a cynical power game, and anyone who thinks that can be avoided is cast as being naive. Cynicism is primarily a defensive mechanism, a way to immunize oneself against emotions related to failing and betraying others and being failed and betrayed, whether in relation to love, ideals, the larger vision or justice. Instead of dealing with the pain and the hurt and working through the grief, one puts up a tough front and denies both the painful feelings and the yarning for love, ideals and so forth.

> Any attachment would be futile, according to the cynic. If a human being seeks it out, the reason is weakness and the fear of loneliness and inde-pendence. Compassion, affliction and pain are no part of the cynic's world. He takes emotional paralysis to the extremes, but the ultimate object is to avoid feeling separation anxiety.
>
> (Eiguer, 1999, p. 671)

Herbert Rosenfeld (1988) has developed the concept of 'the inner gang' to describe a figure in narcissistic patients. Here, 'the game' is unfolding unhampered in the inner world.

> The destructive narcissism of these patients appears often highly orga-nized, as if one were dealing with a powerful gang dominated by a leader, who controls all the members of the gang to see that they support one another in making the criminal destructive work more effective and powerful. (...) The main aim seems to be to prevent the weakening of the organization and to control the members of the gang so that they will not desert the destructive organization and join the positive parts of the self or betray the secrets of the gang to the police.
>
> (Rosenfeld, 1988, p. 249)

However, it makes no sense – as Sievers (2007) points out – to regard 'the game' as the result of a random build-up of individual psychopathologies within a given system. Although 'the game' is also a moral issue, it is above all an issue pertaining to organizational regression. An organization where 'the game' has become the key dynamic has lost sight of its primary task and lost touch with reality. Whether the organization was established on a democratic basis or on the basis of private funds, it has regressed into a tyranny (Visholm, 2006a).

Mark Stein has repeatedly analysed the financial crisis from a psychodynamic perspective and identified tendencies towards demoralized gang leadership using the scandal in the Enron energy corporation in 2001 as an example. Stein & Pinto (2011) examined the fatal development in Enron's executive team through the lens of the 'gang' concept and argues that several other large companies had reached in a similarly demoralized state. Enron was probably a particularly eager participant in the manic culture (Stein, 2011) that characterized Western economies from the collapse of Berlin Wall until the housing bubble burst, and the financial crisis emerged as the new reality. A manic culture is characterized by denial, omnipotence, triumphalism and hectic activity, while criticism or warning signs are perceived as provocations and met with even more acts of extreme and mindless risks. The temptation to join the manic culture and take a break from reality cannot be isolated to particularly psychopathic groups in business, and even if these groups may stand out, this particular mania was virtually a national movement.

From a different perspective, Donald Meltzer has offered a very apt characterization of totalitarianism as a mental state. Totalitarianism is closely associated with feelings of being trapped and with the fear of being destroyed:

> In essence we are dealing with the region of psychic reality where the atmosphere of sadism is pervasive and the hierarchic structure of tyranny and submission forebodes violence. For this reason (…) there is only one value: survival. Although the sadism may vary in intensity as one moves along the spectrum from boarding school to concentration camp, the atmosphere of incipient terror is probably little changed, for one meets evidence that the nameless dread consists in being 'thrown away'. (…) It is absolute loneliness in a world of bizarre objects.
>
> (Meltzer, 1992, pp. 91–92)

> One way or another, the outcome is degradation, not only, of course, in behaviour, but more essentially – being less equivocal in concepts and the ability to think as a basis for action. Truth is transformed into anything that cannot be disproved; justice becomes talion plus an increment; all the acts of intimacy change their meaning into techniques of manipulation or dissimulation; loyalty replaces devotion; obedience substitutes for trust; (…) guilt and the yearning for punishment takes the place of regret.

(…) But the degradation of ethics must have already reached fundamentals before the prisoner is ready to don the uniform and degrade another ('don't do it to me; do it to him/her'). The idea of fear of death has lost its descriptive power in this situation. In fact death is longed for and suicidal ruminations hover in the background continually.

(Ibid.)

The inventiveness displayed by the former American Vice President Dick Cheney and his officials when they were coming up with ways to torture the prisoners at the Guantanamo Base without technically subjecting them to torture sprang from this mental state.

To a large extent, totalitarianism creates its own bad object, both as a fantasy and in the real, external world by means of terror and intimidation. Terrorism is a way to control groups and societies that makes it possible to gain power over the whole group by reducing the individual members to specimens. When a bomb kills or injures a random person, in principle, it injures everyone who has certain shared features with the immediate victim. Terrorism can be seen as a behaviouristic teaching method that has become conscious of the role of the public and the media.

When a Danish bomber terrorized the population of Copenhagen during the 1970s, he placed his bombs in telephone booths and sandboxes with notes that began, 'Hello again, little Denmark' and listed the current bomb as no. 1 in series A to let all Danes know that they had to stay away from telephone booths, waste bins and playgrounds (Lunøe & Visholm, 1981, 1982; Visholm, 1993). The attack on the World Trade Center and the Pentagon in 2001 also made it easy to identify the group that was targeted as the bad object.

While terrorism targets groups and relies on forced identification from individual to group, torture targets the individual. Torture is legitimized as a way of eliciting intelligence that may be used to save lives. The value of the intelligence that is obtained through torture is dubious, however. Thus, it has emerged that American agents uncovered evidence that Iraq had weapons of mass-destruction by torturing more or less random individuals. The truth is, apparently, that one can use torture to make anyone say anything by applying enough pressure and offering hints about what it is one wants to hear in order to stop the torture. To an outside observer it seems both costly, unpleasant and superfluous to use torture for this particular form of discourse fabrication, as it is easily possible to fabricate whatever lies are needed by much more comfortable means. Torture thus requires a different explanation, where the hypothesis will have to be that torture is suited to export one's own inner pain, helplessness and insecurity into the bad object in a 'cleansing ritual'.

Terrorism and torture are thus methods for creating, organizing and preserving the bad partial object in order to create, cleanse, organize and preserve the good, omnipotent partial object. Totalitarianism is therefore not just a mental state, a fixation in the paranoid-schizoid position. In reality, and in connection with the relevant technologies, it tends to construct an outer world that matches the inner world.

Totalitarianism makes collusion tempting where two groups mirror each other and exports their own pain, insecurity and helplessness into each other. The antithesis is the depressive position, where both one's own and the other group are construed as being complex and compound whole objects by focusing on similarities and community between the groups and on differences and contrasts internally within each of the groups. The goal is to embrace one's own helplessness, insecurity and pain without denouncing one's competence and strength. That enables us to be in contact with reality, remain curious and engage in learning processes.

Third subsystem: crowd or mass movement

The mass movement is the sibling group, led by a sibling who has been promoted from the bottom up with the goal of attacking the parental authority and unite or fuse with the desired object. This bottom-up promoted sibling has been given and taken on the role of parent without ever having been a parent and without actually gaining access to the desired object. This sibling is regarded as a hero and a saviour and as someone who will bring the other siblings closer to the desired object. He or she is idealized, and the other siblings idealize themselves and each other. He or she expresses open or masked hate of the parental tier and often also of another group outside the family that is seen as threatening to 'take our place', as sinners or as traitors.

As mentioned earlier, Freud tends to see the leader of this crowd as a father figure, while Chasseguet-Smirgel argues that the leader is rather an agent of the fantasy of a return to and a fusion with the primary object. The father represents reality, while the leader is offering illusions:

> In fact, the paternal figure is expelled and excluded from the group as well as the Superego. All this happens as if the group formation itself should constitute the brotherhood's hallucinatory accomplishment of possessing the mother in the regressive manner of primary fusion. However, the leader may exist (we have only to think of the Nazi crowds). In my opinion, he must not be confused with the father: the leader is he who activates the ancient wish of union of the Ego with the Ego Ideal. He is the one who promotes illusion, the one who lures men away (…). From the point of view the leader – as he who promises the union between the Ego and the Ego Ideal – may be compared to the pervert's mother who makes her son believe that there is no need to wait and to grow up in order to take the father's role and possess his mother.
>
> (Chasseguet-Smirgel, 1984/1985a, p. 61)

The members of the group lose their individuality and begin to resemble ants or termites. This loss of personal characteristics is all the more necessary, because it contributes to the homogenization of the group as a whole. It thus allows each member to feel himself to be, not a minute, undifferentiated particle of a vast whole, but, on the contrary, identified with the totality of the group, thereby conferring on himself an omnipotent ego, a colossal body. (...) The group is at one and the same time ego, primary object, and ego ideal finally intermingled.

(Chasseguet-Smirgel, 1985b, p. 85)

In *Crowds and power* (1960/1981), Canetti develops a new theory of the crowd that is, in some regards, connected with Chasseguet-Smirgel's theory. In this theory, the crowd is the fear of being touched reverted to its opposite. Canetti believes that the fear of being touched by the unknown is universal, and that the crowd situation is the only one where this fear is transformed into desire.

Ideally, all are equal there; no distinctions count, not even that of sex. The man pressed against him is the same as himself. He feels him as he feels himself. Suddenly it is as though everything were happening in one and the same body.

(Canetti, 1960/1981, pp. 15–16)

The crowd is created by the 'discharge'. The discharge is the moment when all who belong to the crowd shed their differences and feel equal. People may feel burdened by these differences (rank, status, property). The discharge provides a huge relief from the burden of differences. The resulting equality is a mere illusion, however. Once the crowd disperses the members return to their usual individual roles and differences. Canetti (1960/1981, p. 16) categorizes crowds based on their dominant affect:

1 baiting crowds, united by the goal of hunting or killing an object;
2 flight crowds, united by the goal of escaping a threat;
3 prohibition crowds, united by the goal of refusing to continue doing what they previously did;
4 reversal crowds, united by the goal of either overturning the social order or preparing for a better life in the afterlife;
5 feast crowds.

Chasseguet-Smirgel sees the mature individual as the only alternative to the crowd, and thus regards the crowd as exclusively regressive. Canetti, on the other hand, associates the crowd with certain reality-oriented tasks. Under certain conditions, the strength that the individuals gain by forming a crowd is not just a regressive fantasy but a very real and necessary power, for example to overthrow a tyranny. Crowds necessarily have to operate from the paranoid-schizoid position, since due to their numbers alone, they cannot handle any real degree of complexity. It is not possible to have discussions with nuanced arguments in a crowd (Simmel, 1908/1992). Hence, 1) there has to be an interchange between the depressive and the paranoid-schizoid position, 2) the crowd's political leadership needs to develop simple messages that are appropriate for the crowd's struggle, 3) the leadership has to be able to be the object of idealization without identifying with it, and 4) other organizational forms, such as the public, newspapers and free elections, can also be brought into play.

Chasseguet-Smirgel tends to overlook that creativity and development necessarily must involve a challenge to the law of the father, the status quo of the reality principle – that, in a sense, there can be no development without an aspect of perversion. Gabriel and Hirschhorn (1999) thus define leadership as the ability to engage others in a dream or vision, in something that does not yet exist, but may succeed.

If a crowd succeeds in overthrowing a tyranny the next challenge, of course, is to establish a democracy, which is not an easy task. There are also situations where the crowd fights to destroy a democracy and replace it with a tyranny. Thus, the establishment of tyranny can occur both as regression in a democracy or an organization and via a crowd taking over the 'parental' power. When an anti-democratic mass movement seizes power and sets itself up as a tyranny it changes from mass seduction to mass oppression.

In totalitarian regimes, crowds can often be mobilized by the regime. Here, the interchange between the paranoid-schizoid and the depressive positions has been halted, and the system is fixated in the paranoid-schizoid position. The crowd's discharge has become a regressive source of pleasure, usually associated with expressing hate or persecuting an outside enemy and diverting attention from the regime's tyranny. Or the crowds are mobilized to take part in mass performances, where the colours on the hats people have been assigned and obediently put on as they sit in their numbered seats form a pattern that celebrates the regime, like when ad makers got the pigeons in Piazza San Marco in Venice to place grains in a pattern that spelled out Coca-Cola.

Religious fundamentalism differs from totalitarianism by pursuing a higher goal than the power of the state. Instead of submission to totalitarian rule the goal is direct submission to God. While national totalitarianism enters into a fight-flight mode, religious fundamentalism is positioned as a basic-assumption group for dependence (Krantz, 2006). The common feature is the paranoid-schizoid constellation: the self and the good breast fuse into a single, omnipotent and omniscient object that projects insecurity, helplessness and pain on the bad partial object: the unbelievers, the sinners, the progressives and so forth.

Fourth subsystem: democracy or association

Democracy seems to represent the opposite of the Oedipus complex. Democracy is the assault on the patriarchal family hierarchy: the abolition of kings, squires and parents and all power to the sibling group, liberty, equality, brotherhood. However, the parents have been replaced by the constitution, that is, the rules for the execution of democracy. We may see the constitution as the law of the father and the law of the mother combined: everyone is equal before the law, but the individual is entitled to being who he or she is. The democratic constitution acts in a parental capacity, helping the children sublimate their mutual hate of each other as siblings.

As Winnicott wrote (1950/1986), democracy requires mature participants who have sufficiently worked through their sibling jealousy to accept playing 'a game of parents and children', including promoting a sister or a brother to the temporary role of parent.

The mental states of a democracy vary between the paranoid-schizoid and the depressive position, where the election campaign with its simplified messages and powerful emotions follows the logic of the paranoid-schizoid position, albeit contained by the law of the father and the law of the mother in the form of the various procedures governing the process. However, the depressive position is the basic state of the democracy. Democracy calls for maturity and the readiness to make sacrifices for a higher cause and is highly motivated by guilt and fear of having done harm. Political processes revolve around the art of compromise, which includes complicated legal texts with significant details and thus requires patience and the ability to connect principles to reality.

Reparative creativity is also a characteristic of democracy, that is, the need to repair damage caused by aggression. The depressive position marks the integration of the two mothers in the paranoid-schizoid position into a whole. Reality is acknowledged: the self has conflicted emotions, the mother is a separate person, and there are other people in the world besides me (and mother). The fear of having destroyed the mother (through the aggressive attacks on the breast) initiates reparative creativity.

The mother is either a dying and ruined figure or a repaired and vital figure. Repairing efforts first of all need to transform former into the latter. The depressive state refers to the certainty that the mother is irreparably damaged. If the feelings of guilt over having destroyed the mother become too overwhelming, the response is a manic denial that any damage occurred, and that aggression even exists. The organizational energy is fuelled by feelings of guilt and the acknowledgement that something is amiss.

Democracy involves guilt and a depressive position. Democracy acknowledges that there is both hate and love between people, and that both need to be kept in check. Democracy acknowledges that people are both uninhibited egotists and caring and selfless fellow human beings. The feelings of guilt stem from the murder of the parents, which is atoned through respect for the constitution, the law of the father and the mother. Democracy is always accompanied by tension: can we expect the others to respect the constitution? Will the majority take actions that pose an existential threat to me?

Democracy has a different time structure from the family. Term periods are not long enough for children to be conceived and born and reach maturity. The sped-up generational change makes it difficult for politicians to act with long-sighted reason.

Democracy cannot be creative in an evolutionary sense. The creative parents exist as a constitution, not as living creativity. Democracy's task is to create the conditions for evolutionary creativity. While families and organizations are rooted in reality-oriented tasks and competencies, democracy is rooted in the notion of individual rights and obligations, regardless of competencies. The democratic ideal honours the person or citizen, and a person's capacity for being a democrat is measured on whether he or she is ready to defend, with their life, the right of even the dumbest person to be heard and allowed to vote.

Democracy is hard work. First, a good democrat needs to accept the fact that there is no father and mother who are going to come to the rescue if something goes wrong; in other words, one needs to accept the role of being both one's own father and mother while also accepting the role of the child. Second, one has to love democracy higher than one's own particular party and feel a certain sense of ownership in the democratically elected administration, even when it represents a party or parties one does not sympathize with (Shapiro, 2003).

Fifth subsystem: panic

According to Canetti (1960/1981), panic is the disintegration of the flight crowd. The organizational elements that have been constructed to modify sibling hate break down, and the sibling hate resurfaces. Disasters at sea and other tragic events where many people are assembled under critical circumstances leaves everyone thinking of no one but themselves. The survivors often struggle to live with the memories of the event.

In his book on the Holocaust, Bauman (1989) mentions the example of passengers after an aeroplane crash who felt compelled to perform acts that would normally be considered unacceptable, such as acting openly selfishly at the cost of others and so forth. Couples who have seen each other under these circumstances are more likely to divorce because they cannot escape the thought that the primitive behaviour reflects their spouse's true character – or, conversely, that their spouse thinks that of them. Bauman's point in this context is that it is a normal aspect of human life that people can be driven to unacceptable acts under certain circumstances – and that the explanation lies more in the situations than in a given individual's personality.

In 'Group psychology and the analysis of the ego' (1921/1955b) Freud mentions the story of Judith and Holofernes, where Judith uses her beauty and guile to sneak up on Holofernes, get him drunk and cut off his head. When the Assyrians discover that their commander has lost his head, they flee in wild panic:

> The loss of the leader in some sense or other, the birth of misgivings about him brings on the outbreak of panic, though the danger remains the same; the mutual ties between the members of the group disappear, as a rule, at the same time as the tie with their leader. The group vanishes in dust, like a Prince Rupert's drop when its tail is broken off.
>
> (Freud, 1921/1955b, p. 97)

In a family, this situation is not uncommon in connection with the generational change, when the last surviving parent dies and leaves the sibling group disorganized, allowing greed and envy to flare up in unheard-of behaviour that leaves onlookers shaking their heads in disbelief.

It could be argued that organization is what maintains civilized and task-oriented behaviour and that an organizational collapse suddenly rescinds all the little unspoken psychological contracts (Hirschhorn, 2000) that keep the organization humming along under normal circumstances. Panic has the opposite effect of the market's liberalist ideal. While the marketplace generates wealth, peace and order as long as all the participants simply pursue their own self-interest, the unreflective pursuit of self-interest leads to one's own and others' doom when panic takes hold. When fire broke out in the Boston nightclub the Cocoanut Grove in 1942, about 450 of the 800 to 1,000 guests lost their lives. The mayhem began when an artificial palm tree caught fire:

> From here, the fire spread rapidly through the crowded room. People panicked almost immediately. All the windows had been covered with plywood boards to keep out the light, so there was no escape that way. And the main entrance was a revolving door that soon jammed up with human bodies as the crowd tried to push through from behind. There were several emergency exits towards Piedmont Street and Shawmut Avenue, and even though fire regulations were broken, the guests should have been able to get out. Afterwards, some of the survivors explained that they had taken a moment or two to orient themselves and then easily exited into the street.
>
> (Dahlberg, 2004, p. 146) [translated for this edition by Dorte H. Silver]

Another example is the hoarding of yeast during the national labour strikes in Denmark in 1998, when many people felt the urge to fill up their refrigerators with yeast to prevent starvation due to strike-induced food shortages.

Sixth subsystem: market

In the market, the organization has no hierarchy, and leadership has no leaders. The market renders all things equal, in the sense that the same law of supply and demand applies to everyone. Market-related inequality, as Marx correctly pointed out, stems from trade in one particular commodity, labour. Apart from that, the market is a hierarchical organization. The ratio of supply and demand is the market's impersonal authority, which gives the market the appearance of being free. Adam Smith (1776) wrote in *The wealth of nations* about the 'invisible hand', the market mechanism, that distributes resources and regulates the economy in a manner that is as well-ordered and beautiful as if done by an invisible hand.

An effective market requires certain basic conditions. Not least, it has been protected against the use of violence or coercion and against agreements that undermine free price formation. In the market, competition is the prevailing regulation principle. For many transactions, the market mechanisms are efficient and rational. The market could be seen as a form of organized panic; in both cases, it is each person to themselves, but while panic only leads to losers, or at least far more losers than necessary, the market produces only winners, at least according to classic liberalist philosophy.

Note

1 Britton (1998) argues that working through the Oedipus complex is similar to working through the depressive position, while Halton (2004) develops a kind of third position: the evolutionary creativity associated with the notion of the creative couple.

Chapter 7

Gender

I Hierarchy and transference

In the first section of this chapter, the focus is on transference dynamics in organizations between the employees, middle managers and top management and between men and women in these various positions. The concept of transference stems from psychoanalysis and refers to a phenomenon where the analysand instead of associating freely, as he or she has been instructed to do, begins to behave towards the analyst as if he or she were the analysand's father, mother or sibling, that is, with feelings of hate, infatuation, betrayal and so forth (Freud, 1914/1958). Transference occurs when the memory has become inactivated due to repression. This causes the person to repeat certain patterns in the interaction that may be traced back, through analysis, to conflict situations earlier in life. In romantic relationships the partners will often push each other into certain roles, which turn out to resemble parental or sibling roles. Thus, we person transfer scenes with significant figures from our own past on our shared life 'here and now'.

In organizations, people come in bringing their individual past, experiences, memories, repressions and transference patterns with them. These are then often mixed together to form more general patterns that contain both something shared and something individual, something from the past and something from the present. It is worth noting that individual patterns of repetition may combine with group processes to be used as fuel for current conflicts and tensions. Even though transferences represent the past interfering with the present, we cannot always assume that they necessarily contribute negatively to the organization's task achievement. As Kernberg (1998) pointed out, it is beneficial for a leader to show a healthy degree of narcissism, meaning that he or she has sufficient self-love to bear not being loved by the employees for a time. A leader who depends on the employees' love will be incapable of leading. The same logic applies to so-called healthy paranoia: a certain anticipatory suspicion and caution is helpful for a leader, since he or she cannot expect everyone to have only good intentions in relation to the leader and the organization – certainly not in the competitive environment that characterizes most organizations today. A dash of idealization directed at the upper and lower levels in the organization can contribute to an energized and engaging atmosphere, but excessive idealization can be lethal. Fraher (2005) points out that the idealization of airline captains is a significant cause in many aircraft accidents and crashes. Excessive idealization leads to the belief that the leader is infallible, even when his or her actions or orders put the team or the organization on a disaster course.

1 Transference in hierarchies

Parents are top executives. They have a creative reproductive capacity. From an organizational point of view, there is no role that would actually qualify as a top executive. Any leader answers to a higher entity, such as a board, the market and so forth. In a sense, only God answers to no one.

In the unconscious fantasy, there is no differentiated, formal and desexualized hierarchy with roles that are filled out by emotionally neutral functionaries with no personality, memory or desire. In the unconscious fantasy, organizations are royal families in kingdoms. In the unconscious fantasy, a top executive is a king who is able to be creative together with a queen, or a queen who is able to be creative with her king, whether the kingdom is a playhouse in the garden, an upper secondary school, a company or a country (cf. Winnicott, 1971/2005, p. 195).

As discussed above, different transference figures are activated when we face top executives and middle managers, respectively. We tend to idealize and admire top executives (Gabriel & Hirschhorn, 1999) and to devalue and feel contempt for middle managers. Transferences on top executives draw on mother and father figures and the fantasy of the creative couple (Meltzer & Williams, 1988; Halton, 2004), while transferences on middle managers draw on our relationship to the parentally promoted sibling (Visholm, 2005a, 2005b, 2006a, 2006b). If the middle manager acts out an idealized role, he or she is the leader of the rebellion against the evil top management and is thus being promoted from the bottom up (ibid.).

In industrial workplaces there is often a big distance between the top executive and the workers on the floor. While the top executive is seen either as smart, courageous and fearless or as smart, evil and selfish, the foreman is seen as someone who thinks he is smart but is in fact often stupid. In hospitals, the consultant and the chief nurse are often idealized as persons who are kind to the staff as well as to the sick and the infirm, while management is seen as self-promoting arrogant bean counters who only care about their spreadsheets.

When we add gender and sexuality to the analytical categories, the parents become fathers or husbands and mothers or wives, while the children become daughters or sisters and sons or brothers – that is, the leader becomes the father or mother figure, while the middle managers become sisters or brothers.

Gabriel and Hirschhorn (1999) have collected stories about top executives from student interns, who were asked to write about their experiences in the workplace. Below, Anna describes her most precious experiences during the internship and her meeting with her top executive:

Anna's story: the most precious experience of my placement
As the manager was extremely busy for days and days, I was becoming even more obsessed with the idea that I had to talk to her and ask her to reveal all the secrets that had guided her to success. Finally one afternoon she was free and pleased to talk to me. (...) We discussed a lot of things, including managerial concepts and attitudes.

The first issue was that of managerial style, in particular the ways in which a manager imposes him or herself on his or her subordinates. Can one win the trust of others by fear or by personal respect? The answer was respect ...

A good manager must also be accessible to his or her subordinates in both business and personal terms. People are indeed the most important issue within the organization and the art of handling them should be one of the major abilities a manager should be endowed with. Nobody starts his or her career as a manager. And if this is the case, they are bound to fail. Only by understanding and considering the position of a subordinate – this is by taking his or her place at least once – can the management of the people and the department be fair and effective.

The discussion continued for a long time and all the issues were mainly connected with the human aspect of the organization. My satisfaction from listening to my manager talk about these issues was indescribable. All these theories I had seen applied in our department with great success were now confirmed by my manager, a person whom I respect and admire enormously. I consider myself very lucky to have worked as a subordinate for this particular manager. I hope that one day I will have the chance to practise all that I have learnt and I am still learning, becoming a successful manager.

(Gabriel & Hirschhorn, 1999, p. 148)

If we were to characterize Anna's experience of her leader here, idealization is the first feature that stands out, with identification as the next.

Anna speaks in almost religious terms, such as 'obsessed', 'precious', 'indescribable' and 'respect and admire enormously'. She appreciates ordinary statements as insights of the highest value. The meeting is almost an epiphany to the young intern. The values Anna focuses on are within the register of accessibility, understanding of the employees, human leadership and so forth. Anna's relationship is one of identification from an oedipal perspective; once she becomes a leader, she too will show this kind of understanding towards her employees. The image that emerges is one of a daughter-mother transference on an employee–top-executive relationship.

Steve's story below deals with an employee-manager relationship, where the idealization of the manager suddenly turns into its opposite. Steve and his supervisor, McKie, work in a section of the company DACRO, which is headquartered in the United States. McKie is the head of CAD, a department within DACRO's branch in the United Kingdom.

> Steve's story: the day I lost faith in Mike McKie
> Initially, I had a lot of time and respect for McKie. He was (in my mind) an unsuccessful [sic] executive who would in time turn CAD around by adhering to his principles and 'sticking it out'. He was very much a 'people' manager with a high profile – always encouraging, and seeing the silver lining in every cloud. All my preconceptions were shattered by the events of and around December 9. The way McKie and his management team acquiesced to Kellner's announcement was spineless. Why didn't McKie have the guts to continue with his strategy for the UK? The sudden change in vision and direction was detrimental to the division's morale and devastating on McKie's authority. Kellner had made the call and McKie had jumped. During the weeks preceding December 9, McKie frequently scurried off to Boston, presumably to ingratiate himself with US senior management (this only served to alienate him further from his UK workforce). I completely lost faith in his authority because it became so second-hand in my eyes. I also experienced a feeling of vulnerability as an employee. The security that a strong management provides had been removed – the UK management team appeared to lack the guts to lead.
> (Gabriel & Hirschhorn, 1999, pp. 151–152)

Steve's experience with his leader is predominantly characterized by disappointment. This disappointment is based on his idealization of the leader that is just as profound as Anna's. Steve is disillusioned, but he does not seem to realize that the basis of this disappointment is his idealizing transferences. He is disappointed that McKie fails to live up to his unrealistic fantasies, rather than being relieved to discover that McKie is a human being in a chain of command where he, like everybody else, has to execute the decisions that are made higher up the chain. Steve almost appears to have perceived McKie as a father figure, as someone who was actually in charge; then he discovers that McKie is really just a promoted sibling, who has been talking a big game but is put in his place when the real father from the United States shows up.

Steve's transference revolves around masculine character traits. Although McKie is a 'people' manager, like Anna's supervisor, the image comes through in concepts and metaphors such as 'guts', 'spine', 'demigods', 'strength' and so forth. (Gabriel & Hirschhorn, 1999, p. 152). It is also interesting to note the nurture aspect when Steve says that he no longer feels the sense of security provided by strong leadership. This drama of struggle and aggression is the antithesis of the qualities Anna is focused on.

Father transferences and mother transferences

Based on an extensive data material, Gabriel and Hirschhorn (1999) have described typical transferences on top executives and categorized these transference patterns along four axes. Each axis contains a plus and a minus variant. The first two have traditional maternal connotations, while the latter two have traditional paternal ones.

MOTHER TRANSFERENCES

1 Caring versus persecution
   This axis is about caring, recognition and support. In a positive variant, this leader resembles the pre-oedipal mother, while the reverse of this fantasy is the leader who is indifferent to the plight of his or her subordinates and who may even be an axeman, willing to sacrifice them in order to achieve his or her ambition.
2 Accessibility versus aloofness
   The second axis pertains to accessibility, where one variant is that the leader is perceived as someone who can be seen and heard, even if his or her appearances constitute special occasions. Conversely, the leader is someone who is mysterious and aloof, distant and inscrutable.

FATHER TRANSFERENCES

3 Impotence versus omnipotence
   The third axis is about omnipotence. The positive variant is a leader who is omnipotent, unafraid and capable of anything, perhaps even omniscient and able to read the minds of his or her subordinates and recognize true loyalty from flattery. The alternative variant is a leader who is externally driven, afraid and fallible.
4 Legitimate claim to power versus impostor
   The fourth and final axis is about whether the leader's claim to power is legitimate or whether the leader is an impostor, someone who has usurped power and whose claims are fraudulent.
                              (Gabriel & Hirschhorn, 1999, p. 155)

However, the transference dimensions increase in complexity when we include gender differences between the individuals making the transferences – the daughters and sons. What transferences would Anna's leader have activated in Steve, and would Anna have been just as disappointed with McKie as Steve was?

Top-executive transferences between people of the same gender are based on identification, according to the oedipal model. One has to oust the same-gender parent by becoming like him or her – and a little bit better. In top-executive transferences between different genders, the typical pattern is not identification but object love.

Transferences on top executives, however, not only draw on the phallic or oedipal phase. Different situations with varying degrees of pressure on organizations, leaders and/or employees draw on scenes from a variety of regressive registers. The more omnipotent a leader appears, the more the fearful subordinate will feel as a helpless child.

Many kinds of leadership in families – many kinds of transference in organizations

If we consider a family from a developmental perspective, from the parents' first encounter until death do they part, we may see it as a catalogue of many different leadership relations, relations that the individual is a part of and relations that he or she may have observed from outside. Children can observe leadership and decision-making practices within the parental couple, who, conversely, can observe who decides what, and how, in the sibling group. Female leadership is also evident in the mother-infant relationship, where the infant experiences both the feeling of omnipotence when he or she fuses with the mother, and total impotence, when the infant is hungry, and the mother is absent. The mother-infant relationship is probably the most intense leader-employee relationship, since the mother decides whether the child lives in a state of bliss or suffers unimaginable dread. The infant has such limited knowledge that he or she has no chance to understand, see through or predict the mother's reactions. Parents may feel the same way about the child, as illustrated by the term 'His Majesty the Baby', which reflects that the notion of the leader's near unlimited power, options and choices is an illusion.

It is difficult to overstate the power that the image of the primordial mother represents. As the most natural thing in the world, she rules over life and death, joy and pleasure, terrifying anxiety and persecution. Powerful leaders do not need to raise their voice or use physical coercion; they have men with weapons and tools to do the work for them. Lucy Kellaway of the *Financial Times*, who for many years wrote a weekly column on corporate culture, finds powerful women scarier than powerful men. Madonna is mentioned as an example:

> [Madonna] has just released a new X-rated video in which she grinds against the wall in bondage gear and lords it over a band of gyrating black men.
>
> (Kellaway, 2012, p. 16)

Female leaders are also big sisters who are busy mothering their younger siblings and deciding what is hot, and what is not, in the girl group.

The notion that big strong men are more powerful only holds true under certain circumstances. Many smaller men with limited muscle mass wield significant influence and have access to substantial economic resources.

Male leaders are fathers who keep burglars and wild beasts away from house and toss the little ones into the air to catch them again as well as men under pressure who cannot make ends meet or are eaten up by their envy of the neighbour's car or the colleague's promotion. They are also sadistic big brothers, who are well-behaved angels when the parents are around and otherwise torment their younger siblings and threaten to cut off their ears if they tell.

There is a great deal of leadership being performed in families. Our experiences from the family setting, including experiences that have not turned to memories but live on as transferences in the authority relations we encounter throughout our lives, influence how we perceive various situations and relationships and thus how we act in them.

This complexity also influences what we reply when someone asks us how we feel about male and female leadership. The reason why it is difficult to reach any convincing conclusions with regard to male versus female leadership is not necessarily because there are no major differences between men and women; the more likely reason is the high degree of *variation* within the same gender and the fact that there are several *different* male and leadership figures. The notions and transference figures that are activated when the issue of male versus female leadership is discussed brings up a variety of leadership images, both good and more traumatic ones, depending on the context and on the speaker's personal experiences. We should also assume an influence from the social context the person is in when someone asks them about male versus female leadership – thus, a given individual may have different and mutually contradictory opinions, depending on whether they are on their own in a same-gender group or a mixed group, whether the supervisor is present and so forth. That does not necessarily mean that the person is a coward or that their personality is disintegrating. It may simply be that different situations call up different scenes from memory.

Top-down transferences

When the aspiring top executive takes on the role for real, he or she either comes into contact with his or her inner creative couple, finds a way somehow to engage with another person or realizes that there is no 'better half' in the office landscape, and, consequently, discovers that it is lonely at the top.

There may be several different motives involved in the desire to be a leader. There may be oedipal motives, such as outperforming the father, the mother or various sisters and brothers, or there may be more perverse motives, such as amassing power in order to cover up inner flaws and shortcomings. Top executives often have very complicated motives for their engagement (Binney, Wilke & Williams, 2003; Hirschhorn, 2001).

The transition from pursuing a leadership position to actually becoming a leader is an interesting aspect of the psychodynamic of leadership. It marks a moment when dream confronts reality. There will often have been many notions, fantasies, thoughts and dreams about what it would be like to finally achieve the goal. Usually, reality is both more and less. It is disappointing to discover that one's inner world does not change. The person may still feel insecure and even powerless at times, which is disconcerting, now that the leadership position has in fact been attained. On the other hand, it can also be surprising to discover the dramatic effect of one's voice on the employees. The leadership position activates the employees' transference. The altered relationship is real, however, not just a transference fantasy, and the new leader will often have to mourn the loss of the former collegial relationships.

If a person (X) has suddenly become a leader and acquired significant power, there is no saying what he or she might do, or so the employees' emotional reasoning seems to be. For the leader him/herself, this magical transformation is notably absent. X is still X. Over time, however, the leader may be caught up in these transferences and come to identify with them.

If the top executive has made it safely through the midlife crisis (Jaques, 1965/1990) and is motivated by evolutionary creativity (Halton, 2004), the employees represent the leader's children, who carry on, also after the parents have had their time. The leader takes care of the employees and imagines that he or she will live on after death in their consciousness and work. If the leader has not worked through his or her midlife crisis, the envy from the younger members of the organization and the fear of their oedipal impulses – whose intensity the leader remembers from his or her own impulses towards his or her parental figures – may lead to a vindictive leadership style.

A top executive who is frustrated, for one reason or another, may easily be tempted into identifying with a love transference from a younger ambitious employee of the opposite sex and imagine becoming truly, or again, part of a creative couple.

It can be very difficult to withdraw from a leadership role, and the leader often has mixed feelings about it. That can make it difficult for the organization and for the new leader, who is not suitably authorized and is continuously undermined by the former leader (who may, for example, be promoted to chairman of the board).

In a family business, the core conflict is that between parents and children. The parents have mixed feelings: if the successor is well qualified and ready to do what needs to be done, they may feel defeated and feel that they have been marginalized. That can lead to envy and feelings of vengeance, unless the parent can turn the scenario around and feel proud of being the parent of this amazing child. However, if the child is only amazing in the eyes of the parents, the organization is facing major difficulties.

The middle manager's transferences

The middle manager will often feel torn between top management and the employees. In high-stress situations, top management will perceive the employees as being more or less psychotic and out of touch with the task and with reality, while the employees, for their part, have exactly the same perception of top management. The middle manager's job is to put both parties in touch with each other and with reality. The regressive temptation is to abandon reality and simply side with one party over the other. Should the middle manager identify with the parents and become the target of hate from the siblings who feel let down and betrayed, or side with the siblings and risk being demoted? Is it possible to find another group to be the target of hate, or can the aggression be sublimated into a focused effort to complete the task? The middle manager may be all too aware that he or she is not much better than the other siblings. To ensure an appropriate distance it may be tempting either to infantilize the other siblings or, conversely, to pretend the difference does not matter.

Examining transference scenes in situations

Regardless of the situation, it will be meaningful to know the different factors that together contribute to the web of mutual transferences. The transferences are the individual actors' unprocessed conflict scenes from the past, which are projected or transferred onto situations here and now. When the behaviour people display in the here-and-now situation seems odd and out of step with the task, it may be helpful to examine whether scenes from the past are interfering with the present. Such an examination may take a variety of forms, including individual coaching, a group consultation, the leader's self-reflection and so forth. The relevant questions to address are 1) which positions in the described three-tier hierarchy the transferences spring from, 2) which gender is at either end of the transference relationship, 3) whether the transference is oedipal or more primitive, 4) what sort of exchange there is between the two parties in the relationship, that is, whether the person who is the subject of the transference identifies with it, objects to it or what his or her response is.

2 The role of the coach

If a top executive feels that it is lonely at the top, he or she may reach out to a coach. The fantasy underlying the desire to engage with a coach or a consultant and the anticipated outcome is to find the other half of the creative couple, the person who has what the leader needs to produce a 'baby'. The coach's well-defined office attracts projections and fantasies about the parents' bedroom. The coach or consultant represents the leader's split-off parts of the creative couple.

Ariane Mnouchkine's (1978) film about the great French playwright Molière has a very elegant way of illustrating that it is really Molière and his wife and partner, Madeleine Béjart, who are the creative couple, more than it is Molière alone who comes up with the plots in brilliant isolation. In the scene in question, things have been going downhill for Molière for some time. He has grown old, and after dumping his wife in favour a young actress (Madeleine Béjart's daughter from a previous relationship), he has become impotent, which has not escaped the attention of local satirists. His troupe desperately needs a new play to perform. Molière is pacing the floor, tearing out his hair. Madeleine suggests that he take a scene from *this* play and combine it with something from *that* play, and soon we see Molière light up and get into the creative process. The scene depicts their original collaboration but also reveals that Molière is probably unaware of Madeleine Béjart's role in the process.

Many leaders identify with one of the poles in the in the much regarded misleading polarity between task-oriented and people-oriented leadership. It is wrong to represent task and people as each other's opposites. When a person is committed to their role and works on the task, he or she relates to a 'third' pole, so it really is not all about feelings and mutual sympathies or antipathies. As Elizabeth Menzies-Lyth puts it:

> Don't nurture people, nurture their primary task! Then you nurture people.
> (Menzies-Lyth in Gustavsen & Magnusson, 1996, p. 113)

Employees are not being paid to like or dislike each other. They are being paid to get the job done. If they are able to work together on the task, they will often develop warm feelings for each other (Hirschhorn, 1988).

However, we tend to attribute the different genders different, specific behaviour patterns and preferences. If the situation calls for action with an obvious aggressive content, such as cutbacks and downsizing, the leader is likely to think that the best choice is a male consultant from a company that does not involve psychologists. Just as Lady Macbeth needs to call on the spirits to steel her will as she plots the murder of Duncan, King of Scots. Her gender is standing in the way of her capacity for cruelty:

> The raven himself is hoarse that croaks the fatal entrance of Duncan under my battlements. Come, come, you spirits that tend on mortal thoughts, unsex me here; and fill me, from the crown to the toe top-full of direst cruelty.
> (Shakespeare, 1606/2005, p. 974)

Task focus, aggression and cruelty seem to have masculine connotations, while the human resources function and psychological issues seem to have feminine connotations and are called into service when the leader sees a need for reparation and healing or when the budget and the schedule seem to allow for some nurture.

In the master's programme in organizational psychology at Roskilde University (MPO/RUC) in Denmark, psychology is often positioned as a feminine field, while economics and strategy are positioned as male topics. Thus, men who choose the MPO programme have a legitimacy issue, as do the women who opt to take an MBA. These students need to be prepared to justify their choice, something women enrolled in MPO and men pursuing an MBA do not have to do.

Although these polarizations lack any rational basis, many men and women are still reluctant to put their gender identities on the line.

3 Vision and commitment

Visions are the domain of parents and top executives. Anyone who has a vision also has an interest in leadership, and anyone wishing to lead needs to be able to tap into a vision. Visionary leaders are driven by gratitude, the desire to pass on the goodness they have received. The time perspective associated with a vision may extend into a future that lies beyond the leader's lifespan, into a time when the leader only exists in the form of ideas or genetic material in his or her successors. The narcissistic aspect of the vision is that it often exceeds the leader's own time horizon and that the realization of the vision, in this sense, gives the leader an afterlife.

Totalitarian visions are driven by envy and the desire to take revenge in order to make up for a loss or a violation that can be repaired through a vision of 'world domination'. The vision is an attack on the parental couple or on a democratic constitution that represents the parental couple, performed by a group of siblings who are led by a sister or a brother who has been promoted from the bottom up.

The concepts of 'vision' and 'mission' have strong associative connections to the *Bible* and Christianity. The notion of a 'mission' can be compared to what the Tavistock tradition calls the primary task, that is, what the company needs to do to survive or be meaningful in relation to its surroundings, while 'vision' is a figure with a more dream-like, passionate and future-oriented character. Visions are about finding the Promised Land or Paradise. It is about coming home to a place where beauty and pleasure reign, and where there is nothing to fear.

Vision means something seen in a dream, a revelation. The world religions contain many of these visions, where God appears in a bright, radiant light, presents an idea to the chosen person, who takes the idea to heart and gets that special light in their eyes whenever they present the idea to their growing flock. The idea is a notion of a particularly beautiful and marvellous future that appeals to the followers' deepest desires and which is precisely open and vague enough to contain the individual followers' more personal dreams.

Phenomena such as revelations, epiphanies, visions, dreams, commitment and passion have parallels to childbirth and to the reunification of the mother and child in the outer world. In their book *The apprehension of beauty* (1988) Meltzer and Williams seek to anchor beauty, vision and passion in that first meeting in the light between mother and child. The mother-child relationship seems to have a special status in visual art as the quintessence of beauty. From a more rational perspective, it can hardly be the formal qualities of the mother and the newborn baby that are the source of this beauty. Childbirth is typically a highly dramatic event. Pain, anxiety, fear, sweat, hope, blood, exhaustion, tears and smiles leave both mother and child in a state that is not exactly catwalk material. Beauty lies in the relationship – or, rather, in our memory of the best and most loving moments in the early mother-infant relationship – and in the emotions and fantasies that are activated when a new human being and all his or her possibilities are born.

The relationship between the mother and the newborn baby puts the general relationship between sensory perception and fantasy into play in a very clear and specific way. Like everybody else, both mother and baby have an outside as well as something underneath it that can only be accessed indirectly. We may guess at what lies behind or underneath the outside, drawing on the clues that emerge through openings in the outside: milk, warmth, rejections, smiles, detachment and so forth. It is the purpose of our creative imagination (Meltzer & Williams, 1988) to generate images and assessments of the whole based on the fragments that are accessible to our senses. The reality we can access with our senses establishes a projective space that our imagination, experience and fantasy are drawn to fill (Visholm, 1993).

For the newborn baby, the encounter with the mother's outside is the quintessence of beauty. The dramatic crisis of childbirth and the entrance into the outer world, where the baby's head suddenly feels too heavy to hold and control, stark noises and light and then the mother's arms, eyes and breasts. In this process, we may use Rilke's definition of beauty in reverse order: 'For scarcely endurable terror is only the infant of beauty'.[1] As the relationship between mother and child develops, the child learns that behind the beautiful outside is both the best and the worst. From the mother's eyes pour loving attention and confusing detachment, and the breast is the source of nourishment that relieves hunger but also the beginning of the frightening process of digestion and defecation.

Meltzer and Williams call this tension between the outside and what lies behind it the aesthetic conflict.

> This is the aesthetic conflict, which can be most precisely stated in terms of the aesthetic impact of the outside of the 'beautiful' mother, available to the senses, and the enigmatic inside which must be construed by creative imagination.
>
> (Meltzer & Williams, 1988, p. 22)

In this sense, beauty is associated with terror, and this connection initiates and motivates the creative imagination and the yearning to understand. The aesthetic conflict generates tension, and this tension is the driving force of passion and commitment. Passion is the combination of love, hate and the desire to know (Bion, 1963, s. 12).

Just as the baby perceives the mother as enigmatic, the baby, too, appears enigmatic to the mother. The parents have not yet learnt to decode baby's sounds and movements, and through trial and error they strive to find and establish situations of accordance (Lorenzer, 1972/1975). Just as the mother presents as an object of overwhelming interest to the child, the child presents as an object of overwhelming interest to the mother. As mentioned earlier, it is not the baby's formal qualities of beauty that activates this intense interest; rather, it is the child's 'babyishness': the child's potentiality to become an amazing human being (Meltzer & Williams, 1988, p. 56). When the mother or the father imagines what this wonderful baby may become, they get a special light in their eyes, and capturing this light, the infant sees the vision for his or her existence and imagines amazing prospects. The parents are likely not imagining any concrete figure; what is so amazing is the endless potentiality itself. And the baby, for obvious reasons, knows nothing of chief fire officers, hairdressers or Nobel laureates.

Anchoring the vision and the commitment in the early parent-child relationship makes it possible to gain a deeper understanding of the potential role of vision and commitment in organizations. The vision is the parents' idea of the child's potential, and the commitment is the baby capturing the parents' vision. A vision is not a specific and detailed discourse about a company that aims, for example, to be one of the top 5 ketchup manufacturers by a certain date. To capture the tantalizing promise of the parents-child relationship's big moments, the vision has to be sufficiently open and leave room for projections. Visions are deep-seated individual motivators, but they are also relational in nature. Just as two people in love envision a wonderful life together when they gaze into each other's eyes, the vision only comes to life in the exchange of gazes between the top executive, the employees and the clients.

4 Managing transferences

Meyrowitz (1986) operates with the concept of the mystification of authority: a mystic relational process unfolding between leaders and followers when certain aspects of social architecture are in place.

Followers should not get to close to their leader. Distance is important for the followers to be able to imbue the leader with authority. One aspect of distance is a difference in height. Leaders gain authority when they position themselves such that their eyes are above the followers, standing on a rostrum, balcony or seated on horseback, for example. The rationale is of course that people have to be able to see the leader for the communication to be effective, but an impactful side effect is that the difference in eye level activates childhood transferences and projections where this height difference applies without the parents needing to climb up to a rostrum.

The second aspect of distance is the relationship between knowing and not-knowing. If we see the leader up close, we are bound to discover that the leader is human – with minor neurotic traits, ordinary human needs and so forth. When there is enough that is unknown, there is room for fantasies and transferences. The distance and the difference in eye level are a free source of authority for the leader. That is what Meyrowitz calls mysterious and characterizes as a kind of magic. He adds that not all magic is black magic (1986). From a psychodynamic perspective the effect is less mysterious. Distance leaves room for the imagination, and the height difference is a cue for the imagination to venture into the realm of authority relations (Visholm, 1993).

However, the visual electronic media reduce this white magic. TV zooms in on the leader's face, revealing the leader's humanity and causing us to reduce the idealization in the authority transference. Distance is reduced, and the height difference is gone. Usually we are disappointed to discover that leaders are simply human. In this context, realism does not foster commitment.

TV, according to Meyrowitz, has altered the relationship between proximity and distance in social relations. TV gives viewers what Goffman calls 'backstage' access, and while text and speech stimulate people to form their own mental images, TV delivers images and conveys an emotional engagement at the cost of discursively structured information. That presents postmodern leaders with an added challenge, as they have less access to the free authority that comes from distance and the resulting mystification of authority.

Based on Meyrowitz's theory we can conclude that staging affects the fantasies and perceptions associated with the leader, and that certain conditions (difference in eye level, distance and so forth) promote an idealizing transference. Using this insight gives us some ability to manage transferences and projections.

This leads us to Goffman, who coined the term *impression management* (1959). In his many descriptions and analyses of social behaviour Goffman has demonstrated how much energy we devote to managing the impression we make on others, among other things by a method he calls 'role distance' (1961). Goffman uses the example of an eight-year-old enjoying a merry-go-round ride. The merry-go-round is clearly designed for younger children, so the eight-year-old feels the need to distance himself clearly from this behaviour by pulling faces, lest outside observers mistake him for a big baby (Goffman, 1961). In certain socioeconomic segments, we can observe a similar behaviour from adults who happen to mention something they saw on TV and then hasten to add, 'Now, of course, I hardly ever watch TV, but …'.

The leader is met with transferences and projections, whether he or she wants it or not. Throughout history, much effort has gone into staging leaders and thus guiding the transferences onto certain tracks. Being interviewed while wearing a sweater, seated in front of one's living room fireplace, is no less staged than speaking from a memorial to the Second World War.

Projective spaces are staged, and perceptual cues are used to guide the fantasies and mental images (Visholm, 1993). It is important not to reveal everything that is inside, in part because it can harm one's image and in part because it does not leave any room for mystery and fantasy.

> At an MPO working conference, the theme was 'Leadership, gender and creativity'. In one of the sessions, women and men were broken up into single-gender groups and asked to share experiences about the conference theme. In the organization exercise, a great deal of mutual curiosity between the genders was expressed, and an 'fish bowl' was created to provide a setting for exchanging stories between the genders. A female participant noted with some regret that the men's stories that were told would be different now that there would be women present. She realized that she would never know what men talked about when women were not present. At the same time, she also seemed a little relieved, as she now knew that the men would preserve some of their mystique. Another observation, which was reported by a female consultant, was that in mixed groups, men who were completely open about themselves were perceived as boring, while men who made it clear that they reserved a corner of themselves that they would not share had a much more attentive female audience.

To understand how information arises and circulates in organizations, it is important to know how 'perceptual cues' define projective spaces that attract our imagination. Fantasies arise when a person enters and exits an office, when two people exchange a reserved smile, or when someone ignores someone else. Pieces of information are put together, and fantasy and experiences are combined with rumours, whether truthful or not, and these rumours are put into circulation.

II Gender differences as splitting

I Gender differences in in-group and out-group dynamics

There is a wide range of opinions about differences between men and women and the nature of these differences. Are the differences universal or culturally determined? Are they open to change? From group psychology we know (Visholm, 2004c) that even minor differences between two groups (for example, groups made up of members with comparable characteristics that differ only with regard to their randomly chosen group names, such as 'the Klee group' and 'the Kandinsky' group) give rise to projection and polarization. The other group is devalued, and one's own group is idealized. During the latency phase, boys and girls go to great lengths to demonstrate that they would love to have no contact with each other whatsoever. Girls pretend they might be infected with 'boy germs' if they touch a boy, just as the boys similarly fear catching the dreaded 'girl germs'. It is fairly easy to recognize this as cover for the opposite desires: curiosity and, in most cases, an attraction that the parties have not yet come to terms with.

The demand for gender equality is based on the assumption that any differences that exist between the genders is of no importance in relation to the area that the specific demand for equality pertains to. There is also the more radical view: that the world we live in now, due to male dominance, is a man's world, and that society will have to be fundamentally remade to enable women to take their rightful place. This latter point of view makes a great deal of sense, since there is no point in a future where the women simply become like men, or vice versa, for that matter. On the other hand, it also makes no sense to assume that everything men have discovered and invented by definition is oppressive to women. The law of gravitation and the invention of the wheel must reasonably be seen to avoid any gender imbalance (cf. Schwartz, 2001).

From a psychoanalytic point of view, it is obvious that there are certain biological gender differences that we need to accept and come to terms with in order to be in accordance with oneself. To engage in human gendered reproduction, the two genders further have to be in contact with each other, and if the parents want the offspring to grow up with a father and a mother, they have to be prepared to become a parental couple. In some regards, realizing that one is not complete in oneself but depends on the other sex to be able to pass on one's genes may be seen to represent a narcissistic injury. One also has to embrace the fact that one does not have access to certain experiences due to one's gender, just as one, conversely, has access to certain other experiences that the other gender is barred from. Thus, there is a risk that we misjudge gender differences due to ordinary in-group and out-group mechanisms, where we attribute qualities to the other gender that are in fact evenly distributed between men and women. On the other hand, there is also a risk of toning down the differences, due to narcissistic injury, to avoid acknowledging the envy stemming from acknowledging the other group's different competencies and one's own dependence.

In texts such as Paula Nicolson's *Gender, power and organization: A psychological perspective* (1996) and Vivian Burr's *Gender and social psychology* (2003), which seem largely representative of the field, a splitting between kind-hearted women and evil men seems quite obvious. All the men seem to like each other and gang up to oppress women, and none of the women compete with each other or have mutual conflicts but are instead united in victimhood. The uneven distribution of power, pay and status is pointed out, and sexual harassment is described and criticized. Mats Alvesson and Yvonne Due Billing (1997), by contrast, are very aware that this gendered focus risks producing a simplified in-group and out-group dynamic. That risk is not only present in research but in any context where people reflect on gender and the organization.

When the gender issue comes to the surface in a group, it is always worth considering whether there actually is a problem in this regard, or whether it represents a more or less unconscious attempt at shifting the focus from unpleasant competition between men, between women or between group members regardless of gender.

> In a supervision group a female participant said she was very stressed by a particular work task. She was the head of an international training programme for women leaders. Twelve women were enrolled in the programme, which consisted of six four-day meetings in a European capital. The theme of the previous meeting had been self-leadership in all the different roles a female top executive has to fill: executive, sex partner, mother, citizen, cook and so forth.
>
> To introduce the theme, the head of the programme had hired a friend and colleague whom she admired for her skill at juggling the many roles. She began her presentation by outlining her main career achievements, including mentioning the award she had received as female leader of the year. Then she showed a slide of her lovely children, and since they were just women together, she also threw in a photo of her handsome Italian lover. Then a photo of herself crossing the finish line at the Berlin Marathon the previous year and finally a shot of her kitchen larder, where she was particularly proud of the French storage jars with home-grilled sweet peppers in different colours, garlic, olive oil and peaches in brandy.
>
> To the surprise of the head of programme, the participants met her with intense hostility. They ignored the guest speaker and addressed all their criticism of the 'completely irrelevant programme' to the head of programme. The following days, participation was low, and some of the participants preferred doing some shopping. At this point, the head of programme was unsure whether she still had a programme or whether she would have any participants at the next meeting.
>
> From an outside perspective, it was easy to see that the head of programme and the guest speaker had mentally organized the world in such a way that everything evil and all unpleasant feelings were placed outside the programme and with the men – hence they were startled and surprised when envy, competition and hostility emerged in a group of women.
>
> The supervision group suggested that the head of programme put envy, competition and hostility among women on the agenda for the next meeting.

Working with issues related to how good or bad one or the other gender is almost always triggers in-group/out-group dynamics. It is not necessarily bad to use broad generalizations occasionally. When it comes right down to it, women have qualities that men do not have, and they are able to do things that men cannot, and vice versa. It is important to develop a certain self-awareness, but it is also important to reflect on the projections that are at play in these activities.

2 The splitting of love in organizational psychology

While both men and women may have reasons to feel narcissistic injury over their dependence on the competencies of the other gender, and both genders may similarly become engaged in one-track in-group/out-group dynamics, Kernberg (1995a, 1995b) has observed a certain stereotypical set of conventional masculinities and femininities that play out in the public domain. The morality at play in public settings corresponds to sexuality during the latency phase and early youth.

In the public sphere, which Kernberg, in extension of Moscovici, also believes that we operate in when we use mass media (the Internet, newspapers, TV and so forth), large-group psychology applies:

> In general, all groups that are unstructured (that is, those that are not organized around some task) foster a restrictive, regressive sense of morality. This type of morality is characteristic of social networks – the small social groups and communities within which individuals communicate with one another but are not intimate and do not necessarily have personal relations with one another. (…) Under such conditions, the members tend to project components of the infantile superego onto the group. They try to establish an unconsciously shared consensus on some basic values – a morality very different from the morality each member operates under as an individual. (…) this morality, which – for reasons that will emerge throughout this chapter – I call conventional morality, is strikingly similar to the morality of children in the latency phase (…).
>
> The characteristics of latency-age group morality include both sexual knowledge and 'innocence,' in the sense that sexuality is something forbidden and has to do with the secret behavior of 'others.' There is also a derogatory devaluation of genital sexuality perceived as condensed with its anal forerunners, expressed in, for example, references to sexual organs and activities as dirty, "dirty" jokes, and the reaction of shame and disgust to sexual behavior, together with a secretly excited and wondering curiosity about sexuality. The simple morality of the latency age divides individuals and causes into good and bad, dissociates genital sexuality from tender affection.
>
> (Kernberg, 1995a, pp. 164–165)

In a comparative analysis of conventional films, erotic art and pornographic films, Kernberg sees a certain confirmation of this pattern of split sexuality in society. Conventional films do not include explicit sexual scenes, and if they do, the audience never sees the heroes' genitalia 'in action', only the villains'. On the other hand, there is a great emphasis on emotions. The opposite is true in pornographic films. Here, love and feelings are taboo, and only the monotonous movements of the organs matter. In films where the erotic content is part of the artistic content, the protagonists are both sexually and emotionally in contact with each other (Kernberg, 1995a).

What is at play here is the split in their love, as Freud (1912/1957) puts it. Freud only saw the split in the male love life, but sexual liberation has made it possible to notice the phenomenon in women too. The object is split into an idealized object, which only has wonderful qualities, but which has nothing to do with sex, and a debased object, which is pure sex and without any spiritual or other qualities besides.

This split state is a sign of immaturity and also a regular aspect of the most common human psychopathology. The splitting is a first attempt at shifting the libido from a parental figure to an 'extraneous object'. The splitting keeps sex and parents safely separated. Adults are able to integrate loving feelings with genital sexuality, but this mature passionate love serves as a protest against or a temporary liberation from the prevailing latency norms of the public sphere and the group.

However, this split is further organized through the splitting between boys and girls and between men and women, which causes both parties to repress a dimension of their sexual desire and project it on the other gender. Thus, the conventional perceptions of masculinity and femininity may be seen as a collusion between boys or men and girls or women that protects both parties from taking on the complex challenges of sexuality and affections.

During the latency phase and early youth, human sexuality is split, with an underlying anal inclination. The sensitive and romantic side of sexuality is split off from the genital and action-oriented side. Intercourse is seen as dirty (like farts, faeces and urine) and associated with fighting and aggression, while tenderness and romance are pure and associated with peace and harmony.

> The fact that early male adolescent groups consciously affirm the latency child's exciting, yet anally tinged concept of genitality dissociated from tenderness and keep to themselves the longing for tender and romantic relations with the other gender contrasts with the development in typical early adolescent female groups. The girl's ideal and romanticized acceptance of an admired male object is part of the 'secret,' private stirrings of genital desires.
>
> (Kernberg, 1995b, p. 179)

The organization of sexuality as collusion means that what boys repress and project on girls is lived out by the girls, while the boys live out what the girls repress and project on them. Morality is a black-and-white concept, as in a children's fairy tale and in the discourse of the conventional public debate. When boys are together with other boys, they speak of the action-oriented aspects of sexuality, and when they are alone they have tender and romantic feelings and dreams. When girls are together with other girls, they focus on a romantic discourse, while the sensuous aspects of sexuality are kept out of the conversation.

The writer and businesswoman Benja Stig Fagerland has collected examples of hateful comments from men who hate women addressed to female participants in the public debate (*Politiken*, 23 June 2012). The quotes are illustrative examples of the anally toned and aggressive sexualization attributed to boys and embrace:

> 'Damn quota feminist whore.'
> 'I know where you live, feminist bitch, you'll taste my cock.'
> 'Fuck off back to Quota Norway.'
> 'I'm sperming all over you, fucking bitch.'
> 'You're just a totally disgusting nasty bitch, you lesbian bitch.'
> 'Look at her eyes: I would like to stick my dick in her mouth, that'll teach her not to challenge!'
>
> (Fagerland, 2012; my translation)

These pathetic utterances position the penis as a weapon and sperm as a substance in the same category as urine and faeces. This is a rather immature perception of an organ intended for pleasure and reproduction and the substance carrying the (probably) young man's unique genes.

Fagerland sees these utterances as harmful to democracy. She points out that she can handle the flak, but she needs to keep the online news sites that she normally writes for out of reach from the two eldest of her three daughters who, she says, understand too much and are scared and upset when someone writes that way about their mother. The result may well be to scare women out of participating in democracy, Fagerland fears.

The interesting topic in the present context is the relationship between the anally or genitally aggressive men and the counter image of the three little sisters, who are scared and upset, that is, between the dirty and aggressive boys and the pure, innocent girls. Fagerland does not write that all men are like the immature commentators, or that they represent all men. She also does not write that her three little daughters are like all women or represent all women. Nevertheless, that is the bottom line of a rhetorical calculus.

As suggested above, these distorted gender images also seem to apply in organizational psychology. The collusion in the discourse does not mention that many men maintain a civil tone and stick to rational arguments, that men may also be aggressive towards men, that women may be nasty towards women, that women may use demeaning language about both women and men, that women may love and feel sexual attraction to men and vice versa, and so forth.

Perhaps there is a postmodern defence in only leaving room for the negative dimensions of the gender difference in organizational psychology discourses. We speak of inequality in terms of executive positions and executive board posts, pay disparities and sexual harassment and keep our dreams of love and creative collaboration to ourselves.

III Love and competition

I Men cannot remember why they compete

According to Schwartz (2001), who bases his work, in part, on the work of Chasseguet-Smirgel (1964/1970, 1976, 1984/1985a), men and women share an unconscious fantasy of a wonderful place that he calls the world of the primordial mother. In this world, there is only love and needs gratification. It is an imaginary place, where reality cannot be allowed to enter, and it is an idealized mother figure who delivers all the goods and the pleasant feelings.

Men and women, however, have very different roles in this regressive utopia. The woman identifies with the primordial mother, but in order to maintain this illusion she needs the man to do hard work in real life and to operate on the boundary, keeping the real world out of the family while also discreetly delivering real-life resources to provide for the family. The man is prepared to do this, because his innermost drive is the desire to be allowed into the world of the primordial mother. It is this idealized female figure that makes him work, achieve, compete and so forth.

But what should the man do to appeal to the woman? How can he gain access to the world of the primordial mother? It cannot be simply through his person, as that is as easily rejected as it is accepted.

> It is through his work that he can make himself appealing to her and at the same time avoid the totally arbitrary caprice of personal attraction and affection. This means that men's work activity is focused on something outside of themselves, on something that exists independently of themselves.
>
> (Schwartz, 2001, p. 45)

The psychological significance of work is to establish an area where the man can be in control. In terms of what he would really like to control, the access to the feminine universe, he is powerless. That is why his relationship with his work resembles the symptomatology of a compulsive neurosis: a reaction formation that is invested with energy through the denial of the powerlessness he cannot consciously accept (Ibid., p. 46).

Schwartz lists a number of dimensions in man's traditional relationship with work. It is characterized by the *displacement of affect*. Emotional meaning or gratification does not spring from work in itself but from the hope

that it may give access to the woman. The displaced desire for control com-
pels the man to try to impose order on his work and on the world and thus
reduce the level of chaos and insecurity. The displacement of affect and the
passion for order come together in the desire for *impersonal rules*. Men do not
associate with each other according to feelings; their feelings for each other
matter less because their feelings are directed at women.

Men are further highly oriented towards *competition*. Since men cannot
openly address the object of their work, as that would remind them of their
powerlessness in the face of women's whims, competition helps them structure
their efforts and act as an alternative source of meaning. Competition offers
success criteria and opportunities for measuring progress:

> Men can measure their rate of progress against each other, and therefore
> avoid having to ask themselves the forbidden question of what the work is
> all about.
>
> (Ibid., p. 48)

During the post-war years, however, it becomes clear that men – perhaps
particularly middle-class functionaries – do not fit this model as representatives of and protectors against real life. There are many 'small' men in big
organizations, each of whom has little say over anything and certainly no say
over what is real in the organization. Psychology comes into the organizations
in the form of motivation theories, McGregor's Theory X and Theory Y, the
human resource perspective, social needs and so forth, which may be seen as
feminization. Television, which spreads throughout the nation during the
1950s, has the effect, as documented by Meyrowitz (1986), of demystifying
and levelling the three axes of child-adult, woman-man and employee-leader.
Men gain access to exclusively female domains: girls chatting, women's conversations in the nursery, powder-room talks and so forth. Women gain access
to boardrooms, locker rooms, on-site builders' huts, lawyers' lunches and so
forth. This process is a huge loss of 'free' authority for male leaders, who lose
mystique on all three axes. But generally, authorities fall to the ground as
human beings, and both the feminine and the masculine universe are demystified, leaving the two genders naked. The projective spaces that had been
created because the two genders led lives that were separate in many respects
now disappear and leave us with everyday life in all its 'disenchanted' realism.

This is illustrated in the literature, such as Sloan Wilson's *The man in the
gray flannel suit* (1955), which describes the dispassionate organizational life
during the 1950s, Richard Yeate's *Revolutionary Road* (1961), which describes
how a young couple's dreams of an exciting life gradually falls apart due to
the temptation of corporate life, with pay and adaptation, while the schizophrenic young man living on Revolutionary Road is the only one who speaks
the truth. In Denmark, Finn Søeborg, who had his debut with the best-selling
novel *Sådan er der så meget* [It's always something] (1950), where the plot

plays out, in part, in the 'Ministry of Reconstruction', where the staff pass time playing Battleships. Søeborg's novels were popular, and he had a keen eye for the absurdities of life during the 1950s. Existentialism, which indivi-dualized the search for the meaning of life, and the advent of absurd theatre are part of the background. The group movement and antipsychiatry leads to the youth rebellion of the late 1960s. Antipsychiatry may be represent the starkest take: the schizophrenic person is the healthy person in a sick society, which the parents and their generation have created within the combined framework of the family, public institutions and society as a whole.

It is difficult for men to find their place in this context, both in terms of finding their direction in life in an emotionally gratifying manner and in terms of being mirrored as important and meaningful. The anger that is manifested in the youth rebellion, the student movement and the women's movement during the late 1960s is characterized by a high degree of internal contra-diction, as men are both ridiculed for their lack of significance and attacked for the global and universal historical evil that they do. On the one hand, men are superfluous pencil pushers, who are so dull that everyone around them suffocates. Just think of Ray Davis' *Well Respected Man* recorded by the Kinks in 1965.

On the other hand, the conspiracy of the patriarchy, capitalism and imperialism is a male endeavour that is to blame for everything that is wrong with this world.

This anger contains a disappointment that is difficult to articulate without shame: a disappointment that the authority figures were revealed to be just ordinary human beings, and that the doors one was kicking were already wide open.

For the men, the situation represents a dual bind, a catch-22: if they show strength, courage and confidence they are bad; if they simply mind their work they are impotent.

2 The feminine mystique

As mentioned earlier, many women identify with the mother in the world of the primordial mother, her magic, power and perfection. Betty Friedan's 1963 book *The feminine mystique*, which helped inspire the women's movement in the 1960s, sprang out of the 1950s and the unhappy life of American women and painted a mobilizing picture of the difficulties these women were facing. The paradox during the 1950s and 1960s was that, even though everyone agreed that the middle-class family, with dad driving his car to work, mum staying at home and three darling children, was about the closest one could get to a blissful existence, the women in the suburban houses were deeply frustrated (see, e.g., the three women in the film *The hours*). The middle-class family of the 1950s was, in many regards, the realization of the world of the primordial mother.

Instead of feeling happy and fulfilled acting as the family's provider of nurture and love, she felt empty and superfluous, suffering from a problem that had no name:

> What were the words women used when they tried to express it? Sometimes a woman would say 'I feel empty somehow ... incomplete.' Or she would say, 'I feel as if I don't exist.'
>
> (Friedan, 1963/2001, pp. 63–64)

What Schwartz calls the world of the primordial mother, seems to be congruent with what Friedan calls the feminine mystique:

> The feminine mystique says that the highest value and the only commitment for women is the fulfillment of their own femininity. It says that the great mistaken of Western Culture, through most of its history, has been undervaluation of this femininity. It says this femininity is so mysterious and intuitive and close to the creation and origin of life that man-made sciences may never be able to understand it. But however special and different, it is in no way inferior to the nature of man; it may even in certain respects be superior. The mistake, says the mystique, the root of women's troubles in the past is that women envied men, women tried to be like men, instead of accepting their own nature, which can find fulfillment only in sexual passivity, male domination, and nurturing, maternal love.
>
> (Ibid., pp. 91–91)

The realization of the feminine mystique and the world of the primordial mother did not work but led instead to frustration. There are several reasons for that. First of all, the world of the primordial mother has always been an illusion, and illusions are not suited to being translated into real life. On a more prosaic note, women had by now attained almost the same level of education as the men and thus had competencies that were not easily lived out in the context of homemaking. As television demystified the male universe, it was also difficult to maintain the fantasy of the husband as the heroic doer of great deeds in the dangerous real world.

Women faced the dilemma that if they were going to engage in society outside the home and do 'real work', they would necessarily destroy their identification with the primordial mother, who is self-sufficient in her omnipotence and thus does not need to work. This was both a perceived inner dilemma and an outer one. Women felt that they jeopardized their femininity by doing 'real work' and imagined they would lose value as love objects.

One compromise would be to accept work that did not have an economic purpose, for example to spend some hours every day in a shop selling pretty objects, while the husband covered the losses; or to renovate and sell manor-house furniture without worrying that the hourly earnings were about one quarter of an unskilled labourer's:

> It is the jump from amateur to professional that is often hardest for a woman on her way out of the trap. But even if a woman does not have to work to eat, she can find identity only in work that is of real value to society – work for which, usually, our society pays. Being paid is, of course, more than a reward – it implies definite commitment. For fear of that commitment, hundreds of able, educated suburban housewives today fool themselves about the writer or actress they might have been, or dabble at art or music in the dilettante's limbo of 'self-enrichment'. (...) These are also ways of evading growth.
>
> (Ibid., p. 474)

Women's liberation presents challenges both to women's self-image and to their notions of men. Women's growing autonomy and authority, in some regards, led to a reduction of men's. Their ability to enjoy this victory is hampered by fact that it diminishes her value in her own and others' perception to pair up with a man who is no longer seen as heroic but is rather a small cog in a big machine. If the woman idealizes the man she herself is diminished, dependent and old-fashioned. If she devalues him, she similarly appears to be a fool. This implies a complex system of inconsistent items in the person's mental accounts, where the same man may be logged simultaneously as both strong and smart, the reason for everything that went wrong in the relationship, the family and the career, a loser, a selfish lout, an extra child, and more.

3 Cinderella and Clumsy Hans knew, their siblings did not

In postmodern society, the traditional pattern, where men compete to accomplish brave and amazing feats, while women compete to be the most beautiful and the loveliest, seems to hide more than it reveals.

If women think that men compete as men, and men think that women do not compete, none of them has discovered what is really going on. The stereotypical image of male competition has to do with visible and measurable skills and possessions: biggest, most, strongest, fastest.

The stereotypical image of female competition is that only losers compete. Disney's *Cinderella* clearly shows that Cinderella – who is as good as the day is long, but who also dreams of winning the prince and half the kingdom – emerges the winner without seemingly competing. Her evil and stupid stepsisters, however, are green with envy and use all sorts of dirty tricks to oust Cinderella. The harder they try, the less sympathetic they appear to the audience. Cinderella wins without us every noticing that she was even taking part in the competition.

Again, women work twice as hard; they have to learn to compete invisibly. They have to look sweet and kind on the outside and do all the dirty positioning efforts without being seen to do so.

When it comes right down to it, men do the same. Unlike his two self-important brothers, Clumsy Hans was not preparing for the competition by puffing out his chest or rehearsing all sorts of useless pseudo knowledge. Men who compete too openly are entertaining, while the cleverer ones operate behind the scenes. Organizational power and influence are about building alliances and strongpoints and being ready to seize the moment when it arises.

IV Work and family

1 Job, gender, age and a person's value as love object

There seems to be empirical support for the notion that pairing today generally takes place between a man who is older, taller, better paid and higher status than the woman (cf. Christoffersen, 2004). This implies, at least, a partner problem for high-performing women and low-performing men, but since the pattern appears to be so irrational, it also calls for a psychological explanation. The question is whether men are incapable of loving (are afraid of) women who have more power than they do, or whether women are incapable of loving men who have less power than they do?

Since the education system places same-age boys and girls in the same class, the pairing pattern where the man has higher status implies that girls and women direct their attention upwards in the age-group hierarchy and make boys and men who are on their level feel invisible until they turn their gaze downwards, where they meet the admiring gaze of the younger girls and women. This may be partly explained by the fact that girls develop faster than boys, so that same-age boys will seem more immature. Another aspect has to do with the role of physical appearance for women's value as love objects, and that our general perception associates beauty with youth, while the man's value as love object depends on money and status, which are typically only attained later in life, unless the man is a rock star, a footballer or similar. Men's and women's respective value as love objects thus peak at different times in their life.

However, this gives girls and women a competitive advantage in the job market, compared to same-age boys and men, since relationships with older boys and men provide access to important information, contacts in working life and social life overall – what Bourdieu (1998) calls 'social capital'.

2 An aesthetic reflection

The workplace is the carrier of what is conventionally associated with masculinity, and the home is the carrier of what is similarly associated with femininity. Two grey-green plants in the reception at the office is the only feminine touch in the workplace, while all traces of work in the home are exiled to the home office, the basement or the garage. The family sociotope becomes the setting where success or failure in the workplace is manifested in the form of consumer goods with no relation to the workplace, while it is somehow sinful (Protestant work ethic, LEAN, cost reduction or optimization and so forth) to associate beauty or aesthetics with work.

Gullestad has a good description of men's difficulty finding their own place in the home:

> When you visit a family in the evening, you often see the dad or the male partner sitting on the sofa watching TV. In the weekends he often has a glass of beer or a drink in front of him. Some of the men are big, heavy workers, who rest heavily on the sofa, legs splayed. Men who work in the service sector are often slender and have a different physique and physiognomy. They might sit with their legs crossed, more like the middle-class men. But generally, they appear to be uncomfortable in their own home. They often look out of place, bored perhaps.
>
> (Gullestad in Nielsen & Rudberg, 1994, p. 301) [translated for this edition by Dorte H. Silver]

Gullestad's observation probably has to do with the fact that the woman will have had many thoughts and ideas about what the home should look like and perhaps less about what activities the couple should be able to engage in at home, until the children arrive and make this a moot point. The man will rarely have put much thought into the aesthetic challenges of the interior design and probably also has not thought much about what he and his wife are supposed to do with their time when they are not eating, having sex or sleeping. On Sundays, however, they might find appropriate places for him to show off his car and his partner to an audience who is out to do the same.

There is a straight line from the invention of 'manliness' during the inter-war years to Gullestad's observations from the 1980s. In his analysis of the history of men, Kiselberg (1979) connects the Boy Scout movement, Jack London's books about 'real' men in the wilderness and a certain potential for Nazi mobilization. The men have no say on the factory floor. Women rule the small home, where she has to spend her time looking after the children. How is he supposed to make a good impression on the woman under these circumstances, where the smartest move, from a functional perspective, is for him to hand over his pay cheque as soon as he has cashed it. Similarly, the woman and the family as a whole depend on the man not only earning a liveable income but also bringing it home, carrying it safely past the local pub and the betting shop.

The culture of manliness grows out of fantasies and literature revolving around the dangers one encounters in the wild, where there are no women and no factory owners, and describing how these real men tackle the problems. Kiselberg captures the problem well when he describes the activities of the Boy Scout movement as aimed at solving self-imposed challenges in nature. In Germany, an Association of Men was launched in 1930. An organizer advocating for it wrote:

> In accordance with her nature, the woman must always be the guardian of the relations on which the life of the family and the genders rely, while the man pursues a life that combines equal with equal [i.e., man with man, Ed.] to a heightened expression of life and a potentiated awareness of life. (...) Here lies a deep and probably irreconcilable contrast between man and woman that may result in tragic conflicts but which also permeates everyday life and which in Germany appears mainly in the eternal split between family life and the man's regular table at the bar to reach a zenith of bourgeois comedy in the struggle over the front-door key.
> (Schütz in Kiselberg, 1979, p. 228) [Translated for this edition]

A key point in Kiselberg's work is that the notions of 'manliness' and 'real men' only become an issue in connection with the invention of the wage earner. Previously, one's office or rank was one's source of identity, but now gender is suddenly put into play. Employment in big public or private companies does not make heroes of most men. In a sense, this sort of working life, may be said to castrate men and – since the rationale seems to be that the man is able to attract the woman based on what he achieves in his working life – thus his love life.

For a housewife who is dependent on a frustrated man it seems obvious that she should want freedom and closer contact with the world. Women's movements begin to campaign for equal pay, support for unmarried mothers and decriminalization of abortion. The yearning for freedom is also expressed in a public relation happening in 1926, where Edward Bernays linked freedom and autonomy to cigarette smoking. Adrian Curtis's documentary on advertising and psychology in the 20th century, *The century of the self*, explains how Freud's nephew in the United States, Edward Bernays, both came up with the term 'public relations' as a more genteel term for propaganda and developed the strategy aimed at making women smoke. He contacted a psychoanalyst to gain an in-depth psychological understanding of the topic; the analyst explained that if cigarettes could be made to look phallic, women would embrace them as symbols of freedom and independence. With a cigarette within reach, women did not need to envy men for their potency and independence. Bernays contacted a group of suffragettes and asked them to discreetly carry cigarettes during the Easter Parade and to light up on a given signal, when the parade passed by a large group of press photographers. Bernays also spread the nickname 'torches of freedom' for cigarettes, in a subtle reference to the powerful Statue of Liberty in the bay.

With the breakthrough of modernism after the Second World War, a large number of new homes were built for the workers. Architects fought an important battle for light, fresh air and hygiene, but in a derived consequence that is well aligned with modernism overall, decorative items, personality and personal characteristics are regarded as being either effeminate, bourgeois or both. The Danish designer Poul Henningsen was busy ridiculing allotment cottages resembling miniature versions of Rosenborg Palace, and the progressive choice was to be cremated after one's death and insist on an anonymous interment. In not-for-profit housing associations, everything was to be exactly according to the architect's designs. New York's skyscrapers may be phallic, but only a few clients – and not all the ant-like men who do the actual construction work – can boost their profile by claiming to have built the tallest building. Modern architecture reduces people to particles in a universe where all particles are equal and interchangeable (cf. Chasseguet-Smirgel, 1984/1985a). Modernism's hatred of symmetry is also manifest in the abolition of a more feminine, welcoming architectural expression, where the main house greets arrivals by extending its two side buildings in an embrace, and where the courtyard contains and protects everyone, big and small. The youth rebellion's long hairstyles, Indian clothes, second-hand and DIY style is a revolt against modernism's anti-personal style, with the squatters' free town of Christiania in Copenhagen as one of the most colourful examples.

Meyrowitz (1986) links the general spread of television with women's liberation in the 1960s. Television brought the big wide world – which women had previously only had access to via the radio, newspapers and the husband's tales – into the living room. They discovered that the world outside the family home might not be as complex and challenging as their husbands had led them to believe. Meyrowitz's media analysis concludes, overall, that television becomes a medium of levelling and demystification. He offers a detailed analysis of the three dimensions, leaders and employees, children and adults, men and women. Television breaks down the former divisions between men's and women's worlds, and equal opportunities in the workplace and in the family dismantle the rest. The mystique disappears and the gender spell is lifted.

The new social media, however, hand the capacity for network-based self-staging back to ordinary people. A challenge in this context is that in many disciplines, a person competes with the entire world. While in the traditional village communities, many more were able to enjoy being the prettiest, the strongest, the cleverest and so forth, today we can continuously compare ourselves to the world champions online. On the other hand, there is always the possibility that one's mother will post one's musical accomplishments on YouTube, which may result in instant fame and fortune.

TV shows about endangered and oppressed men have begun to try to give men the courage to have their say in the decoration of the home. There has to be room for big loudspeakers, sports trophies and reindeer antlers. Most workplaces are also beginning to show a certain feminine touch. Art associations hang paintings on the walls, and the open-office landscapes are home to more than just potted plants.

3 Reintegration into postmodernity

In the postmodern era the boundaries between family and work seem to be under continuous reconstruction. IT work stations and management lingo make their way into the home, while the workplace culture is feminized, and the genders mix (Hochschild, 1997). Men and women may discuss children, cooking and cleaning during their breaks at work, and husband and wife may talk about work issues over dinner. A form of reintegration is taking place. This provides improved opportunities for mutual inspiration, learning and help but also increases the opportunities for comparison and, thus, for competition.

Changes to family and working life have created a situation where both the man and the woman are in the service of two organizations, one workplace each and the same family with divided leadership. In the old model, where the man was the breadwinner and the woman was the housewife, both had to do their best within their respective organizations in order to optimize family life. Today, many, both men and women, experience an inner split in connection with the prioritization of work versus family. If one of them sacrifices their career and has to make do with a reduced pension in order to stay at home with the children for prolonged periods, he or she may justifiably feel cheated if the couple later divorces. While marriage was once organized in a way where what benefited one partner would benefit them both, today, things are more complicated.

4 The family as evaluation team

Children shape their ambitions through identification and counter-identification with their parents and through the need to find independent profiles in relation to their siblings. The parents supplement the process with the projections of their own needs and wishes. There is a wide range of literature about how projection, identification and projective identification in the family shapes ambitions and career aspirations for the members of the family (cf. Laing 1967; Stierlin, 1982; Shapiro, 1978; Lunøe, 1987, 1988; Jakobsen & Visholm, 1987; Scharff & Scharff, 1987/1991; Scharff, 1989; Visholm, 1993, 2005a). Some parents project their own unrealized ambitions on the children, while others project unmanageable 'parts' of themselves on the children in order to get rid of them. It is an important task for parents to help their children differentiate from one another, so that they do not have to compete in the same discipline from morning to night.

In the family context, where both competition and in-group solidarity unfold, the members are continuously evaluating each other's performances.

The family, which is the first 'organization in the mind', influences the individual member, both as an open conversing system that comes together for birthdays, holidays and so forth, and as an inner evaluation team. The term evaluation team was developed by Hirschhorn at an MPO working conference in 2003 intended to evaluate the master's programme MPO (Master of Organizational Psychology at Roskilde University, Denmark). The idea is that all groups, in addition to their role in relation to the primary task, are also evaluation teams, the latter role taking on added prominence at certain times – at the beginning of a process, in case of crises – and has little prominence at other times. We are always all evaluating ourselves and each other, but the role of evaluation takes on varying prominence, in speech and thought, at varying times.

Building on Hirschhorn's model, we may say that all families also constitute an evaluation team or an evaluation family. What is unique about the family is that it is both the oldest and the primary evaluation team. It has both an inner existence, as part of the superego, and an outer existence, as an interaction form at family gatherings, where each member can relate their own successes while the siblings will regale the group with stories of his or her failures, to put things bluntly.

Note

1 'For Beauty is only the infant of scarcely endurable terror, and we are amazed when it casually spares us. Every Angel is terrible.' Rainer Maria Rilke (1912): The first elegy. In *Duino Elegies* (Trans. S. Cohn, p. 21). Northwestern University Press.

Chapter 8

Role analysis

Psychological processes in organizations can be understood and analysed from a variety of different perspectives. The focus may be placed on the organization as a whole, relations between leadership and employees, relations between different departments or between the different tiers in the hierarchy, the group as a whole, relations between the individual and the group and so forth. Which focus is the most relevant depends on the task at hand. In any case, however, it is worth underscoring the wide range of approaches to choose among. Both the coach or supervisor working with an individual manager and the organizational consultant or manager working with the organization at large is – or should be – aware of how the understanding of an issue can change when it is viewed and examined from a different angle. Clare Huffington (2008) has presented an illustrative case.

The case of Sarah, vice president in an investment bank

Sarah was vice president in an investment bank, leading the operations side of the unit. Her line manager had criticized her for having poor presentation skills and being ineffective in getting her points across to senior colleagues. The bank recommended that she take a course to improve her presentation skills.

Sarah was puzzled by the matter. She was convinced she had better presentation skills than most of her colleagues, and she also did not feel that she ever had any problems communicating with senior colleagues.

Sarah did not feel the criticism was apt. The situations that presented difficulties were meetings with senior colleagues from the bank's Trading department. She felt that was probably where the criticism came from. She decided to see a coach.

Trading represented the exciting and risk-taking unit in the investment bank, with the traders as the ones who closed the deals. Operations was the boring unit that handled the practical aspects of the deals after the fact. Traditionally, Trading was seen as the leading party in meetings with Operations.

Currently, the bank was facing faltering confidence in the market due to the fallout from the collapse of a large bank. Sarah and Operations had been instructed to take a more proactive stance on risk management in relation to Trading.

The analysis of the issue concluded there was a functional split in the organization between risk-taking and risk management. The change in strategy made the traders more aware of the risk or anxiety aspect of their part of the job, which made it harder for them to dare take risks. Unconsciously, they sought to project his anxiety on Sarah and Operations.

The traders were all male and had no experience working with a proactive and demanding woman from Operations. The immediate expectation was for Operations to be passive, and for women to be more passive than men. That theme was taboo in the organization, because the organization tried to cover up gender issues in political correctness.

Sarah had been raised by strict parents, who criticized her for every mistake. This made her afraid of addressing authority figures unless she was 200% sure she was right, which only made her appear even more intimidating to the traders.

Sarah was very surprised to hear that she might be making the traders anxious. She changed her style to adopt a more cooperative approach. She spoke to other vice presidents and found that they had similar difficulties. A meeting was planned for managers and employees from both Trading and Operations to discuss the new strategy and share their concerns instead of being split.

Sarah's coaching showed that the bank recommended that Sarah take a presentation course because Trading and Operations were unable to work together to handle the new situation with its raised anxiety level – a perfectly pointless solution to the problem. A polarization emerged between Trading and Operations, which was further fuelled by gender positioning. Sarah became the scapegoat because her personal background made her the most intimidating woman or representative of Operations.

Role analysis identifies the client's current roles in an organization in light of hidden family dynamics in his or her personal life history. The method can help clients or conference participants identify any repetition compulsion, examine how the past is influencing the present in conscious and unconscious ways and discover the freedom to choose when to repeat a habituated pattern and when to try something else.

There are different approaches to role analysis. Thus, Gordon Lawrence (2006) emphasizes the need to steer clear of the Oedipus complex, infantilization, interpretations, psychopathology and privacy and instead focus on roles and environment and offering working hypotheses. Lawrence sees this as being congruent with Bion's distinction between Sphinx and Oedipus (Bion, 1961). At the Grubb Institute, Bruce Reed and John Bazalgette (2006) focus on roles and work with a triad of 1) finding the role, 2) making the role and 3) taking the role. Susan Long (2006) is more aligned with the method outlined in the present book. She uses both role biography and role history and is thus interested in both how a role is shaped from the outside by the organization's expectations, the way the incumbents meet these expectations over the years (role history), and how the individual shapes and is shaped by the roles he or she gets and takes in the various organizations he or she is a part of over time – from the childhood home to the current workplace.

The model presented here is one I first used in my review and application group at the Leicester Conference in 2005. The best-known group relations conference in the world, the Leicester Conference is also known as the Tavistock Conference. The participants at these conferences, which will be described in more detail later in this chapter, are leaders, consultants and others who wish to learn and develop in the field of leadership, groups and organizations. The role analysis model was subsequently developed and tested in conferences and supervision groups in the programme for organizational psychology at the Institut for Gruppeanalyse (Institute of Group Analysis, OPU/IGA) and in the master's programme for organizational psychology at Roskilde University (MPO/RUC). The method was inspired by John Newton, Susan Long and Burchardt Sievers's 2006 book *Coaching in depth: The organizational role analysis approach* and by Halina Brunning's *Executive coaching: Systems-psychodynamic perspective*, also from 2006. Further, it draws on Hirschhorn's understanding of the relationship between person and role (Hirschhorn, 1988; Jakobsen, 2004) and systems psychodynamics (Visholm, 1993, 2004a; Shapiro & Carr, 1991) but also on family and couple therapy (Jakobsen & Visholm, 1987; Carvalho, 1994; Dicks, 1967; Ruszczynski, 1993; Scharff & Scharff, 1987/1991; Scharff, 1989; Shapiro, 1978; Shapiro & Zinner, 1971).

I Role and personality

From the perspective of modern psychoanalytic and psychodynamic thinking, personality is a result of the individual's life history, as it plays out in different sociotopes in society (family, preschool, school and so forth). Human beings are not born as blank slates but come into the world with genetic dispositions, strengths, weaknesses and vulnerabilities, which influence their individual personal development. Personality is the individual seen from outside, while the identity is the individual's self-perception, seen from inside. A psychiatrist may diagnose a personality disorder, while the person may report having identity issues. Identity concerns the perception of the relationship between self and self-image.

Modern sociology (Giddens, 1991, 1992; Beck, 1986/1992) underscores that individuals living in postmodern society are continuously tasked with making decisions about their lives while also continuously formulating and editing a narrative or life story that establishes meaningful connections between the events and, ideally, presenting their careers as a result of rational and well-motivated choices. In a sense, this aspect of life corresponds to Goffman's 'impression management' (1959), which, as described above, concerns the lengths we go to in order to present material about our lives and our social situations to others in such a way that we like what they see. However, our life story should also make sense seen from inside. While Goffman's perspective captures the manipulations and lies we perpetrate in order to look good in other people's perception, the psychoanalytic perspective deals with the unconscious manipulations of and lies about reality we engage in to be able to put up with ourselves. Throughout our childhood and youth, we will occasionally end up in conflict situations that are too difficult for us to handle consciously and directly. In this case, the unconscious aspect of ourself responds with defence mechanisms, including repression, denial, projection and projective identification. In relation to our life story, the situations that are handled by our defence mechanisms turn into gaps in our narrative. Naturally, we can weave stories to cover up these gaps, but the repressed material returns in the form of repetition compulsion, regardless how many stories we tell ourselves to rationalize it. What is repressed exists beyond language and manifests relationally, as scenes in real-life situations. For example, we may repeat a repressed family situation in the middle of a work situation, like Sarah from the investment bank, who prepares and double-checks everything as if she were about to face her strict parents rather than the fleet-footed traders.

Personality is thus a system of strengths and weaknesses and of conscious and unconscious aspects. A person's life story is, on the one hand, an identity narrative where the person organizes him/herself within a coherent meaningful, and on the other hand, a mix of regular memories, generous interpretations and distorted and repressed conflicts.

Role is a key concept in sociological theory. It applies to the set of social expectations, norms, rules, duties and rights associated with a given social position or a task. The role represents what the situation, the system, the organization or the structure demands and expects of the person who has taken or been allotted the role. Roles complement each other in a variety of ways: as reciprocal role pairs, such as the doctor and patient or diner and waiter relationship, in functionally connected roles in working life or in biologically connected roles within the family.

There are two main approaches to role theory. The school of structural functionalism, formulated by Talcott Parsons and Robert King Merton, views roles as institutionalized bundles of rights and duties associated with an ideal type of a given social position. Any individual holds multiple roles (for example mother, wife, daughter, sister, psychologist, member of a political party, member of a tennis club). Every role is associated with a number of role-partners. A teacher's role-partners include students, colleagues, superiors, politicians, parents and others, all with their own different expectations of each other's role behaviour. The sum total of these mutual expectations is a 'role-set'. From this perspective, society can be seen as a giant network of roles, peopled by individuals. When these expectations are in disagreement, they give rise to role conflicts or role strain, something that anyone who is simultaneously a spouse, an employee and a parent frequently experiences.

The other approach is symbolic interactionism, its role theory formulated by Erving Goffman. His focus is on the active interaction processes, where individuals shape, take and perform roles. In this tradition, acting is used more or less consistently as a metaphor for interaction processes in social life.

However, the association between the concept of roles and acting has made some people feel that role theories are alienating, since the notion of performing or taking on a role may be seen as pretending or play-acting, hiding one's true self behind an act. That is the stage or film actor's job, to become and represent a character who is not the actor him/herself. However, the role concept associated with play-acting differs from sociological role theory, as stage or film actors represent a particular person's way of filling a set of roles, while the theoretical role concept does not preselect a particular person to fill the role in a particular way.

Larry Hirschhorn (1988) has studied the psychodynamic processes associated with taking a role. From a psychoanalytic perspective, taking a role can be understood as confronting a challenge or a task, and these encounters between role and person produce varying degrees of pleasure and anxiety. In this sense, the role can be seen as specification imposed by the primary task on the individual members of the given system or organization (cf. Visholm, 1993, 2004a). Organizing a group around a given task involves distributing the roles the individual members need to perform to complete the task.

When a person encounters a role, the anxiety and pleasure produced by that encounter depend on both the person and the role. Every role has aspects of anxiety and risk, but everyone is different, and challenges that may seem quite manageable to one person may activate high levels of anxiety in another. Taking the role of husband is pleasurable, on the one hand, as it typically involves marrying one's sweetheart and looking forward to the happiness the two are going to share. On the other hand, the husband will also be aware that many marriages end in divorce, that divorce can lead to profound suffering and grief, and that quite frequently, one of the two is going to run off with an apparently more attractive partner, despite declarations of eternal love. Anyone who ventures into a marriage accepts living with this risk. The same applies to roles in working life. To do one's job and perform one's assigned duties, one sometimes has to do things that are unpleasant and anxiety-provoking. For example, a CEO may have to let a large group of employees go in order to save the company from bankruptcy; and the role of police officer may include having to inform a mother and father that their 18-year-old son, who has just acquired a university place, has been killed in a traffic accident.

In these situations, the person can either embrace the role and perform the unpleasant but necessary task or use defence mechanisms and step out of the role, which may be characterized as unconscious role-distancing. Defence mechanisms are initiated by the unconscious part of the self and serve to dampen or eliminate anxiety. Defence mechanisms work by distorting, simplifying or denying aspects of reality. If the CEO denies the company's dire economic straits, he or she may soon have to lay off even more people. The police officer may come up with an excuse, such as needing to finish some paperwork, in order to hand the task of informing the next of kin to a younger and less experienced colleague, who may not even have had anything to do with the case – and so forth. The cost of this anxiety reduction is the harm it does to the person's reality perception and the detrimental impact it has on the quality of the person's job role performance. When the anxiety becomes overwhelming, and we withdraw from the role, we also withdraw from reality and enter a surreal fantasy world. This in turn depersonalizes the people we work with. Instead of seeing them as they are and basing our actions on this perception, we come to see them as figures in our own fantasy and treat them accordingly. Since roles are not isolated incidents but are always embedded in a system of roles, interconnected in some sort of mutual dependence, when someone steps out of their role, projective and introjective processes trigger a chain of anxiety in the system where real uncertainties and risks combine with threatening inner voices. Thus, we depersonalize each other when we step out of our roles, and we persona-lize each other when we (re-)take our roles and face reality (Hirschhorn, 1988).

In this understanding, where roles are defined as aspects of a primary task, they could also be called formal roles, in contrast to informal ones. Most formal roles today offer some latitude for us to shape the role in our own way without completely stepping out of role. One teacher may be accommodating and help-ful, thinking that the students need all the help they can get, while another tea-cher may be more reluctant to intervene and encourage the students to follow their own path, thinking that grappling with real life is the only way the students can learn anything. These different approaches to teaching both fall within the scope of the role. However, if a teacher gives the students higher marks than they deserve because he cannot bear seeing their disappointment, he has stepped out of role, is undermining the system and has triggered an anxiety chain.

Informal roles do not spring from the primary task and may indirectly hamper or promote task performance. When people come together in a group, they seek to make the group resemble something familiar by attempt-ing to assign each other familiar roles from their childhood family. These processes are unconscious and driven by projective identification (cf. Visholm, 1993, 2004a). As a result, the roles of the mediator, nag, scapegoat, snob, lis-tener, party organizer, insightful, funny and so forth are 'automatically' dis-tributed among the members. The roles provide identity and thus a sense of security, but they also limit the latitude we allow ourselves and others in the group. It is these types of roles in particular that role analysis aims to describe. Formal roles too are not psychologically neutral. For example, one's choice of occupation is influenced in many regards by the distribution of roles in one's childhood family.

II Role analysis

Role analysis generates insight by examining the roles individuals have taken and been assigned in various systems: childhood family, current family, organization, working conference. The participants produce drawings or diagrams of their family relations and organizational position and describe the main roles they have taken and been assigned at the working conference. Often, people are found to repeat familiar role patterns in new systems.

Role analysis was originally developed as a particular approach to review and application groups at group relations or working conferences. Review and application groups serve to, first, summarize and share personal learning at the conference and, second, connect the conference learning with the individual participants' workplace roles in their 'home organizations'. In her 2009 book on psychodynamic coaching, U. C. Beck provides a very narrow definition of role analysis, arguing that, in contrast to psychodynamic coaching, it only applies to work roles. This narrow definition will undoubtedly have its proponents, but in my experience, the full potential of role analysis is best realized when the comparison between roles becomes a triangulation of family roles, organizational roles and conference roles.

A working conference (see Beck & Visholm, 2014a, 2014b, 2014c; Visholm, 2011b) is a temporary organization, whose primary task is to generate experiential learning on organizational psychology for the participants. At OPU and MPO, working conferences are an important part of the curriculum. They last three to five days and are held off-campus. They typically include big and small process study groups, where the participants and a consultant facilitator examine what is happening in the groups in real time. In addition, there is usually a main exercise where the participants and staff organize in various ways and then work on an assignment, typically examining the processes of organizational psychology that are going on in the exercise, with a particular focus on whatever is the current conference theme, for example 'Authority, leadership and organization', 'Leadership and innovation', 'Gender and creativity'.

These conferences typically give rise to many experiences of frustration, tension, enthusiasm, mania, conflict, boredom and so forth. The task for the review and application groups is, first, to identify the roles the members have taken and been allotted during the conference; second, to identify their own experiences, feelings and thoughts in connection with that; and third, from an application perspective, to associate these experiences with challenges in their own organization. An important educational point in these groups is that it is important to be quite specific in the effort to connect the learning with one's work in the home organization, as the conference otherwise risks being perceived as a great experience with no connection to the participants' everyday life.

In a Role Analysis group with six participants, at least 60 minutes should be allocated to drawing and then 3×30 minutes per participant to work with each of the three elements of the role analysis: family, home organization and conference. The purpose is to gain insight into unconscious patterns and maladaptive defence mechanisms and thus create latitude to choose among different types of behaviour. The method is to find links and connections between the roles the individual participants have taken and been allotted in their respective childhood families, current families, home organizations and the conference that the Role Analysis group is a part of. During the first session, the participants are introduced to the purpose of role analysis and encouraged to draw both a family diagram and an organizational diagram (see illustrations on the following spread) (Figures 8.1 and 8.2).

The family diagram should actually combine three diagrams, as each participant should draw both their own and their partner's childhood family diagrams and a diagram for their current family. Each person in the diagrams should be noted by first name, gender, age and occupation as well as three characteristic personal qualities – ideally added spontaneously and without deliberation. At this point, it is already possible to establish links and connections between the two childhood families and the current adult family.

The organization diagram is drawn using the same procedure. Significant others, at both the personal level and the system level, are noted by first name, gender, age and job title, and three spontaneously generated qualities

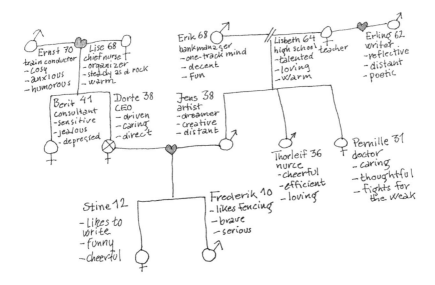

Figure 8.1 Family diagram.

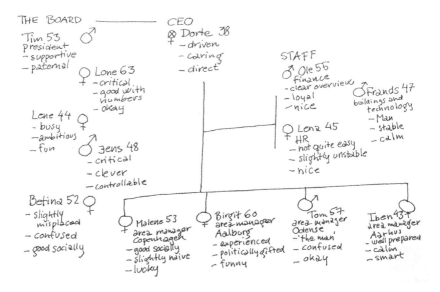

Figure 8.2 Organizational diagram.

are added. Often, family and organizational relations are rather complicated in postmodern societies; when that is the case, it is necessary to be suitably creative and find room for the essential aspects.

The method can be varied by using drawings instead of diagrams or by a combination of the two formats. Contrary to what one might expect, drawings will not generally bring out more emotions than diagrams. Experience shows that diagrams are most effective, but often, drawings can provide additional, interesting material.

When the participants have finished the diagrams, they present them to the group. The consultant directs the process, asks questions and receives help from the other participants. First, the group does a round on family dynamics, then it discusses the 'home organization' and finally, it addresses the conference experiences. The increasingly clear patterns are put into perspective in relation to the individual participant's role in the 'home organization'.

The organizational psychology angle focuses on the issue of why the organization needs to place tension and conflicts in or between systems in the form of persons, groups and so forth. The issue of why this person or that person, these two individuals or this group or that group are allotted these roles is also central. When dealing with individuals, it is relevant to apply a more individual psychoanalytic approach, and the field moves into the area where psychotherapy also operates. Bion's (1961) concept of valence specifically addresses what organizational or group processes a given individual has the valence to get unconsciously involved in. Coaching and supervision should be able to address both questions: why does the system need to allocate this role to you, and why did you (again!) take on that role? In role analysis, the latter question is figure, while the former is ground.

Example: Anne and the women

Anne, a participant in a working conference who worked as an engineer in the Technical Administration of Region 'Z', had established a certain reputation for being able to hang out in the bar as long as the toughest blokes.

One thought-provoking aspect of her presentation of her childhood family was that she hated her mother for constantly letting her know that she had ruined the mother's life by being born. The mother had had to give up a promising career as a classical musician in order to be a mother and also seemed to feel that neither her husband nor Anne's two brothers lived up to her standards.

Anne found it difficult to deal with women, so she enjoyed her work in a Technical Administration where she might go weeks without seeing another woman. She loved her husband and was deeply grateful for having had two sons.

In the organization exercise at the conference she had followed a group of participants into a room where a woman had soon taken charge. Anne was able to tolerate that for exactly 25 minutes, then she walked out and toured the corridors a little until she ran into Tommy and Harry and formed a group with them with a strong emphasis on the creative aspect of working on unauthorized ground. They enjoyed their interactions in the group and relished running down the self-righteous female managers. They were invited to join several other groups, just as the staff also encouraged them to find a workspace within the authorized area. The consultants were only able to offer help if the group worked in an unauthorized room.

Anne's problem was clearly that she automatically avoided other women, both because it meant missing out on the resources they had to offer and because she, less visibly, carried a self-hate that occasionally led to self-destructive behaviour.

The other participants in the organization exercise were unable to integrate the group – the 'unauthorized', as they came to be known – in the exercise. Like Anne in her own system, the group derived a certain self-destructive pleasure from being a thorn in the side of the well-functioning system; conversely, the larger group was unable to let go of its own perfectionism in order to reach out to the 'unauthorized'.

Example: Sean and acknowledgement

Sean worked as an HR assistant in a large municipal administration. He felt an intense lack of acknowledgement from his supervisor and – it turned out – from the consultant in the supervision group.

He was the middle child of five, with two older brothers and two younger sisters. He had grown up in the countryside, where the family had been farmers for generations and had considerable amounts of self-esteem invested in this lifestyle. One day, there was a fatal accident, where the grandfather knocked down the second-eldest brother with the tractor in the middle of the yard. He was never able to forgive himself and slowly withered away and died a year after the accident. The atmosphere in the family became cramped and strained, and the mother began to focus more on the dead brother than on the remaining siblings. On the small coffee table, she kept a lit candle in front of his picture at all times, and she would often comment that now, Neil would have started school or how Neil would have loved this strawberry dessert. The father grew even more withdrawn and silent than before and only showed an interest in farm-related issues. Sean withdrew and went on long bicycle rides around the local area. He did well in school and gradually became determined that he was not going to be a farmer. He took a business degree, developed an interest in organizational psychology and added consultancy training on top of his master's degree.

At some point, he realized he was gay, and a few years later he worked up the courage to tell his mother that he was in love, and his partner's name was Steve. His mother's comment was that it was a good thing he had moved to Copenhagen where that sort of thing would not stand out as much.

In the supervision group Sean addressed the theme of how unfair it was that his manager rarely acknowledged his contributions, while his two younger, female colleagues received frequent praise. In professional terms, he felt he was at least as competent as the better of the two women. The two females felt it was quite natural to stop by their supervisor's office whenever they had accomplished something, while Sean found this cheap and preferred not to sing his own praises like that. With this behaviour, Sean was unconsciously recreating situations where others received the acknowledgement he yearned for – just as it had been in his childhood family.

Chapter 9

Mergers

In merger processes between organizations it is clear to see how family dynamic figures are activated and make it extra hard for managers and employees to focus on the task at hand. Feelings of deep injustice, canonization of the managers who were thrown overboard in the process, passive aggression directed at the new management, brotherhood and solidarity between the employees from the now dismantled organizations and contempt for the new colleagues are frequent and powerful emotional binds in post-merger organizations. These feelings are very human, and they come up whether they are welcome or not. They block the employees' commitment to the task and can drive the new management mad.

I Mergers and blended families

The social and emotional dynamics of merger processes have many features in common with the family dynamic processes involved in divorce and subsequent new family constructions. Blended families, where both parents come from previous relationships, are often much more complex and difficult to manage than traditional nuclear families. The blended family was first used as a metaphor for the post-merger organization by a CEO who had seen more than most – both in organizational and family life. Over the 1970s he developed a small high-tech company. After five years, the company was purchased by a bigger company. Over the following six years, he had been through three mergers with increasingly big companies, and in addition he had gone through a divorce and subsequently established a new family with children from the two marriages. He proposed:

> Maintaining motivation after a merger involves looking for the right balance between corporate control and SBU autonomy in a merged company. It's a little like trying to motivate a teenage stepchild. You've got to know what's important and not hassle too much or an adolescent will become completely demotivated and do nothing ... or rebel and do something really bad. It is especially tough if you're not the natural parent and your values are both different and new.
>
> (Gilkey, 1991)

If we first briefly review the processes taking place in the social system that an ordinary nuclear family constitutes, we can subsequently examine what happens when we put two of these small social systems through divorces and into new family structures.

As we have already discussed several times above, sibling rivalry as well as alliances among siblings against the parents or external enemies are part of everyday life in ordinary families. Every child in the sibling group wants to be a respected member of the sibling group while also secretly hoping to be the parents', or one of the parents' favourite child (Coles, 2003). Triangles consisting of two persons who are 'in' and one who is 'out' operates both in and between the generations. An important challenge for the family is the generational change: the transfer of power from one generation to the next and the pairings that need to take place as part of this process (Figure 9.1).

Just as the children have an ambivalent relationship with the parents, whom they love and admire and occasionally despise and hate, the parents also have an ambivalent relationship with the children. They are proud of the children's skills, good marks in school and outer beauty, but they also envy their youth, strength, bodies, opportunities and future. As mentioned, this intergenerational tension is what Freud considers the engine of society's cultural development (Freud, 1905/1953). The family dynamics also include the parents' feelings for each other, love, hate, admiration, contempt, gratitude, envy and so forth. In the family, the members discreetly jockey for position through competition and alliances. On the other hand, like any other group, families are prepared to stick together whenever they face an external threat. Briefly put, the family is a melting pot for all sorts of feelings and relations – not out of the blue but in relation to the family's primary task (Figure 9.2).

In 1988, Ed Shapiro offered the following definition of the family's primary task: to facilitate age-appropriate development for all the members of the

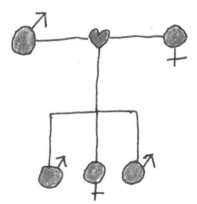

Figure 9.1 An ordinary family.

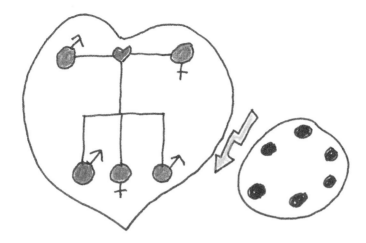

Figure 9.2 Family sticking together in the face of an external threat.

family (Shapiro, 1988). Perhaps it looks as if Shapiro is simply passing the buck to the developmental psychologists, but in fact, the definition is very apt, not least because a key characteristic of dysfunctional families is that the parents have regressed to an immature level of functioning, forcing the children to shoulder far too big a responsibility far too soon. The definition also implies an insistence on the need for 'age-appropriate development' for family members of all ages.

A merger process between two organizations begins with two managers or parental figures falling in love. If the mother from the Blue family and the father from the Green family fall in love they will soon build a common vision of a blended family which they imagine as a state of bliss. Initially, the whole affair is secret, and neither the children nor the betrayed spouses are told what is going on. The more sensitive, however, can tell something is happening and wonder about the many errands that the clandestine lovers have outside the organization or home (Figure 9.3).

When the clandestine affair is revealed, or the love-struck managers present their plans, the response from the betrayed spouses and children is anxiety and resistance. Naturally, the betrayed partners are opposed to the merger project, since they know from stories of other divorces that there is not really a place in the new structure for the parent who was betrayed and abandoned. This is parallel to organizational mergers where it is often the CEO from one company and the COO from the other who become the new management couple. The children are not enthusiastic either. Often, the only ones who can see the creative potential of the new construction are the new couple. The excluded partners and the children find the endeavour destructive and sick. If the new couple goes on to produce a child, the situation worsens. Although

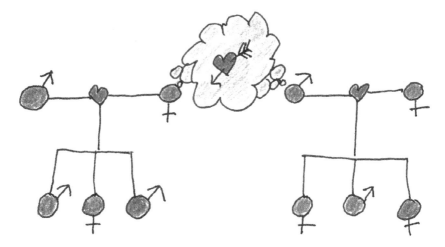

Figure 9.3 Rose-coloured merger fantasies.

this may give rise to alliances among the blended children, the alliances are built on a foundation of hate.

In such a reorganization process, the family does not have access to the powerful resource of family unity since the threat is coming from both outside and in. The children may try to blame the outside parent for seducing the father or mother, who would really have preferred to stay with his or her original family, but that explanation rarely holds up for long. Sometimes a parent may try to turn the children on the other parent, whom they then try to exclude. However, children dislike having to side with one parent over the other. They often relate to the breakaway adult with passive aggression, to his or her new love with slightly less passive aggression and to the betrayed adult with a nurturing and protective stance.

This is closely aligned with the employees' reaction to new management. The employees' sympathy is reserved for the abandoned managers, who are idealized along with the former organization. This is difficult to discuss, as it feels disloyal towards the manager who paired up with a new manager colleague. Consequently, these feelings are instead expressed indirectly in the form of distancing, passive aggression, strange behaviour that is annoying to the manager and intensely annoying to the manager who, in a dynamic sense, occupies the step-parent's role and so forth (Figure 9.4).

There are three main reasons why children do not enjoy divorces and reorganized families. First, if the father has found a new love, she has taken the place that the daughter secretly desired for herself. The son may temporarily take the father's place by the mother's side, but even though this is labelled an oedipal triumph (cf. Chasseguet-Smirgel, 1984/1985a) and as such provides some pleasure, it also takes time and energy away from the son's own development. The same applies – with the relevant modifications – when it is the

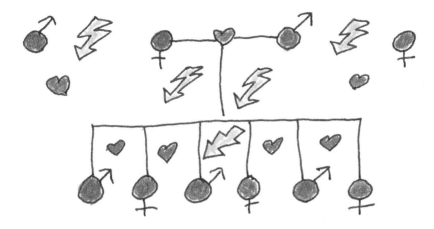

Figure 9.4 Complex feelings in connection with mergers and blended families.

mother who finds a new love. From an organizational perspective, the new co-habiting partners can be said to be placed in positions that the employees may had been vying for themselves.

Second, if the project calls for the children to share a home with the new constellation of father and mother and stepfather and stepmother, either part-time or full-time, it is not hard for the children to figure out that the resources will be notably reduced, particularly if the step-parents bring in their own brood of children. The step-parent's children are not seen as new potential playmates and network opportunities but as existential threats and competitors for limited resources. The result is hostility between the two groups of children. From an organizational perspective this corresponds to hostility and sometimes sabotage among the groups of employees.

Third, if the family's primary task is to facilitate the age-appropriate development of all the members of the family, the merger represents an inversion of the parental and child roles. In the family's development, the original 'plan' was for the children to leave home and find partners, thus representing renewal, while the parents are expected to form a stable and conservative antipole that the inventive and innovative youth can challenge and lean on. When a parent breaks away and starts up something new, that represents an assault on the new generation's positions. The children feel their development is pushed back, and that they are being subjected to forceful infantilization. They have to stay in the background while the new couple handles all the serious matters. In organizational mergers, working procedures often become more formalized because they now have to work in a big and often international organization. This formalization is perceived – and could reasonably be said to be – a demotion of the employees' own leadership responsibility.

Many of the irrational aspects of 'resistance to change' have their roots in these processes and emotional binds. The change activates opposite feelings, and as a result, feelings are often repressed instead of being expressed and worked through. All change implies both loss and gain, and in order to feel free to enjoy the gains one has to mourn the loss (Freud, 1917/1957; Visholm, 2004d). However, mourning the loss looks and feels like disloyalty towards the new reality, while celebrating the new feels and looks like a betrayal of the old. As Bion put it:

> As if the new development were a rival to be destroyed.
>
> (Bion, 1965/1984b, p. 98)

As outlined here, corporate mergers activate many of the same patterns as a divorce with the subsequent establishment of a blended family. Often, the manager comes from one organization, while the second-in-command comes from the other. The physical office space and plant often belongs to one organization, so the employees from the other organization have to relocate.

> A participant in a supervision group, who was a consultant on a merger between two geriatric psychiatry wards, described a merger that had unfolded in precisely that way. One ward had provided the physical setting but lost their director, while the director of the other ward became the director of the post-merger unit and brought her former staff with her. During a session with a group reflection on the merger and the transformation process it became clear that the employees who worked in their familiar setting were in no real hurry to help out the newcomers. For example, they might not remember where the nappies were stored when the newcomers asked.
>
> The session revealed that the merger process had activated very powerful feelings. The employees who had lost their director felt real hate towards the new director, her staff and her ideas, while the former director grew in stature as time went by. On the other hand, it also became clear that these powerful feelings to a high degree were wildly exaggerated and fairly irrational.

The comparison between a corporate merger and a divorce and new family formation is apt in many regards. Mergers clearly activate emotional reactions and processes that may be seen as a transference of family patterns to companies. However, while the children often manage to establish meaningful relations with both parents, and while the abandoned parents may also later successfully establish their own new families, the employees and leaders who are made redundant in the merger will usually be scattered into many different companies or perhaps even end up in the isolation of unemployment. While the 'victims' in a divorce thus remain in play, the contact between those who were let go and those who stay on in the new post-merger organization fades out fairly quickly. Some divorced families may be stuck in very 'toxic' relationships for years, while others reconcile and form new constellations. In organizational life, the tension does not receive new fuel from reality, and so it fades away or lives on as nostalgia and wounded feelings waiting for redress.

It should also be noted that in fact, the process that brings the new management couple together usually has little in common with falling in love. A more apt analogy would probably be a shotgun wedding arranged by the board or a higher level of corporate management. When the employees realize this, their anger against the management couple may be lessened, while the higher level of management instead is seen as bad.

II Organizational leadership in a merger

Organizational changes activate many strong and conflicted feelings. The management guru John P. Kotter makes this very clear in his books on change, including his 1996 book *Leading Change* and *The Heart of Change*, 2002, the latter co-authored with Cohen. The amount of power and energy that comes from a strong task commitment is matched by the amount of organizational deadweight and depressiveness that can spring from unprocessed feelings over loss and violation.

Change processes are often initiated by an organizational crisis, for example in the form of an altered assessment of the organization's market position. In relation to the family dynamic merger psychology above, extramarital affairs often spring from depressiveness or frustration over the couple's relationship. When a CEO becomes aware of a critical situation, that gives rise to what Bion calls 'catastrophic change' (Bion, 1965/1984b; Visholm, 2004d) occurs, the CEO may discover that a competitor has come up with something that is twice as good as his organization's own top-op-the-line product, and at half the cost. He puts two and two together, envisions how the company's turnover over the coming months is going to plummet, how layoffs will be necessary, how he is going to get the cold shoulder first from the board and then from his wife, who cannot stand being married to a laid-off CEO, and how the world generally turns into a barren landscape with permafrost, eternally overcast, where he stumbles around, starving, cold and alone. The CEO's world becomes fragmented, and anxiety and emptiness fill his mind.

If the CEO masters 'negative capability' (Bion, 1970/1988; French, 2001; French & Simpson, 2003) he holds on without acting in panic and waits until a so-called selected fact appears (Bion, 1963). A 'selected fact' is an idea that is capable of picking up the pieces of the former self-image and world picture and put them together in a new way that may contain a higher degree of complexity than before and also suggests a solution to the current problems. This may involve, for example, pulling an old project out of the drawer, one that was originally abandoned because the necessary technology had not been developed yet, or perhaps taking the opportunity to restructure and shift the 'labour-heavy' tasks to countries where labour costs are lower. Together with the other members of the management team and the chairman of the board, the CEO develops a plan that not only solves the current problem but also sets the organization on a good path well into the future.

The feelings that the CEO is now experiencing are pride, joy and excitement, and he is looking forward to sharing these feelings with the employees, whose workplace he has managed to save. He is therefore profoundly disappointed at the big meeting with the staff when he is met by suspicion and stony-faced shock instead of applause and enthusiasm. It irks him that now, just as everybody has to get into gear to salvage the situation, he is surrounded by opposition, mistrust, questions and confusion.

The source of the problem is that, in a sense, the employees are reacting precisely the way the CEO originally did. The CEO overlooked the fact that while he sees the plan as the answer to a psychological catastrophe, it does not represent that to the employees; instead, it represents a 'psychological catastrophe'. Who gets to stay on? Who will be laid off? Will I be offered a job in Poland? Will I still be able to leave early enough to pick up the kids from day care? Am I going to have to work in accordance with some idiotic American concept? The change raises many urgent questions, which can hardly be dismissed as irrelevant, seen from the individual's perspective. The fragmented self-image and world picture and the accompanying anxiety and sense of meaninglessness have now been shifted to the employees.

The anxiety they feel will likely generate all sorts of fantasy scenarios among the employees. Sending out informative letters with facts and reassurance does little to assuage their fears. The employees will probably insist that they are generally being kept in the dark. The CEO despairs; after all, he made a big effort to keep everybody informed via daily updates throughout the process. The point is that the employees are incapable of taking in new information as long as their minds are plagued by horror fantasies. However, the more these horror fantasies remain bottled up within the individual employees, the bigger and more threatening they become; if they are instead related and shared in a calm atmosphere, they will assume a realistic scale. In this phase of the process, leadership involves listening and thus making room for a real exchange of information.

As it becomes possible to establish a realistic picture of the consequences, losses and gains resulting from the change, it becomes time to make room for mourning the loss of the old reality. Some employees and some of the managers may have been with the organization for years and have incorporated its culture, logo and values as part of their own identity. It takes time to learn to use the new name instead of the old, and initially people tend to confuse the new colleagues with clients or guests. Since the mourning over the loss of the old situation may be perceived as a rejection of the new, it is important to make room and allow for the employees to express their grief. Good mourning thus makes it possible to engage in the new reality. Freud has described the work of mourning as follows:

> Reality-testing has shown that the loved object no longer exists, and it proceeds to demand that all libido shall be withdrawn from its attachment to that object. This demand arouses understandable opposition (...). This opposition can be so intense that a turning away from reality takes place and a clinging to the object through the medium of a hallucinatory wishful psychosis. Normally, respect for reality gains the day. Nevertheless its orders cannot be obeyed at once. They are carried out bit by bit, at great expense of time and cathectic energy, and in the meantime the existence of the lost object is psychically prolonged. Each single one of the memories and expectations in which the libido is bound to the object is bound up and hypercathected, and detachment of the libido is accomplished in respect of it. (...) The fact is, however, that when the work of mourning is completed the ego becomes free and uninhibited again.
>
> (Freud, 1917/1957, pp. 244–245)

The acknowledgement of the loss of the organizational object happens gradually, just as it takes time to work through a divorce and come to terms with the failure to preserve a complete family picture and a continuous narrative. Every time one encounters holidays or anniversaries, there is a psychological mourning to be dealt with, but once one has, for example, come to terms with the notion of celebrating Easter in a particular way, new ideas will gradually begin to emerge that suggest alternative ways of celebrating.

Failing to work through the mourning process leads to a situation where large groups of employees hold on to the image of the old organization as a golden era, where everything was better, people were more competent and friendlier and so forth. As long as there are employees and managers in the new organization who have been given notice and are waiting to leave, it will be difficult to unleash any enthusiasm for the new organization. It seems inappropriate and insensitive to be looking forward to something that some of the others are not going be a part of. This might make it tempting to use an approach that was used in a large American software firm during the 1990s, described by Howard F. Stein in 2001. A woman – called 'Betty' in the story – says,

> The strangest thing happened last Monday, Howard. I was off sick Friday. I came into work on Monday morning and the office next to me was cleared out. (...) It's like there's a big hole in this place. I knew the guy ten years. (...)
> At 9:00 a.m. Friday, security guards showed up all over the plant at the offices and workstations of people who were going to be fired. They

escorted them to the big auditorium over in the corporate conference center. They didn't even tell them why they had to go, except that it was an important announcement. After they walked them in, they left and locked the doors behind them.

The way I heard it secondhand, the CEO then went in after everybody was there, delivered a little speech on how the company had to downsize radically in order to survive and be competitive. He told them not to take it personally, and thanked them for their service to the company.

The security police escorted them back to where they worked, helped them clear out their belongings, then took them down to administration to hand over all their keys and receive their last paycheck. The police walked them to their cars, and that's the last they saw of this place.

(Stein, 2001, pp. 55–56)

The impact of such an approach is not to unleash enthusiasm but rather to establish a – justified – paranoid atmosphere with some of the characteristics of concentration camp. The process dehumanizes both the ones who are retained or hired and the ones who are laid off, corresponding to downsizing metaphors such as cutting 'excess fat' or 'dead meat'. In these situations of loss, people react both by identifying with the persons who were let go and by being affected by the loss of having them as colleagues. The process thus leaves a big gaping hole for those who are left behind, a hole that is filled with anxiety and terror. There is probably also an amount of survivor's guilt matched, in equal amount, by the fear of being the next to be 'deported'.

Although it is unpleasant, both for those who are laid off and for those who stay behind, it is important to say goodbye in a way that lets both parties look at themselves in the mirror the next day. It is also important not to keep those who have been dismissed sitting around for too long. The way dismissed employees are perceived by those employees who are focused on the task leads to the departing employees being treated as socially dead (cf. Hirschhorn, 2000). They are not future competitors or allies. It is not pleasant and probably serves no purpose to be subjected to being regarded as socially dead.

There are two kinds of polarization among the employees. The first, most obvious one is mutual hostility between the employees from the two organizations that have merged. Ordinary primitive group processes kick in, and each of the two groups of employees attribute nothing but bad qualities to the other, ranging from a lack of morals to a lack of adequate competencies. Underneath, there may be a fear that in fact the other group is the more competent and that their superiority will soon be revealed. It is important to name and interpret this mutual hostility as a reflection of loyalties and ordinary group processes in contexts where two groups feel that they are competing for limited resources.

In most cases, the employees from both organizations are probably competent and committed, but the uncertainty of the merger process makes polarization tempting. A good way to move past the polarization is to estab-lish task forces, project groups and similar work groups staffed with partici-pants from both organizations and equipped with appropriate competences to get the task done. It is important that the task is a necessary and important one for the organization, not something that may be perceived as a diversion initiated by the HR department.

The employees in these task forces will soon discover that the employees from the other organization are just as competent as they are. In this process, the manager may make him/herself available to anger projections, for example by imposing the group make-up on the employees as a way to facilitate col-laboration among the two groups of employees. If management succeeds in making opinion leaders from both groups engage in a committed task-driven effort there is a good chance that the merger will be successful, including establishing effective teamwork in a good working climate.

The other form of splitting that may occur is that the employees split up into saboteurs and sycophants (Hoyle, 2004). While the sycophants in principle welcome everything management does as intelligent and good, the saboteurs have the opposite view, which is that everything management comes up with is bad and evil. If the most eager proponents of both camps manage to organize the employees around their two positions, the result will be conflict and trouble rather than efficient collaboration and a productive working climate. To avoid this, management should seek to isolate the extremists of both wings and focus on addressing both the moderately enthusiastic and the moderately critical. It is in these two groups that there will be real thought processes related to the merger that will be worth paying attention to. Instead of polarization, man-agement needs to promote integration by exploring how both sides might have valid points.

It is important to allow and legitimize complex (negative) feelings in relation to the change – for example by sharing one's own reservations. This involves ensuring continuous reflection on the process, for example by interpreting and pointing out – in a relaxed and humorous way, ideally using one's own experi-ences as an example – how the emotional binds of the merger process interfere with a rational approach to the task.

Chapter 10

Innovation

Don't imitate, innovate.

(Ad for HUGO by Hugo Boss)

Everybody starts by imitating their heroes. (…)
>   First off you just copy, then eventually you start to find out
>   if you can add your own thing to it.

(Keith Richards in West, 2009)

The concept of innovation is on everyone's lips in this new millennium. Innovation appears to be the answer to globalization and the growing international competition.

The definition of the concept of innovation is widely debated. In this context, I am going to stick to a broad and simple definition. Essentially, innovation means renewal (Oxford English Dictionary online). Innovation is both a process and a product. A successful innovation process leads to innovation, which does not need to be a product in a narrow sense. The process aims to create something new and better and has to address both concept and realization. Whether it is actually new and better is determined by the context.

In this chapter I will first discuss C. O. Scharmer's theory of innovation, which is widely used in Denmark. This will be followed by a brief review of psychoanalytic creativity theories concluding with a presentation of a three-phased psychodynamic innovation model and a related concept of pseudoinnovation or perverse innovation. The chapter closes with a review of how creatively intended organizational psychology approaches offer a 'creative' cover-up of conditions in the public administration that cannot bear the light of day by dismissing such concepts as reality and truth.

1 Scharmer – presentation and criticism

C. O. Scharmer's book *Theory U: Leading from the future as it emerges: The social technology of presencing* was published in the United States in 2007 and appeared in Danish in 2009. Scharmer is a senior lecturer at the

Massachusetts Institute of Technology in Boston, USA, and collaborates, among others, with Peter Senge, who is known for his theory of the learning organization (1990). In an innovation context, the key concept is 'precensing'. The 'U' in 'Theory U' illustrates a process where precensing is at the bottom of the 'U', as the way to that point is about opening up and leaving the past behind, while the way back up describes the movement from idea to product. One particular life event plays a key role in Scharmer's theory. I will introduce Scharmer's interpretation of this event and demonstrate how his understanding of it leads to a flawed theory of innovation, creativity and leadership.

In the book, Scharmer describes how his thinking leading to Theory U began in his youth, as he stood in front of his burnt-out childhood home, a 350-year-old farm north of Hamburg, Germany. One day, in the middle of a lesson, a schoolteacher said to the young Scharmer that his parents had phoned the school and ask him to hurry home. She did not tell him why but he got the message and opted for a taxi from the station rather than wait for the usual bus. The teacher's eyes were slightly red, Scharmer recalls.

As he stood in front of the smouldering ruins, Scharmer initially felt that the ground had been ripped from under his feet:

> The place of my birth, childhood, and youth was gone. (…) As my gaze sank deeper and deeper into the flames, the flames also seemed to sink into me. Suddenly I realized how attached I had been to all the things destroyed by fire. Everything I thought I was had dissolved into nothing.
>
> (Scharmer, 2007, p. 24)

However, now Scharmer discovers that he himself is still alive:

> Everything I thought I was had dissolved into nothing. Everything? No, perhaps not everything, for I felt that a tiny element of me still existed. Somebody was still there, watching all this.
>
> (…)
>
> I felt my mind quieting and expanding in a moment of unparalleled clarity of awareness. I realized that I was not the person I had thought I was. My real self was not attached to all the material possessions smoldering inside the ruins. I suddenly knew that I, my true Self, was still alive. I was this 'I' that was the *seer*. (…) I was no longer weighed down by all the material possessions the fire had just consumed.
>
> (Ibid.)

Scharmer's grandfather, who was 87 years old and had lived on the farm his whole life, visited the site, and without even turning his head to the smoking ruins he went up to his son, Scharmer's father, and said,

'Kopf hoch, mein Junge, Blick nach vorn!' 'Keep your head up, my boy, look forward!' Then he turned, walked directly back to the waiting car, and left. A few days later he died quietly.

(Ibid., p. 25)

Scharmer discovered that we have two selves:

One self is connected to the past, and the second self connects to who I could become in the future.

(Ibid.)

Twenty years after this event, Scharmer is still grappling with the issue of what is his true self and how it relates to the other temporal dimension, that is,

The one that seemed to draw me from the future that wants to emerge.

(Ibid.)

Theory U is constructed as an attempt at cleansing the mind of the past and opening it to the presence and then – in a magic moment – tapping into the 'source' behind 'the blind spot' and embracing 'emergent' presencing: the idea that points to the future.

But what is this struggle that Scharmer is having with the past? Why is it pulling him away from somewhere he wants his focus to be? And how is Scharmer's struggle with the past relevant to leadership and innovation? These are the questions I will attempt to answer in the following.

Scharmer's interpretation of seeing the burnt-down family farm is that he is able to turn a trauma, a traumatic event, into an epiphany that inspires him to develop Theory U. It is, however, worth examining whether Scharmer actually manages to replace his trauma with an epiphany.

The ordinary reaction in the face of this sort of traumatic experience is a crisis response that includes the phases of shock, reaction, adaptation and reorientation. In a classic psychoanalytic perspective, after a loss the person has to complete the mourning process to be able to break free from the loss, so that 'the ego becomes free and uninhibited again', as Freud puts it (1917/1957).

Failure to mourn the loss makes it impossible to break free. Breaking free does not mean cleansing the mind of memories or destroying them but integrating the traumatic experience of loss into one's life history as something one can reflect on and learn from. If Scharmer is haunted by the past, as he puts it, it is thus reasonable to assume that he has failed to mourn the loss of the family farm properly.

Indeed, Scharmer's description seems to include repression. A family farm is not just a material entity. In the story we meet Scharmer's father, who is comforted by his father with the encouragement to look forward and keep his head high. We learn that the grandfather dies a few days after the fire, but we hear nothing about whether Scharmer's mother consoled Scharmer, or whether Scharmer's own father said something uplifting to the young Scharmer.

One imagines it must have been a pretty sad time for the Scharmer family with the grandfather's funeral – without a wake at the family farm – the family being put up in a hotel, a young man alone with his parents. The parents are cut off from everything their personas, competencies and strength depended on. Farmers without a farm would seem about as meaningless as a skipper without a ship.

The tragedy takes place in Scharmer's youth, when the psychological developmental task is to challenge and break free from the parents. It appears that the young man has defeated his father without a battle, as the fire beat him to it. Scharmer's description contains both a triumphant note and an element of loneliness, isolation and emotional flatness: I, I, I he writes.

Freud (1905/1953) argues that 'cultural development' or creativity draws its energy from intergenerational tension. To make an impression on the opposite-sex parent, one tries to outperform the same-sex parent. The fire extinguished this tension for the young Scharmer.

The razed family farm may be seen as the sort of oedipal showdown where the father has been struck down too hard, and where it was not his son's creativity that ousted him. There is nothing grand or beautiful that the son has accomplished, no manifestation of ingenuity, skill, efficiency or greatness that the father needs to acknowledge. Scharmer seriously seems to believe that the fire unleashes his creativity. It is probably closer to the truth to say that he remained in the shock phase of his crisis response and never actually worked through or adapted to his loss.

The key figure in Scharmer's theory is that if we can only stop constantly downloading patterns from the past we can get into contact with our true selves, which potentially hold good ideas for shaping the future – the way he did after the fire. Scharmer almost seems to express regret that not everybody can be so fortunate as to see their childhood home razed by fire:

> The challenge is how to access the deep territory without burning down the family farm.
>
> (Ibid., p. 180)

The past is actually standing in the way. Scharmer devalues the past. The emptiness that the lost past leaves behind is to be replaced by precensing, the new social technology.

Scharmer does not offer a very precise definition of his concept of 'presencing'. Terminologically, it combines 'presence' in the moment and 'sensing'. What we are supposed to sense is not the outer world but a source that springs behind the 'blind spot' in our authentic selves:

> Presencing happens when our perception begins to happen from the source of our emerging future. The boundaries between three types of presence collapse: the presence of the past (current field), the presence of the future (the emerging field of the future), and the presence of one's authentic self.
>
> (Ibid., p. 163)

This somewhat overwrought emphasis on presence, depth, authenticity and so forth raises suspicion that Scharmer is constructing a projective space, a magical box from whence the magician, holding us in thrall with his hypnotic gaze, can pull out one innovation rabbit after another.

On the one hand, we have Scharmer's staunch and rigid criticism of the past, in all its guises, and on the other, we have the vaguely defined, semireligious concept of presencing.

If we take a closer look at Scharmer's illustrative examples from the Presencing chapter, however, we find several metaphors from the domains of struggle, love, reproduction and family life. The following are statements by participants in innovation seminars:

> When this moment of change comes, it is no longer me, alone, who is creating. I feel connected to something far deeper and my hands are co-creating with this power.
>
> (Statement by the sculptor Eric Lemcke, ibid., p. 168)

> After we reconvened, the project leader pressed on through an endless list of checkoff items. I glanced up at David (…) someone who had initially struck me as probably the most hardnosed guy in the group. An iron man (…) he was also the most focused and serious guy on the team. (…) His question came from his source, and that was the turning point. (…) The project leader was furious.
>
> (Ibid., pp. 169–170)

> It felt as if I was breaking through a membrane.
>
> (Ibid., p. 171)

> Well, in a way I experienced the day as a wedding. In the end there was a solemnity in the room, like in a cathedral, and an intimacy, like you only have when you know one another as well as you do in a family.
>
> (Ibid., p. 172)

Letting go and surrendering can be thought of as two sides of the same coin. Letting go concerns the opening process, the removal of barriers and junk in one's way, and surrendering is moving into the resulting opening.

(Ibid., p. 181)

These examples abound in metaphors for competition, attack, conception, liberation, sex, dedication, childbirth, delivering a baby and so forth: themes associated with relationships and passion. Scharmer's presencing concept only operates with his ever-present 'I'. In the examples, the repressed returns, intergenerational tension, creativity as generativity: conception, childbirth and raising a child.

Scharmer's theory comes to a dead end, in part because the point is not to burn the past but to challenge it and in part because the conceptual marginalization of the past means that Theory U is inadequate when it comes to addressing the relational challenges of creativity. Scharmer represses the relational aspects – desire, power and upwards, downwards and lateral competition – unconsciously positioning it behind the blind spot, at the source of the authentic self, where we can only glimpse the origins of the repressed material by looking at the metaphors provided in the examples.

III Innovation and psychodynamics

While research and literature on innovation viewed from a psychoanalytic or psychodynamic position is limited, there is a wider range of concepts and theories about creativity.

A psychoanalytic or psychodynamic theory on innovation can be divided into three stages: 1) the conception of an idea, 2) nurture and protection – testing and development and 3) realization. The theory outlined here draws on ideas and observations by, in particular, Freud, Klein, Bion, Chasseguet-Smirgel, Hirschhorn, Meltzer and Halton.

In this context, Freud is best known for his sublimation concept, which views creative activity as a way to translate impulses into a socially accepted form (1905/1953). He claimed elsewhere that 'cultural development' was driven by the tension between the generations (1905).

Melanie Klein (1957/1975b) places creativity in the depressive position in the form of reparation work, the effort to put the mother together again and repair her after the attacks from the paranoid-schizoid position.

This theme is also found in the work of Bion, who regards creativity as the exchanges between the 'container' and the 'contained', which he denotes by male and female symbols, respectively, and between the paranoid-schizoid position and the depressive position (1963). In extension of the Keats's poetry, Bion (1988) also writes about 'negative capability', the ability to tolerate uncertainties, mysteries and doubts without giving in to the pressure to decide one way or another.

Janine Chasseguet-Smirgel (1984/1985a) also uses the reproduction process as an image of creativity. True creativity is based on an acknowledgement of the genital universe, the universe of differences, while perversion and pseudo-creativity unfold in the anal universe, the undifferentiated universe.

Larry Hirschhorn (2001) sees the passionate person as someone who has a hole in their identity. To the passionate person, the realization of the project is equal to repairing the hole in the identity. The relationship between the passionate person and his or her idea is compared to a romantic relationship, where the passionate person believes their love is so amazing and unique that they are above the rules that the other group members have to abide by. The rest of the group may well find this attitude to be problematic.

Building on Klein's work, William Halton (2004) has described three kinds of creativity that are associated, respectively, with the paranoid-schizoid position, the depressive position and a third position: the evolutionary position. Initiatory creativity, which is based on omnipotence as a result of fusing with the mother, is associated with the paranoid-schizoid position, while reparative creativity, which aims to repair the damage that has been done, is associated with the depressive position. Evolutionary creativity is based on gratitude and the desire to pass on what has been received and is associated with the notion of the creative couple (Meltzer & Williams, 1988) and of tradition. An important part of Halton's contribution is to point out how creativity activates envy, and that envy can take on many guises.

Stage one conception

The process of conceiving ideas is similar to an artist's process of inspiration and to the stage of conception in reproduction. In some case, the ideas appear uninvited; in other cases, a person might pace the floor for months without being able to conceive any new ideas. Sometimes a woman gets pregnant without wanting to or having made any special efforts. However, if a woman determines to become pregnant, it may take years before it happens. In short, we cannot force good ideas to come into the world.

The challenge is to combine respect for tradition with the courage to challenge it. In order to renew something, we need to know the current situation, since otherwise there is no way to know if we simply invented something that had already been invented or perhaps even confuse progress with setbacks. A Hugo Boss ad that many will remember said, 'Don't imitate, innovate.' Keith Richards of the Rolling Stones does not agree. He says imitate first, and then innovate:

> Everybody starts by imitating their heroes. (…) First off you just copy, then eventually you start to find out if you can add your own thing to it.
> (Keith Richards in West, 2009, p. 104)

In this sense, creativity is associated with the Oedipus complex. Being creative means challenging the parents, in competition with a group of siblings. It thus involves competition both within and between the generations. In their first attempts at tackling the Oedipus complex at the age of three to five years, the boy ideally realized that he cannot defeat the father and, for now, has to give up trying to take the mother away from him. He realizes that it is going to take time and effort to become like the father and instead identifies with him, learns, improves and grows, that is, he imitates. Similarly, the girl has to realize that she has to be an adult to master the mother's role and she too has to learn, improve and grow. In this process, there are occasional alliances with siblings and peers, where they enjoy discussing the parents' weaknesses and the flaws and shortcomings of the older generation at large. In this exchange, they may also test new ideas and discuss how they are superior to the ideas of the older generation. Ganging up to criticize 'the old folks' gives them a break from their mutual competition. Finally, the young adults have become so adept that they can actually challenge the parents. Then it is time for innovation. They no longer blindly take over the parents' opinions or automatically oppose them but are able to provide an independent assessment, respect and admire certain things, criticize others and being open to what is different, for example a partner who is not mum or dad.

In large companies that are not family-owned, this dynamic is less apparent, but fragments are often identifiable, and it is important to establish the key aspects at play. At stage one of the innovation process, where the conception of ideas is on the agenda, the leader's focus is on creating an atmosphere that combines the playful, erotic, exploratory and experimental elements with serious challenge in and between generations. The leader has to make and provide room, avoid allowing him/herself to be seduced for more than a brief moment and be able to display 'negative capability' (Bion, 1970/ 1988), that is, being able to tolerate being in a situation with no answers or solutions without giving in to the pressure to find a solution before its time. This involves having the courage to say and to realize for oneself that stuffing a pillow under your jumper is not equal to an actual pregnancy. In creative processes, it is important that the necessary decision-making authority is present or at least comes into the picture at a prearranged time. After all, one is not going to reveal one's best ideas before the game is on, and one has an actual chance of winning. Here, it can be tempting for the leader to see him/ herself as being above the competition, but the leader is not above envy and may ultimately prove to be the worst enemy of the new little ideas.

There is an aggressive aspect to competition and rivalry, and envy even has destructive aspects. The opposite of envy is gratitude. That feeling clearly permeates Keith Richards's relationship with his predecessors ('heroes'). In good scenarios, gratitude can become an engine of creativity: the desire to pass on the goodness one has received. The new generation may feel gratitude for what they have received from their predecessors, and the old generation may feel pride and gratitude over their offspring's accomplishments. No competition, no development, but development springs both from what has been passed on and how it has been processed, so there is reasons for both parties to feel pride.

Stage two: nurture and protection – testing and development

When new ideas arrive, there is an important leadership task in protecting them against attacks from the ones who did not have them and also in seeing through perverse creativity and to reject ideas that are not viable. It is obvious that there is something at stake in coming up with new ideas. The brainstorming technique, which instructs the participants not to assess the individual ideas at first but simply bring up anything that comes to mind was clearly developed to damp down our spontaneous tendency to put down other people's ideas. Other techniques involve rotating the ideas throughout the group to be developed further, probably in the hope of toning down individual ownership and boosting common ownership. We are not that easily fooled, however. The originators of the ideas are not going to forget which ideas were their own.

The parents have to keep the 'child' safe. Envy is rarely direct and obvious but comes in many clever disguises. Little creative ideas may be subjected to attacks disguised as praise with just one tiny little reservation that is soon blown up to proportions that would overpower and kill any new idea. Leadership in this case is not about exposing or shaming the envious attackers but instead about rescuing the good ideas. It may be helpful openly to define envy as a commonly occurring feeling.

The leadership task at this stage is to distinguish between rational and envy-driven criticism and to contain and neutralize the envy that successful ideas activate. Containing involves attributing meaning and proportion to experiences and feelings. By daring to be present and taking an interest in the individual participants' experiences when there is a conflict in the group, the leadership demonstrates that there is room for conflict and for disparate experiences and that these differences and this tension can be productive.

Stage three: realization

In many cases, the realization stage marks the time when the idea is presented to a wider circle where it has to prove its worth. Here, it is going to encounter resistance for several reasons. One is that other people's creativity generally triggers envy. Another is that new ideas imply a criticism of the existing state of affairs that they aim to replace. They are thus an attack on and, in a sense, a devaluation of the existing situation and they may pose a threat to employees and others whose competencies become superfluous or whose jobs, privileges or positions disappear. Changes mean losses for some, gains for others and both for most people. If the organization is to welcome the new idea there has to be a burning platform – a palpable, comprehensible and existential threat to the organization that the change can save it from – or it will be necessary to initiate containing and mourning. When employees are presented with change – or merely to rumours of change – their anxiety levels increase considerably, and they begin to imagine all sorts of horror scenarios.

It is important for the leader to listen to these fantasies and take them seriously, so that their demonic content can gradually be dismantled. Once the demons are out of people's minds, there will be room for information and thus for addressing the changes in a realistic manner. If we fail to say good-bye to the old reality, it is going to return as fantasies about a golden era when everything was better – which is also an effective way to undermine creativity and innovation (Visholm, 2004d).

IV Pseudoinnovation

In *Creativity and perversion* (1984/86) Janine Chasseguet-Smirgel attempts to develop a theory of creativity, where perversion features as pseudocreativity: something that parades as creativity but is not. In her book *The perverse organisation and its deadly sins* (2008) Susan Long attempts to apply the concept of perversion on organizations. Here, I will attempt to connect this thinking with the theory of innovation.

As mentioned earlier, according to psychoanalytic theory the child is not supposed to have his or her oedipal desires fulfilled. Instead, the child is sup-posed to realize that he or she is too small to be better than an adult and thus instead focus on becoming an adult and learn what it takes. If this development fails, the child may achieve an oedipal triumph (Chasseguet-Smirgel, 1984/1985a), gaining the opposite-sex parent and getting rid of the rival, which does sometimes happen, to a greater or smaller extent, in connection with divorce or death. However, this triumph is not beneficial, as the child loses the motivation to mature and become a competent adult. After all, the child has already achieved what he or she wanted. The other possibility is perversion. Chasseguet-Smirgel (1984/1985a) distinguishes between the genital universe of differences, where gender and generational differences are acknowledged and respected, and the anal universe, where differences are denied and attributed no meaning. Faeces is undifferentiated matter. Our digestion turns different kinds of food into the same mass before it is returned to the ecological cycle of nature. The perverse possibility exists in the anal universe, where anything can be made equally well by undifferentiated matter (faeces), if it is decorated a little and described in inventive terms. A turd wrapped in tin foil, for example, is far superior to a real penis, and stuffing a pillow under one's jumper is superior to a real pregnancy. Gender and generational differences thus become unsubstantial. Anyone can make children who are just as good, if not actually better, out of undifferentiated matter. The benefit of being in this undifferentiated universe, according to

Chasseguet-Smirgel (1984/1985a) is that we escape psychological pain on several levels:

> Differences having been abolished, the feelings of helplessness, smallness, inadequacy, as well as absence, castration, and death – psychic pain itself – also disappear.
>
> (Chasseguet-Smirgel, 1984/1985a, p. 13)

In Chasseguet-Smirgel's theory, however, the origins of the creative transgression remain unclear. To acknowledge gender and generational differences simply implies accepting reality, while being creative or innovative means coming up with something that is not real yet, to renew and improve aspects of reality. Within regular reproduction, creativity is ensured by the system of the combination of different DNA strings. Still, this doesn't guarantee, that every individual child is a gift to humanity. In the creative process, where the parental generation is both respected and challenged, there are constant whispers, such as 'Is this "the Emperor's new clothes" or an amazing innovation?' or 'Is it perversion or innovation?'

Those who are challenged and who are not too happy about being overtaken, are more inclined to think 'perversion', while the challengers hope to demonstrate that it is true innovation. Innovation is based on cunning and skill, engagements with the matter, hard work, the urge to compete, dreams of big achievements or clever solutions, while perversion is basically built on deception – self-deception and the deception of others – and aims to cover up one's own flaws and shortcomings. The common factor is the effort to find easier and better ways. One takes on the struggle, while the other cheats.

If the innovation is true innovation, it works, and it works better than the solution or approach that it challenged. It becomes a new reality. With pseudoinnovation, the renewal falls short; for example, the tin foil may peel off, and it is a big effort to keep acquiring new tin foil to cover up the turd.

New Public Management (NPM) with its goals, performance standards and output controls, could be said to have a built-in structural requirement for pseudoinnovation. For example, in Sec. 52 of the Danish Act on Social Services, it reads,

> The municipal council shall decide on measures under subsection (3) where such measures must be deemed to be essential to a child's or young person's special need for support. The municipal council shall choose the measure or measures, which are best suited to resolve the problems and meet the needs identified in the course of the child protection examination under section 50.

If we combine this rule, which imposes no upper limit on costs, with the fixed economic allocation, anyone can see that situations are going to occur where the municipal administration does something wrong, whatever it decides. It either complies with Sec. 52 and overspend or stay on budget and act in violation of Sec. 52. Within the legal framework, it is not possible to determine that the needs of a child or a young person cannot be met because the coffers are empty. On the other hand, overspending is not politically viable.

The former Chief Executive of Furesø Municipality in Denmark, Klaus Majgaard said in an interview in *Berlingske Tidende* on 12 February 2012 that he was not pleased to admit that the public sector stays on budget by using dual messaging that passes the buck downwards, to lower tiers in the hierarchy:

> Maintain strict control and stay on budget, but make sure the quality is impeccable. Or, trim down the bureaucracy, but make sure to be able to document everything you do.
>
> (Majgaard in Frank, 2012)

One is reminded of Bateson et al.'s (1956) double-bind hypothesis, which claimed that a young person who is caught in a double bind – a situation in which there is no right choice – can be driven to schizophrenia. Bateson's hypothesis cannot be confirmed, but within public leadership it is easy to determine that NPM's built-in double binds lead to pseudoinnovation and perverse leadership.

Here is an anonymized example from a Danish municipality. When the head of department discovers that the coffers are about to be empty, he instructs the psychologist who recently made professionally motivated referrals to special-needs education for children and parents, to draw up new referrals with fewer hours without mentioning budgeting constraints. Another example is the ample documentation that exists that families appear to have much greater need for treatment during the early months of the fiscal year than towards the end.

It is well known from the press that municipalities often fail to respond to indications of child abuse and incest in a timely fashion. They turn a blind eye, because the other can see that an appropriate response would blow the budget.

The built-in double bind in NPM thus pushes leaders and employees into a perverted universe where people have to call things by another name in order to obscure illegal administration practices.

V Positive thinking, political correctness, social constructionism and more

In closing, I will demonstrate how various approaches to the field of organizational psychology with actual creative intentions end up offering 'creative' cover-ups of aspects of reality (not least in public administration) that do not seem to be able to bear the light of day.

Positive thinking

In her 2010 book *Smile or die: How positive thinking fooled America and the world* Barbara Ehrenreich offers a critical take on positive thinking. Ehrenreich wrote the book after undergoing cancer treatment. During her treatment she had been provoked by the many encouragements she had received to embrace positive thinking and to look for 'the bright side of cancer'.

She traces the roots of positive thinking to the Calvinists, whose gloomy and self-denigrating thinking caused them to have headaches, insomnia and digestive problems. In response to this mindset, positive thinking was posited, its most persistent idea being the law of attraction, which holds that focusing intensely on something will bring it into being. From this, it follows that positive thinking will attract good things, while negative thinking will result in bad things. Ehrenreich has two objections to this idea, the first being that it is an illusion that our thoughts can affect the physical world. In the long run, illusions do not lead to good outcomes. Ehrenreich mentions several examples from George W. Bush's administration, where employees who felt that reality ran counter to the President's optimism in certain areas were fired. Similarly, she points out the intimate connection between the financial crisis and positive thinking.

Ehrenreich's second objection is the amoral and down-right mean aspect of this thinking. People who are in unfortunate circumstances are automatically assigned the responsibility for having put themselves into the situation and for thinking their way out again. Thus, positive thinking makes people responsible for events they have no responsibility for and absolves them of responsibility for events that they are responsible for. Naturally, Ehrenreich does not advocate defeatist, powerless and pessimistic thinking. The alternative to positive and negative thinking is thinking and realism.

While positive psychology has taken on growing prominence in recent years, appreciative inquiry (Cooperrider & Srivastva, 1987) has been around for a long time, in recent years in a somewhat unclear fusion with appreciative leadership. I personally recall a brief leadership course in a county administration, where the leaders were quite relieved not to have to tell the positive story about their organization for the third time in two years. They were also relieved that they were now allowed to voice their thoughts and feelings about the employees and about other leadership levels, even if that was initially about irritation and anger. Working with the thoughts and feelings that were actually there led to a better understanding of the organization's current situation and generated new energy for improving task performance. Feelings – positive as well as more difficult ones – hold valuable information about the state of the organization (Koefoed & Visholm, 2011).

Political correctness

In a series of essays and articles that have now been collated in the books *Revolt of the primitive: An inquiry into the roots of political correctness* (2001) and *Society against itself: Political correctness and organizational self-destruction* (2010) Howard Schwartz addresses the topic of political correctness.

Political correctness is a form of positive thinking with a purpose that is, at first sight, positive and humane (maintaining a civil tone and avoiding racist or discriminatory language). Roughly put, it aims to avoid bringing up anything that might harm the perception of minorities in society.

However, as the term itself reveals, political correctness has to be something other than basic correctness or truth. Prejudice is the basis of political incorrectness, a group psychology phenomenon where a group expresses wrongful and denigrating perceptions of another group, either because the members do not know better or because they are ignoring the truth.

Political correctness thus refers to positive prejudice. There is a problem, however, if political correctness denies or distorts the truth. The fear of saying or doing the wrong thing can undermine our curiosity and our search for knowledge, which are conditions for learning. That would prevent us from examining or including undesirable experiences and facts and thus compel us to repress them.

Schwartz's latest book includes a chapter co-authored with Larry Hirschhorn: 'The Jayson Blair scandal at the *New York Times*' (Schwartz & Hirschhorn, 2010). In this case, it took the newspaper several years to dismiss Jayson Blair, although it had ample evidence and examples of him circumventing the paper's high and identity-shaping ideals about journalism and instead fabricated his own stories out of whole cloth. Schwartz and Hirschhorn conclude that the reason the editors did not suspect Jayson Blair of this sort of fraud and deception was that he is Black.

Social constructionism

The dismissal of reality, including the rejection of the question of whether some 'social constructions' are more in step with reality than others, is one among many other problematic phenomena, a double-edged sword.

If an employee rejects his employer's argument that pay rises are impossible because of budget constraints by dismissing this argument as merely a social construction, the employer can, with equally compelling logic, argue that the employee's failure to make ends meet is itself a social construction.

Social constructionism deauthorizes itself, since, if it is valid it is merely one social construction among others. The social constructionist urge is the urge to play and provoke. Gergen quotes Rorty in the following:

> This playfulness is the product of [the] shared ability to appreciate the power redescribing, the power of language to make new and different

things possible and important – an appreciation which becomes possible only when one's aim becomes an expanding repertoire of alternative descriptions rather than The One Right Description.

(Rorty in Gergen, 1991/2000, p. 193)

The postmodern player exists, after all, in a symbiotic relationship with 'serious culture'. Without others to play the part of 'foolish fools', there are no opportunities for the heroic one.

(Gergen, 1991/2000, p. 194)

Gergen, who occasionally has access to the oedipal universe of differences himself, is able to constrain himself:

How are we to respond, for example, to the death of a child, life in a caner ward, crack houses in D.C., the condition of South African blacks, or the Holocaust? Does one wish in these instances simply to let signifiers frolic and go piss in the wind? Even the most jaded postmodern would stop short of such a conclusion.

(Gergen, 1991/2000, p. 194)

It is reassuring to know that Gergen, as a person, is able to constrain himself, but there is nothing in social constructionist theory that can actually bring it out of its non-committal playfulness. Phrases such as 'There is not one truth, there are many' or 'Nothing is more true than anything else' can have a liberating effect when one works with social relations, but they do not alleviate the need to make up one's mind, prioritize, argue and decide what is better than something else. That is not possible within the framework of social constructionism. And so the deconstructive joke is on the person who told it. It is fun to challenge authority, but unless one is prepared to embrace authority, it remains an empty gesture.

What was originally intended to have a critical and creative potential is now used to legitimize pseudoinnovation and perverse leadership. While it was once possible to challenge by offering alternative descriptions and new constructions, leaders who are under pressure now resort to storytelling, positive thinking, also known as hot air.

Chapter 11

Globalization and modernization

> At the turn of the millennium, the king and the queen, the state and civil society, are both naked, and their children-citizens are wandering around a variety of foster homes.
>
> (Castells, 1997/2010, p. 420)

To Winnicott in 1950, Britain was a self-evident, well-defined whole surrounded by the sea on all sides. To Krarup, when Denmark voted to join the EEC (now the EU) in 1972 and later, in 2006 (cf. Chapter 4), when he saw the need to quote himself, Denmark was a similarly well-defined and self-evident entity that could be compared to a house:

> The national border is the wall of the home. There are doors and windows in the wall, so people can look and travel in and out.
>
> (Krarup, 2006) [translated for this edition]

Krarup's house metaphor and Winnicott's natural borders for the people and nation have been severely challenged since the statements were made. Since then, the boundaries around nations, organizations and families have changed radically in many regards. The wholes and boundaries that once seemed fairly natural have come under pressure, reshaping and reorganization, primarily as a result of technological development spearheaded by information technology.

I No sense of place

In the traditional premodern family enterprise, work and family life unfolded within the same well-defined geographical locality. The modernization process, with industrialization, urban growth and intensification of global trade, led to the formation of nation-states and separated work and family temporally and territorially. Everyday life was a carefully choreographed rhythmic activity. After breakfast, the family dispersed, as the members travelled to their respective workplaces, schools and preschools where they, along with members from multiple other families, took on the tasks the various workplaces, schools and preschools had been put into this world to handle. At the end of the day, the same rhythmic activity repeated itself, only in reverse. Now the students, pre-school children and workers returned home to their families and had dinner, some of them shopping on the way home.

In sociology, around this time, the 'situation' emerged as a concept the social sciences could use in studying modern people's social behaviour (cf. above, Chapter 5). In this concept of the situation, the physical location plays a key role, as demonstrated by Joshua Meyrowitz in his 1986 book *No sense of place*:

> Situations are usually defined in terms of behaviours in physical locations. Goffman, for example, describes a behavioural region as 'any *place* that is bounded to some degree by barriers to perception.' (...) Lawrence Pervin defines a situation as 'a specific *place*, in most cases involving specific people, a specific time and specific activities'.
>
> (Meyrowitz, 1986, p. 35)

Until recently, these situated face-to-face meetings were the only ways we could gain access to the sights and sounds of each other's behaviour.

> The physical barriers and boundaries marked by walls and fences as well as the passageways provided by doors and corridors directed the flow of people and determined, to a large degree, the number, type, and size of face-to-face interactions.
>
> (Ibid.)

Meyrowitz's book, subtitled *The impact of electronic media on social behavior*, analyses how the electronic media, particularly telephones, radio and TV have altered our social lives. The interesting point, theoretically speaking, is that these electronic media have compelled the social sciences to abandon its brick-and-mortar metaphor and replace it with the concept of information systems. The core aspects of the situational concept is not bricks and doors but delimitation via perceptual barriers, as Goffman notes. The electronic media break down both the physical place and, in some regards, clock time as perceptual barriers. The radio reporter sends his or her report from the football match live into the living room, where the telephone rings with a call from mother-in-law in a city across the country. A person can watch Princess Diana's funeral on TV while enjoying their evening coffee, become moved by the event, leave the house to buy some flowers, lay them down in front of the British embassy where a TV crew is filming; they might ask the person why they have come, and the reply will be transmitted live into thousands of Danish homes and so forth.

Since Meyrowitz's 1986 book, smartphones, email and the Internet with the new social media have only further intensified the process. In Meyrowitz's definition, information systems are

A given pattern of access to social information, a given pattern of access to the behavior of other people.

(Ibid., p. 37)

The expanded concept suspends the limited perception of a particular information system and thus also suspends the traditional contrast between face-to-face interaction and mediated interactions. The phrase 'a given pattern of access' is crucial in its emphasis on boundaries: someone has access, others do not, and that is what distinguishes one information system from another.

The key aspect of the social processes that drove the change to the concept of the situation can be described as the development of the possibility of being present in more than one place at the same time. When this possibility is realized, it is no longer possible to determine unambiguously where a given person is located. One might ask whether she is at home, online or at work, and the correct answer may turn out to be 'Yes!'

The family's new boundaries and their impact

The possibility of being present in two places at once generally leads to an opening of society and to a relative levelling of differences between women and men, children and adults and managers and employees. Meyrowitz draws on Goffman's dramaturgy metaphor that distinguishes between 'frontstage' and 'backstage' domains. In a restaurant, the staff's frontstage is the dining room, while the kitchen is their backstage. For the guests in relation to the staff, the frontstage is when the waiter is within earshot, and backstage is when the waiter is out of earshot. When the waiter interacts with the guests, he is smiling and being polite and respectful, just as the guests pretend to understand the complexities of sophisticated food and wine; on the other hand, when the waiter is in the kitchen he may make disrespectful comments about guests, who, left to themselves, may be disparaging the waiter and the establishment overall. Meyrowitz's point in this connection is that TV gives us access to each other's backstages, and that this takes the mystique out of the differences. TV shows us what the lawyers do on their lunch break and what they talk about. Surprisingly, the wig and gown-wearing judges eat ham sandwiches and have marital problems. This removes some of their authority mystique, become human and look just like the rest of us. Men gain access to women's backstages and vice versa. Children gain access to the parents' backstages, and ordinary people gain access to the authority figures' backstages.

In this manner, TV opens the family to the world and to society's various subgroups, and authority figures are demystified and come to appear human. Parents lose the ability to control the flow of information to the family, because it is in practice impossible to censor the family's TV consumption. TV generally conveys an experience that everything could be done differently. What happens in one's own family clearly is not the only way to be a family.

The Internet contributes to the ongoing democratization of the access to information, so the authority figures' superior knowledge is gradually being reduced. In the authority relations generally, the weight is shifting from role-based towards a more person-based authority (Visholm, 2004b). The parents' authority is further weakened as the state and the market are taking over some of the family's dependence relations, and because the parents' influence on their children's choice of occupation and partner disappeared throughout the 1960s and 1970s. The relative levelling of the differences between men and women was also promoted by the fact that more women moved into the labour market, which reduced their dependence on the man, along with improved contraceptives.

The technologically facilitated modernization in the form of changes to the family's boundaries means both that the boundary between the family and the rest of world becomes highly permeable and that the parents' function as gatekeepers becomes difficult, bordering on impossible, in several regards. The difference between parents and children is reduced and demystified, just like the difference between father and mother, men and women. The man's authority and the parents' authority are weakened. It becomes difficult to establish clear roles, and the normativity of heterosexuality comes under pressure.

The network society in the information age

During the post-war years, the Western democracies stabilized and additional democracies emerged outside Europe and the United States, The European Union began to take shape. In 1989, the Iron Curtain came down, and attempts began to build new democracies in the countries in the former Soviet bloc. It soon becomes clear that the post-war assumptions about the foundation of democracy were beginning to change. The social life that the nation-states' democracies were supposed to manage began to evade the control of the nation-states in a growing number of domains.

The nuclear bomb was not seen as a weapons technology that protected nation-states against each other but instead as a global threat. Environmental and climate issues could not be addressed within the borders of the nation-states. The new means of communication also escaped the control of the nation-states and the parents, and images and information began to pour over the national borders through networks of computers and into living rooms and nurseries. Production processes were scattered over several continents, and the concept of organization increasingly eluded an understanding that was based on walls, windows and doors. Financial flows intensified and were less and less slowed down by national borders. These changes, which can be summarized under the concept of globalization, increased the rate and intensity of the modernization process. In his trilogy *The information age*, Manuel Castells introduced the notion of the network society as a concept to describe society's altered organizational structures. Castell's network concept is similar to Meyrowitz's modified concept of the situation, which is bounded by the access to information:

> Networks are open structures, able to expand without limits, integrating new nodes as long as they are able to communicate within the network, namely as long as they share the same communication codes.
>
> (Castells, 1996/2000 p. 432)

In his trilogy from the 1990s, Castells tended to see networks as the elite's and the globalized economy's space for the flows of wealth, where the capital in principle acted as a global phenomenon, while labour was tied to the local setting:

> Informationalism, in its historical reality, leads to the concentration and globalization of capital, precisely by using the decentralizing power of networks. Labor is disaggregated in its performance, fragmented in its organization, diversified in its existence, divided in its collective action. (...) Capital and labor increasingly tend to exist in different spaces and times: the space of flows and the space of place, instant time of computerized networks versus clock time of everyday life.
>
> (Castells, 1996/2000, p. 436)

However, experiences from recent years demonstrate that the space of flows is not the reserve of the elite, the financial interests and power at large. Political opposition across the spectrum also use the Internet and smartphones and produce new types of political public realms that are often difficult for nation-states to control.

> The space of flows coexists with the flow of spaces, and both express contradictory social interests.
>
> (Castells & Ince, 2003, p. 58)

At times, the network society can appear to be completely without borders and boundaries. Sonia Abadi (2003) claims that the network society has dissolved virtually all boundaries in the global village:

> There are worldwide networks that cut through geographical, political and cultural frontiers: art, scientific or technological discoveries and, increasingly, the internet and communications in general. But there is also trafficking – in drugs, arms, currency, power, women, children, organs – and the malignant implementation of globalisation. It seems that where before there was a border, now there is a network. In its luminous aspect, it is a symbol-generating and containing fabric that

modulates, diversifies and expands. In its ominous aspect, it spells dis-location, disintegration and degradation.

(Abadi, 2003, p. 223)

However, Abadi is probably not right in her claim that 'where before there was a border, now there is a network'. The network society is not without borders, whether in its positive or its negative aspects. Rather, there is a growing occurrence of 'mismatches' between border systems. One of the main sources of tension in the globalized world is that communication in some regards flows quite freely across borders, which also means that images of Western affluence circulate freely in poor countries, where they may provoke envy and provide the inspiration to emigrate, which in turn is why the borders around 'Fortress Europe' grow ever thicker and increasingly impenetrable. Another source of tension is mismatches between national democracies and globalized processes: economics and environment.

The network concept has certain connotations: flat structures with a democratic atmosphere, no obligations and freedom from hierarchical authority relations. Networks also have connotations of open boundaries in a wider sense. Anyone can join; everyone is welcome, and you can take it or leave it. In addition to all this freedom, there is also care and nurture; net-works also signal a safety net and a sense of connectedness for the uprooted postmodern individual. There is a strong utopian charge in the network con-cept. When we then, like Abadi, realize that the lack of boundaries also applies to the 'powers of darkness' the utopia suddenly seems frightening.

The network society also contains elements that are difficult to handle from a democratic approach. Democracy requires us to be careful about who belongs to the group that is bound up in mutual rights and duties as members of the democracy. Every citizen has a vote and only one vote. Persons can stand for election when they have been a member of the given group for a certain period of time and have reached a certain age. It is usually not possible to belong to more than one group within the same domain (for example nations or trade unions).

In contrast to democracy, no one can have a complete overview or grasp of the entire network. I know someone who knows someone, whom I do not know, but maybe I can get to know them via the person I know and so forth. The network has boundaries, but unlike democracy, the network cannot relate to itself, because the network does not contain any organizational centre that represents the whole network and respects its boundaries.

The nation-state and the network society

The situation of the nation-state has many similarities to the family situation. More and more of the activities and processes that are important to citizens' life and happiness take place outside the control of the nation-state: climate and pollution, financial flows, crime flows, weapons technology and communications technology. These changes demonstrate that our democratic institutions are inadequate. Like it or not, we have become participants in a global economy, and consequently we have to consider ourselves citizens on several levels – no longer just citizens in a parliamentary nation-state but also EU citizens and citizens of the world. The catch is that we have not developed democratic institutions to match the globalized economy. The new network organization of modernization thus leads to the development of a growing democratic deficit.

Organizations and work in the network society

Globalization is changing the boundaries of organizations and institutions. Organizations are changing from entities that had a domicile, an area that they served and a locally connected labour force to fragmented production processes, where each step of the process is carried out in the country that offers the most favourable economic conditions, often spread over several continents. Marketing and sales take place on the global market with the necessary local adaptations. Labour unions are gradually losing both influence and meaning, as the entity they face is spreading and moving its partial organizations around the globe. The labour movement thus finds itself in the same situation as the family and the nation: the domain where it is supposed to exercise its influence and exert its power is crumbling.

Generally, the radicalized modernization process elevates the level of anxiety in life. The pace of organizational development in the form of mergers, outsourcing, division into sections and so forth is in no way in sync with the time structure of family life. A modern family is an organization that has to coordinate two 'adult careers' and two or three 'children's careers'. Women and children are no longer accessories to the man but independent agents in education and working life. This imposes new vulnerabilities on the family but also opens new choices and opportunities.

The changes in the authority relationship that we described in connection with the discussion of the electronic media and the family also apply in organizations and institutions. The development from the early 20th century until today in some regards involves a humanization of working life but that is not all there is to it.

The bureaucracy that Max Weber described was organized with a view to exercising control through rules and roles and to keep personality and emotions out of the picture (1922/2003). This marked a break with monarchy and autocracy, where the all-powerful leader's personal whims made governance unjust and erratic. In the ideal bureaucracy, every issue would be receiving the same (correct!) treatment, regardless of who decided it. In many regards, the system corresponded to Taylor's 'scientific management' (1912/1997), which claimed to be able to calculate 'the one best way' via a scientific approach to the working process. The authority system was role-based and top down, and the edict was 'do not speak unless you are spoken to'. As Ritzer described it in his 1993 book *The McDonaldization of society*, a later instalment of this system is still in operation in many organizations.

The Hawthorne experiments (Roethlisberger, 1941/2001; Mayo, 1949/1997) and the group and democracy movement uncovered the social life unfolding alongside the roles and the rules, sometimes hindering and sometimes helping task performance, and also showed that the employees had other, more complex motives than pay. The role- and rule-based organization systems often proved to leave untapped resources in the employees, who for their part also showed an interest in more content and more influence on their work. Personality, feelings and opinions began to be allowed back into working life (Hirschhorn, 1997).

Companies increasingly aim to mobilize more and more of the employees' resources: their creativity, capacity for self-management, feel for what is happening on the market and so forth. This makes managers increasingly openly dependent on the employees and requires them to find a way to lead in a situation where the employees may know best. This makes both the managers and the employees more psychologically vulnerable, but it also gives them a chance to bring their personality and competencies into play in a way that is more developing and exciting. However, there seems to be a catch. On the one hand, companies are less loyal than ever, and on the other hand they demand a stronger emotional commitment (cf. Sennett, 1998).

The polarization between workers and capitalists or management is less prominent today, and the dismantling of the automatic hostility that long characterized this relationship means improved opportunities for learning. The parties do not necessarily have to interpret every initiative from the other party as an assault. On the other hand, as Lawrence and Armstrong suggest (1998), it is worth considering whether the weakening of the trade unions that is happening throughout the Western world, not least facilitated by former British Prime Minister Margaret Thatcher, may not have displaced the anger and depressive feelings related to working life from the familiar conflict between work and capital to

> an increasing incidence of withdrawal, overt or covert complaint, and so-called 'stress'.
>
> (Lawrence & Armstrong, 1998, p. 60)

It would be appropriate to add workplace bullying to the list. The employees direct their aggression against themselves and each other instead of examining the sources of their depressive and aggressive feelings and dealing with them.

II From interest and places to identity

To a high extent, radicalized modernity can be described as technologically and economically driven shifts of boundaries in and between systems:

families, organizations and nations. A sense of homelessness seems to be spreading as a result of the ongoing reorganizations of the systems. Volume 2 in Castell's trilogy on the information age, which is titled *The power of identity* (1997/2010), addresses how people increasingly form groups based on identities rather than near where they live or the organizations they work for.

> In such a world of uncontrolled, confusing change, people tend to regroup around primary identities: religious, ethnic, territorial, national. Religious fundamentalism – Christian, Islamic, Jewish, Hindu, and even Buddhist (in what seems to be a contradiction in terms) – is probably the most formidable force for personal security and collective mobilization in these troubled times. In a world of global flows of wealth, power, and images, the search for identity, collective or individual, ascribed or constructed, becomes the fundamental source of social meaning. This is not a new trend, since identity, and particularly religious and ethnic identity, has been at the roots of meaning since the dawn of human society. Yet Identity is becoming the main, and sometimes the only, source of meaning in an historical period characterized by widespread destructuring of organizations, delegitimation of institutions, fading away of major social movements, and ephemeral cultural expressions. People increasingly organize their meaning not around what they do but on the basis of what they are, or believe they are.
>
> (Castells, 1996/2000, p. 3)

The transition from interest to identity politics gives rise to new conflict axes in society. In a society where people regroup around identities instead of interest, democracy faces new challenges. Interest politics is, after all, generally based on an acknowledgement of mutual dependence among the parties as well as a common interest in the larger whole, while identity groups often derive their identity through a negative demarcation in relation to out-groups, view themselves as the whole and the others as aberrations, sinners, heathens, inferiors and as people who have taken or plot to take our place.

Resistance to modernization and globalization

Far from everyone approves of the globalization-driven radicalized modernization process. That became clear to everyone after the terrorist attack on the Pentagon and the World Trade Center on 11 September 2001. This attack gave rise to simplistic interpretations of the conflict as a global clash of civilizations or a war between 'democracy and Islam' or even 'the West and the rest', as the American commentator Samuel Huntington put it (Barber, 1995, p. xv). However, this view misses the point that the resistance is not only externally positioned but also exists internally in the Western nation-states (it should be noted that a bomb attack against the Alfred P. Murrah Federal

Building in Oklahoma City was carried out in 1995 by two American-born White nationalists). It also misses the point that the Islamic fundamentalists and 'holy warriors' are far from representative of the entire Muslim world.

In his book *Jihad vs. McWorld* (1995) Barber attempts to analyse the relationship between globalization and modernization on the one hand and the resistance against these developments on the other. On the one hand, we have Jihad, which in Barber's terminology is not an exclusively Islamic phenomenon but a combination of disintegral tribalism and reactionary fundamentalism, while McWorld, which in Barber's terminology is not an exclusively American phenomenon but characterizes integrative modernization and aggressive economic and cultural globalization. At first glance, these two opposite forces may appear to be representatives of 'the good old days' versus the hypermodern world, but, as Barber demonstrates in detail, the militant groups of 'the good old day' relied on the McWorld communications and infrastructure McWorld uses to market itself, just as McWorld markets its products by using images and symbols of the 'good old days'. The two powers are dialectically interconnected. In the preface from 2001 – written after the 11 September attack – Barber argues that in addition to fighting the terrorists directly we should also isolate them from their base by addressing the reasonable aspect of the criticism of McWorld, including, not least, the democratic deficit globalization is producing.

Nationalism and religious fundamentalism

The antiglobalization movement – fx ATTAC – has discovered its own globalized identity and changed its programme from antiglobalization to economically equitable and democratic globalization, while nationalists and religious fundamentalists are still labouring under the illusion of a lost golden age, where one could enjoy the pleasures of one's own religion and national characteristic unmolested by immigrants and multinational franchises. A thinking which implies that if we could only get rid of the disturbing elements and rebuild the nation, we could return to a more 'appropriate' way of living.

Religious fundamentalists are more dangerous in some regards, since the goal of their aspirations is not of this world and their struggle serves as a pass to heaven. One thing nationalists and religious fundamentalists have in common, though, is the totalitarian quality of their thinking. They know what there is to know; there is nothing new to learn. The Bible or the Qu 'ran has all the information they need. There is no need for curiosity, nothing new to learn.

Inverse totalitarianism

There are signs that the leaders of the democracies of the 'free world' are themselves regressing and moving in a totalitarian direction. Several scholars (Krantz, 2006; Khaleelee, 2004; Rothstein & Rothstein, 2006) have documented a tendency toward Evangelical fundamentalism in the political leadership of the 2000s in the United States and the United Kingdom. President George W. Bush and Prime Minister Tony Blair seemed to listen more to the messages they believed they received from God than to their respective political bases.

Antiterror legislation appears to be removing more and more sections from the constitution ('the law of the father and the mother') and the values that they are allegedly seeking to defend. The pressure to sign up for a paranoid-schizoid logic, where one is either for or against a given position, seems intense in many countries and is further intensified every time there is a new terrorist attack.

Lawrence (2005) argues that the United States is approaching a state of inverse totalitarianism, where it is not, as in Nazi Germany, the totalitarian state that is taking over private companies but the big corporations that are taking over the government, controlling the media and, via the media's construction of the risk of terrorism, passivizing the population in a state of paranoid anxiety and the struggle for survival.

The way in which the 2008 financial crisis was handled seems to confirm Lawrence's thesis. It is difficult not to see the financial crisis as a humiliating defeat for the neoliberals, who have been virtually giddy since the Berlin Wall came down in 1989. The dismantling of the Eastern bloc was seen not just as the failure of realized socialism but also as evidence that capitalism was unproblematic (cf. Stein, 2011). That the latter is not true was demonstrated convincingly by the financial crisis (Hendricks & Rasmussen, 2012).

There are no meaningful political groups that dare formulate an alternative to the international capitalism, which is clearly operating under fairly loose frameworks and without real sanctions from potent collaborative machineries of government that could ensure fair and proper conditions – also on the financial markets.

Intellectual antimodernism

In this situation, the intellectual mainstream – social constructionists, Foucaultians, postmodernists and other post-structuralists – are of little use. It is a shame, euphemistically put, that they focus their energy on 'demonstrating' that the truth is local and situated (bricks-and-mortar and clock time) while ignoring the globalization without subjecting it to a critical examination, so that the local and situated element of the information systems is left free-floating and unprotected. It is also a shame that the language turn is occurring during a time when written culture is falling apart, the temporal and spatial organization of social life is changing radically (Meyrowitz), and a flow of varying images is flickering on every available surface. Indeed, the question is whether postmodernists should not actually be regarded as antimodernists. In a sense, the poststructuralist rejection of the differences between language and reality denies reality in the same way as Christian fundamentalists reject the enlightenment project and makes do with the Bible, and Islamic fundamentalists reject secularization and live their lives by the Quran or Sharia, in a world with cars, moon rockets, Internet and smartphones. In any case, political correctness and American post-modernism (Schwartz, 2001; Chassegeut-Smirgel, 2005) seem to match the negative self-image of both Christian and Muslim fundamentalists. By failing to acknowledge reality and the tension between concept and object, every-thing is the same. Mistakes are not possible, when nothing is more true than anything else. There is no accountability, curiosity disappears, and learning processes cannot take place (Chasseguet-Smirgel, 1984/1985a, 2005; Schwartz, 2001; Visholm, 2002, 2012).

However, there is no indication that curiosity and critical responsibility and thus the tension between discourse and reality are coming back – not as something that, in a totalitarian perspective is to be elevated to final and eternal truth but as a driver of research and critical intellectual accountability. In Henning Bech's *Kvinder og mænd* [Women and men] (2005), which offers interesting analyses of the relationship between discourse and reality, the author plucks up the courage to say, 'I'm not too worried about talking about reality' (p. 12, translated for this edition). He adds, 'Even the mightiest discursive constructions are not, it seems, immune to reality – there were no weapons of mass destruction [in Iraq, Ed.], and there was no contact [between Saddam Hussein's regime and Al-Qaida, Ed.]' (p. 13, translated for this edition by Dorte H. Silver).

III Conclusions

Globalization implies a democratic deficit, as more and more processes in social life elude the influence of national democracies, and so far, democratic institutions have not really emerged that are fully capable of operating in relation to globalized capitalism. This democratic deficit is in some regards undermining trust in democracy, which in relation to globalization has proved ineffective so far. It is quite a task to alleviate this democratic deficit, but perhaps it is no bigger than the original task of establishing the national democracies. In a sense, what we are facing now is the same procedure, only geared to a higher systemic level.

If we apply the family dynamic metaphors to this systemic level, the nations may be seen as orphaned siblings looking for a way to regulate their mutual relationships and create the conditions for leading a reasonably free and creative life within their own borders. They need to be mature enough to play 'a game of parents and children' under the law of the father and the mother. We have to imagine that the bigger stronger nations can lead the way and act as examples to the smaller, weaker nations. Ultimately, for example, we need to establish the United Nations as a global democratic institution with a monopoly on the use of force and install 'the law of the father and the mother' for the planet and its inhabitants.

I am not imagining that we are going to dismantle the nation-states or, for that matter, the municipalities. However, I do think that the EU, like other regional institutions, needs to be strengthened, both as a step in the development of global democracy and as an institution in its own right. The point is simply that our democratic institutions need to be geared and upgraded to match the globalized market and the developmental flows. From the individual's point of view, being a 'citizen of the world' should thus not be seen as an alternative to being, for example, a Dane or a Copenhagener. We should see ourselves as local, regional and global citizens at the same time.

About forgetting Lewin

In Chapter 4, we discussed Lewin's and Winnicott's perceptions of the psychology of democracy. Both authors consider democracy important and argue that it cannot be taken for granted but must, in a sense, be learned and reclaimed from generation to generation. This posits democracy as something somehow unnatural, not something that emerges and is maintained on its own, while at the same time regarding it as the result of natural maturation.

Lewin may be right that a clear task formulation and acknowledgement of the employees' skills and experiences both contribute resources to the organization and promote the employees' development and their readiness to exercise authority. However, Lewin is not right that an ambiguous authorization structure under the name of democratic leadership promotes the employees' development or democracy in the long run. Instead, it deludes people into thinking, on the one hand, that it is possible to determine the truth by voting on it and, on the other hand, generates unhelpful utopian and paranoid perceptions. It is thus important that we forget about Lewin's concept of democracy.

Winnicott's insistence that democracy requires that we identify with the larger group and that we take care not to create scapegoats or groups that are targeted for persecution is more relevant than ever but no easier given the boundaries in the network society. The same applies to the demand to be mature enough to play 'a game of parents and children', that is, to be able to handle electing and promoting an equal to be the leader.

Winnicott's thinking on the young person's murder and the parents' survival or their abdication (cf. Chapter 4), may be read as a critique of Lewin's notion of democratic leadership. Pseudodemocracy and manipulation are hardly going to promote the development of democratically engaged citizens. Clear authorization, whether from the top down or from the bottom up, has to be preferable. Hirschhorn (1997) has considered the notion of a postmodern hierarchy:

> The chain of command is a time-tested tool for delegating authority while not abdicating leadership. Today, the word 'hierarchy' conjures up images of control and suppression. A hierarchy has another aspect,

however. Although it creates a system in which some roles are vested with more authority than others (this is the 'antidemocratic' aspect), it also facilitates delegation. It allows leaders to 'lend' their authority to subordinates, thereby enabling the subordinates to participate in the leadership process.

(Hirschhorn, 1997, pp. 57–58)

A quality of the postmodern hierarchy is openness and thus vulnerability. People are required to personalize their roles. The increased vulnerability that arises in this process makes it tempting to abdicate and to resort to various defence mechanisms instead of confronting the threats the organization is faced with.

If a leader is worried about external threats to the company, he or she may resort to micromanaging the employees or develop an unconscious fantasy of involving the employees in the challenges facing the company through shared influence and ownership without acknowledging the full extent of his or her dependence on them.

Thus, by abdicating, either an apparently overcontrolling or an apparently democratic [leader], may be tackling his own vulnerability.

(Ibid., p. 58)

Hirschhorn further argues that bureaucracy, in contrast to hierarchy, is a powerful procedure for facilitating abdication and masking what is going on. Bureaucracy, in the sense of rules and procedures, renders the decision-making process impersonal, meaning that the leader becomes anonymous, which is the first step towards abdication, and he or she loses the ability to delegate tasks and responsibilities. Authority now springs from rules instead of springing from relationships (Ibid., p. 76).

The introduction of the concept of the promoted sibling (Chapter 2) makes it possible to distinguish between transference patterns at the level of top and middle management and also to distinguish between the authorization process in democracies and associations, where the elected officials derive their authority from the voters, whom they represent, and the authorization process in organizations (and families), where the leaders and employees are recruited, authorized from the top down and represent the organization's authority system.

With Bion (Chapter 5) it became possible to address regression within groups and organizations, instead of regarding groups, organizations and crowds as being regressive per se. Via abdication, organizations and families may regress to tyranny and totalitarianism on the one hand or to 'democracy' and 'bureaucracy' on the other. The delegation of authority, clear task distribution and the acknowledgement of employees is not regressive, however, but in fact methods that facilitate development in both the organization and its employees. Similarly, associations and democracies may regress to tyranny and totalitarianism if they compromise on 'the law of the father and the mother'. It is an obvious task for psychology to examine how regressive processes in systems arise and develop and how systems may halt this regression and find their way back to the task.

Arguably, the initial ambiguity of Lewin's democratic leadership concept contributed to a movement that helped individuals and groups, who were otherwise not heard, find their voices and their authority. Today, however, this approach actually has undemocratic effects, because it undermines the authority of democracy by calling a pseudodemocracy, wrapped in unclear authority relations, a democracy.

Instead, we should underscore the difference between democracies and associations, on the one hand, and families and organizations, on the other. Democracy – whose deficit is not only due to globalization but also due to the existing unequitable distribution of possibilities that stems from economic freedom – is the only sensible framework for regulating the harmful effects of the economy. Without individuals, families and organizations, however, democracy would have no content and no one to execute what the democracy decides. The two different organizational forms need each other to be different.

The good postmodern citizen should thus be able to serve both as a leader and as part of a followership. He or she has to be able to elect and be elected, consider his or her own interests in the short and long terms, balance these interests with those of the larger whole and bear in mind that it is perfectly legitimate for other citizens to think similarly. As Kant has pointed out, the citizen should be ready to obey in situations where it is appropriate while still having his or her own independent thoughts and not being afraid to share these thoughts in public (Kant, 1783/2009).

Interpersonal curiosity or pathological certainty

The new authority relations create the possibility of developing social curiosity, a condition for learning and development. Ed Shapiro and Wesley Carr (1991) introduced the concepts *interpersonal curiosity and pathological certainty*. In extension of Freud and Bion, they consider curiosity and the desire to examine and get to know oneself and the world a fundamental aspect of human developmental psychology. Social curiosity is the desire to listen to other people's thoughts, feelings and fantasies and the ability to engage in another person's personal experiential universe without feeling threatened if the other person perceives the world quite differently.

It is important for the child that the adults make room for and take an interest in the child's experiential universe – not least because it will help the child establish appropriate boundaries between self and world. When the parents ask about the child's experiences they simultaneously authorize the child to have his or her own experience, even if it differs from the parents'. That is a condition for being able to engage in flexible interactions with others and negotiating a common understanding and interpretation when that is important. The 'pathological certainty' has no respect for the other person's experience. For someone who claims to have complete certainty there is nothing new to learn, no discernible curiosity. These parents believe they know exactly what children and young people think and feel and have no problem telling them what they need to do to be successful in life. This pathological certainty serves to protect the parents against their own anxiety and offers no understanding of children's needs and problems. Instead, it generates feelings of isolation, emptiness and depressiveness in the family.

The altered authority relations thus offer an opportunity for developing more curious, independent and critically responsible citizens who dare embrace their own authority and take responsibility for the larger whole – also in the form of the duty to criticize the reality we live in.

Large-group traumas and grief work

In a series of interesting works, Vamık D. Volkan (1997, 2004, 2006; Visholm, 2007) has studied psychological processes in so-called large groups: nations, population groups and so forth. He regards large groups as entities that have a life of their own and may be subject to regression, which may in turn unleash huge potentials for violence. One example is Milošević (cf. Chapter 5), who was able to mobilize the Serbs by reviving ('the chosen trauma') the traumatic defeat of the Serbs at the Battle of Kosovo in 1389. Large groups, like all other organizations, need to work through traumas and mourn their losses, Volkan argues.

The question is whether the same logic might not be helpful in relation to the modernization and globalization process. As often happens in change processes in organizations (Visholm, 2004d), we may be quick to categorize people as either agile, progressive, trendy modernists or conservative, old-fashioned, reactionary relics. A result of this categorization is that the losses and traumas related to radicalized modernity are not worked through and mourned (Krantz, 2006). Losses and traumas in the radicalized modernization process happen continuously on an individual, an organizational and a national level – the loss of jobs, professional identity, the coherent family picture, networks in local communities and workplaces – and without processing and 'mourning' they manifest as resistance to change in general. Grief and anger that are not articulated and worked through develop into depression, schizoid withdrawal or compulsive rebelliousness. People withdraw from life here and now into idyllic constructions of a golden age. Instead of engaging in a common mourning process, a polarized relationship with a dangerous potential for violence emerges between modernists and antimodernists.

Homelessness and exile

In psychological terms, the feeling of homelessness and the implied notion of a 'home' seem to be the central dynamic of social life. Globalized internationalists incarnate the manic defence. They feel equally at home or not at home in New York, Tokyo, São Paulo, London and Berlin. The nationalists imagine that there once was a home, and that there is a chance it might be recreated, either here or in the afterlife.

In a very interesting reading of Freud's 'Moses and monotheism', Lilian Munk Rösing (2006) argues that in this text, Freud, so to speak, constructs Moses as a postmodern patchwork figure of Egyptian, Jewish and all sorts of 'non-identity' and thereby advocates for universalism. This is to say that we are all 'non-identical', and that our shared humanity stems not from belonging to a people, a race, a religion and so forth but that we are 'patchwork' figures in cultural and genetic terms. If we for example were to examine an Aryan in depth, we would probably find a sizeable share of 'Jewish genes', a pinch of French, a dash of Turkish, a spoonful of Ethiopia and so forth. And if the Danish right-wing politician Pia Kjærsgaard, who is highly critical of immigration and cultural diversity, were to look closely, she would find that the Danish national budget features pages and pages covered in Arabic numerals. We all have the alien factor in our core, and if I read Rösing correctly, I second her recommendation to abandon the notion of a home and instead begin to work on feeling at home in our exiles.

References

Abadi, S. (2003). Between the frontier and the network: Notes for a metapsychology of freedom. *International Journal of Psychoanalysis*, 84(2), 221–234.

Allport, G. W. (1948). Foreword to the 1948 edition. In K. Lewin (Ed.), *Resolving social conflicts and field theory in social science*. American Psychological Association 2000.

Allport, G. W. (1954). The historical background of modern social psychology. In G. Lindzey (Ed.), *Handbook of social psychology* (pp. 1–80). Addison Wesley.

Alvesson, M., & Billing, Y. D. (1997). *Understanding gender and organizations*. Sage.

Anderson, B. (2001). *Forestillede fællesskaber: Refleksioner over nationalismens oprindelse og udbredelse* [Imagined communities: Reflections on the origins and spread of nationalism]. Roskilde Universitetsforlag.

Andkjær Olsen, O. (1988). *Ødipuskomplekset* [The Oedipus complex]. Hans Reitzels Forlag.

Arbejdsmiljøinstituttet (2004). *AMI's korte spørgeskema om psykisk arbejdsmiljø* [Questionnaire about mental working environment from the National Institute of Occupational Health].

Armstrong, D. (2005). Emotions in organizations: Disturbance or intelligence. In R. French (Ed.), *Organization in the mind*. Karnac.

Barber, B. R. (1995). *Jihad vs. McWorld; Terrorism's challenge to democracy*. Ballantine Books.

Bateson, G., Jackson, D. D., Haley, J., & Weakland, J., (1956). Toward a theory of schizophrenia. *Behavioral Science*, 1, 251–264.

Bauman, Z. (1989). *Modernity and the Holocaust*. Cornell University Press.

Bech, H. (2005). *Kvinder og mænd* [Women and men]. Hans Reitzels Forlag.

Beck, U. (1992). *Risk society: Towards a new modernity* (M. Ritter, Trans.). Sage. (Original work published 1986)

Beck, U. C. (2009). *Fokus og dybde: Psykodynamisk coaching* [Focus and depth: Psychodynamic coaching]. Hans Reitzels Forlag.

Beck, U. C., & Heinskou, T. (2011). Ledelse og mentalisering [Leadership and mentalizing]. In T. Heinskou & S. Visholm (Eds.), *Psykodynamisk organisationspsykologi II. På mere arbejde under overfladerne* (pp. 175–196). Hans Reitzels Forlag.

Beck, U. C., & Visholm, S. (2014a). Authority relations in group relations conferences and in 'real life'. Group relations conferences – Danish design I. *Organisational and Social Dynamics*, 14(2), 227–237.

Beck, U. C., & Visholm, S. (2014b). Learning from experience. Group relations conferences – Danish design II. *Organisational and Social Dynamics*, 14(2), 238–249.

Beck, U. C., & Visholm, S. (2014c). Working with new designs. Group relations conferences – Danish design III. *Organisational and Social Dynamics*, 14(2), 250–263.

Berke, J. H. (2012). *Why I hate you and you hate me. The interplay of envy, greed, jealousy, and narcissism in everyday life*. Karnac.

Bettelheim, B. (1975). *The uses of enchantment*. Vintage Books.

Binney, G., Wilke, G., & Williams, C. (2003). *Leaders in transition: The dramas of ordinary heroes*. Ashridge.

Bion, W. R. (1961). *Experiences in groups and other papers*. Tavistock.

Bion, W. R. (1963). *Elements of psychoanalysis*. Basic Books.

Bion, W. R. (1988). *Attention and interpretation*. Karnac. (Original work published 1970)

Bion, W. R. (1993). *Second thoughts*. Karnac. (Original work published 1967)

Bion, W. R. (1984a). *Learning from experience*. Maresfield. (Original work published 1962)

Bion, W. R. (1984b). *Transformations*. Karnac. (Original work published 1965)

Bonnerup, B., & Hasselager, A. (2008). *Gruppen på arbejde: Organisationspsykologi i praksis* [The group at work: Organizational psychology in practice]. Hans Reitzels Forlag.

Bourdieu, P. (1998). *Practical reason: On the theory of action*. Stanford University Press. (Original work published 1994)

Britton, R. (1998). Oedipus in the depressive position. In R. Britton (Ed.), *Belief and imagination: Explorations in psychoanalysis* (pp. 29–40). Routledge.

Brotheridge, C. M., & Lee, R. T. (2006). We are family: Congruity between organizational and family functioning constructs. *Human Relations*, 59(1), 141–161.

Brunning, H. (2006). *Executive coaching: Systems-psychodynamic perspective*. Karnac.

Burr, V. (2003). *Gender and social psychology*. Routledge.

Canetti, E. (1981). *Crowds and power* (V. Gollancz, Trans.). Farrar, Strauss and Giroux. (Original work published 1960)

Carvalho, S. (1994). History of family therapy. In S. Box (Ed.), *Crisis at adolescence: Object relations therapy with the family*. Jason Aronson.

Castells, M. (2000). *The rise of the network society: The information age: Economy, society and culture* (Vol. 1). Blackwell. (Original work published 1996)

Castells, M. (2010). *The power of identity: The information age: Economy, society and culture* (Vol. 2, 2nd ed.). Blackwell. (Original work published 1997)

Castells, M., & Ince, M. (2003). *Conversations with Manuel Castells*. Polity.

Chasseguet-Smirgel, J. (1970). Feminine guilt and the Oedipus complex. In J. Chasseguet-Smirgel (Ed.), *Female sexuality. New psychoanalytic views* (pp. 94–134). Karnac. (Original work published 1964)

Chasseguet-Smirgel, J. (1976). Freud and female sexuality. The consideration of some blind spots in the exploration of the 'dark continent'. *International Journal of Psychoanalysis*, 57(3), 275–286.

Chasseguet-Smirgel, J. (1985a). *Creativity and perversion*. Free Association Books. (Original work published 1984)

Chasseguet-Smirgel, J. (1985b). *The ego-ideal: A psychoanalytic essay on the malady of the ideal*. Free Association Books.

Chasseguet-Smirgel, J. (2005). *The body as mirror of the world*. Free Association Books.

Christoffersen, M. N. (2004). *Familiens udvikling i det 20. århundrede: Demografiske strukturer og processer* [The development of the family during the 20th century: Demographic structures and process]. Socialforskningsinstituttet/VIVE.

Cohen, D., Mitchell, J., & Britton, R. (2009). Siblings in development: towards a metapsychology. In V. Lewin & B. Sharp (Eds.), *Siblings in development. A psychoanalytical view*. Karnac.

Coles, P. (2003). *The importance of sibling relationships in psychoanalysis*. Karnac.

Coles, P. (2011). *The uninvited guest from the unremembered past*. Karnac.

Cooperrider, D., & Srivastva, S. (1987). Appreciative inquiry in organizational life, parts 1 and 2. In R. Woodman & W. Pasmore (Eds.), *Research in organizational change and development* (vol. 1, pp. 129–169). JAI-Press.

Curtis, A. (Director). (2002). *The century of the self* [TV documentary series]. BBC.

Dahlberg, R. (2004). *Den menneskelige faktor: Historiens svageste led* [The human factor: History's weakest link]. Aschehoug.

Daldry, S. (Director). (2002). *The hours* [film].

Dicks, H. V. (1967). *Marital tensions. Clinical studies towards a psychological theory of interaction*. Basic Books.

Dommermuth-Gudrich, G. (2004). *50 klassiske myter* [50 classic myths]. Aschehoug.

Ehrenreich, B. (2010). *Smile or die: How positive thinking fooled America and the world*. Granta.

Eiguer, A. (1999). Cynicism: Its function in the perversions. *International Journal of Psychoanalysis*, 80, 671–684.

Erdheim, M. (1988). Adoleszenz zwischen Familie und Kultur [Adolescence between family and civilization]. In *Psychoanalyse und Unbewusstheit in der Kultur*. Suhrkamp Verlag.

Erikson, E. H. (1959). *Identity: Youth and crisis*. Norton.

Fagerland, B. S. (2012, 23 June). *Kvinder betaler en høj pris, når de blander sig i debatten* [Women pay a high price when they take part in the debate]. Politiken.

Fisher, J. (2007). A father's abdication: Lear's retreat from 'aesthetic conflict'. In P. Williams & G. O. Gabbard (Eds.), *Key papers in literature and psychoanalysis*. Karnac.

Fraher, A. (2005). *Group dynamics for high-risk teams: A 'team resource management' (TRM) primer*. iUniverse.

Frank, L. (2012, 13 February). *Kommunaldirektør om inklusion: Vi sendte aben videre* [Municipal chief executive on inclusion: We passed the buck]. Folkeskolen.

French, R. (2001). 'Negative capability': Managing the confusing uncertainties of change. *Journal of Organizational Change Management*, 14(5), 480–492.

French, R., & Simpson, P. (2003). Learning at the edges between knowing and not-knowing: 'Translating' Bion. In M. Robert, R. M. Lipgar & M. Pines (Eds.), *Building on Bion: Branches* (International Library of Group Analysis 21). Jessica Kingsley.

Freud, S. (1953). Three essays on the theory of sexuality. In J. Strachey (Ed. & Trans.), *The standard edition of the complete psychological works of Sigmund Freud* (Vol. 7). Hogarth Press and the Institute of Psychoanalysis. (Original work published 1905)

Freud, S. (1957). On the universal tendency to debasement in the sphere of love. In J. Strachey (Ed. and Trans.) *The standard edition of the complete psychological works of Sigmund Freud* (Vol. 11). Hogarth and the Institute of Psychoanalysis. (Original work published 1912)

Freud, S. (1955a). Totem and taboo. In J. Strachey (Ed. & Trans.) *The standard edition of the complete psychological works of Sigmund Freud* (Vol. 13). Hogarth and the Institute of Psychoanalysis. (Original work published 1913)

Freud, S. (1955b). Group psychology and the analysis of the ego. In J. Strachey (Ed. & Trans.) *The standard edition of the complete psychological works of Sigmund Freud* (Vol. 18, pp. 65–144). Hogarth. (Original work published 1921)

Freud, S. (1957). Mourning and melancholia. In J. Strachey (Ed. and Trans.). *The standard edition of the complete psychological works of Sigmund Freud* (Vol. 14). Hogarth and the Institute of Psychoanalysis. (Original work published 1917)

Freud, S. (1958). Remembering, repeating and working through. In J. Strachey (Ed. & Trans.) *The standard edition of the complete psychological works of Sigmund Freud* (Vol. 12, pp. 145–156). (Original work published 1914)

Freud, S. (1961a). The ego and the id. In J. Strachey (Ed. & Trans). *The standard edition of the complete psychological works of Sigmund Freud* (Vol. 19, pp. 1–308). The Hogarth Press and the Institute of Psychoanalysis. (Original work published 1923)

Freud, S. (1961b). Civilization and its discontents. In J. Strachey (Ed. & Trans). *The standard edition of the complete psychological works of Sigmund Freud* (Vol. 21, pp. 57–146). (Original work published 1929)

Freud, S. (1963). Introductory lectures on psycho-analysis (Part III). In J. Strachey (Ed. & Trans.) *The standard edition of the complete psychological works of Sigmund Freud* (Vol. 16). Hogarth. (Original work published 1916–1917)

Friedan, B. (2001). *The feminine mystique.* Norton. (Original work published 1963)

Furnham, A. (2005). *The psychology of behaviour at work. The individual in the organization.* Psychology Press.

Gabriel, Y., & Hampton, M. M. (1999). Work Groups. In Y. Gabriel (Ed.), *Organizations in depth: The psychoanalysis of organization* (pp. 112–138). Sage.

Gabriel, Y., & Hirschhorn, L. (1999). Leaders and followers. In Y. Gabriel (Ed.), *Organizations in depth: The psychoanalysis of organization* (pp. 139–165). Sage.

Gergen, K. J. (2000). *The saturated self: Dilemmas of identity in contemporary life.* Basic Books. (Original work published 1991)

Geronimi, C., Jackson, W., & Luske, H. (Directors). (1950). *Cinderella [animated film].* Disney.

Giddens, A. (1991). *Modernity and self-identity: Self and society in the late modern age.* Polity.

Giddens, A. (1992). *The transformation of intimacy: Sexuality, love and eroticism in modern societies.* Polity.

Gilkey, R. (1991). The psychodynamics of upheaval: Intervening in merger and acquisition transitions. In M. Kets de Vries et al. (Eds.), *Organizations on the couch* (pp. 331–360). Jossey-Bass.

Goffman, E. (1959). *The presentation of self in everyday life.* Doubleday.

Goffman, E. (1961). Role distance. In E. Goffman (Ed.), *Encounters: Two studies in the sociology of interaction* (pp. 85–141). Ravenio Books.

Gould, L. J., Stapley, L. F., & Stein, M. (Eds.) (2001). *The systems psychodynamics of organizations.* Karnac.

Grinberg, L., Sor, D., & Tabak de Bianchedi, E. (1993). *New introduction to the work of Bion.* Jason Aronson.

Gustavsson, L., & Magnusson, I. (1996). En modell för ledar- och ledningsutveckling [A model for the development of leaders and leadership]. In S. B. Boëthius (Ed.),

Den svårfångade organisationen. Texter om medvetna och omedvetna skeenden. Natur och kultur.

Halton, W. (2004). By what authority: Psychoanalytical reflections on creativity and change in relation to organizational life. In C. Huffingtonet et al. (Eds.), *Working below the surface: The emotional life of contemporary organizations* (pp. 107–125). Karnac.

Hein, H. H. (2009). *Motivation: Motivationsteori og praktisk anvendelse* [Motivation: Motivation theory and practical applications]. Hans Reitzels Forlag.

Heinskou, T. (2004). Den lille gruppe på arbejde [The small group at work]. In T. Heinskou & S. Visholm (Eds.), *Psykodynamisk organisationspsykologi* (pp. 49–68). Hans Reitzels Forlag.

Heinskou, T., & Krasnik, H. (2008). Mentalisering: Evnen til at forstå sig selv og de andre – og mentaliseringsbaseret terapi (MBT) [Mentalization: The ability to understand oneself and others – and mentalization-based therapy (MBT)]. *Ugeskrift for Læger*, 170(45), 3688.

Heinskou, T., & Visholm, S. (Eds.) (2004), *Psykodynamisk organisationspsykologi. På arbejde under overfladen* [Psychodynamic organizational psychology. At work under the surface.] Hans Reitzels Forlag.

Heinskou, T., & Visholm, S. (Eds.) (2011), *Psykodynamisk organisationspsykologi II. På mere arbejde under overfladen* [Psychodynamic organizational psychology. More work under the surface.] Hans Reitzels Forlag.

Hendricks, V. F., & Lundorf Rasmussen, J. (2012). *Nedtur: Finanskrisen forstået filosofisk* [Downturn: A philosophical analysis of the financial crisis]. Gyldendal.

Hinshelwood, R. D., & Winship, G. (2006). Orestes and democracy. In P. Coles (Ed.), *Sibling relationships.* Karnac.

Hirschhorn, L. (1988). *The workplace within: Psychodynamics of organizational life.* MIT Press.

Hirschhorn, L. (1997). *Reworking authority. Leading and following in the post-modern organization.* MIT Press.

Hirschhorn, L. (2000). Changing structure is not enough: The moral meaning of organizational design. In M. Beer & N. Nohria (Eds.), *Breaking the code of change.* Harvard Business School Press.

Hirschhorn, L. (2001). *Passion and group life: Examining moments of creativity and destructiveness.* CFAR. Retrieved from www.cfar.com.

Hirschhorn, L. (2002). The modern project and the feminisation of men. In R. D. Hinshelwood & M. Chiesa (Eds.), *Organisations, anxieties and defences: Towards a psychoanalytic social psychology* (pp. 35–64). Whurr.

Hirschhorn, L. (2003). Tasks, affects and evaluation [PowerPoint presentation]. MPO/RUC Workshop, Tune, Denmark.

Hirschhorn, L., & Gilmore, T. (1980). The application of family therapy concepts to influencing organizational behaviour. *Administrative Science Quarterly*, 25, 18–37.

Hirschhorn, L., & Gilmore, T. (1992). The new boundaries of the 'boundaryless' company. *Harvard Business Review*, May–June issue.

Hjortsøe, L. (2008). *Græske guder og helte* [Greek gods and heroes]. Politikens Forlag.

Hochschild, A. (1983). *The managed heart: The commercialization of human feeling.* University of California Press.

Hochschild, A. (1997). *The time bind: When work becomes home and home becomes work.* Metropolitan Books.

Holy Bible, New International Version. (2011). Biblica. Retrieved from www.biblega teway.com/versions/New-International-Version-NIV-Bible/.

Hopper, E. (1997). Traumatic experience in the unconscious life of groups: A fourth basic assumption. *Group Analysis*, 30, 439–470.

Hoyle, L. (2004). From sycophant to saboteur: Responses to organizational change. In C. Huffington, D. Armstrong, W. Halton, L. Hoyle & J. Pooley (Eds.), *Working below the surface: The emotional life of contemporary organizations* (pp. 87–106). Karnac.

Huffington, C. (2008). The system in the room: The extent to which coaching can change the organization. In D. Campbell & C. Huffington (Eds.), *Organizations connected: A handbook of systemic consultation.* Karnac.

Huffington, C., & Miller, S. (2008). Where angels and mere mortals fear to tread: Exploring 'sibling relations' in the workplace. *Organisational and Social Dynamics*, 8(1), 18–37.

Jaques, E. (1976). *A general theory of bureaucracy.* Heinemann.

Jaques, E. (1990). Death and the midlife crisis. In *Creativity and work.* Int. University Press (Original work published 1965).

Jakobsen, P. (2004). Rolle og person [Role and person]. In T. Heinskou & S. Visholm (Eds.), *Psykodynamisk organisationspsykologi* (pp. 109–126). Hans Reitzels Forlag.

Jakobsen, P., & Visholm, S. (1987). *Parforholdet: Forelskelse, krise, terapi* [Couples: Falling in love, crisis, therapy]. Politisk Revy.

Jessen, H., & Hvenegaard, H. (2001). *Arbejdsmiljøfaktorer i gruppeorganiseret arbejde: Litteraturstudie: Dokumentationsrapport, Del 2* [Work environment factors in group-based work: Literature study: Documentation report, Part 2]. CASA.

Joyce, A. (2011, October). Why the ugly sisters and Cinderella? [Conference paper]. EFPP Conference, Krakow, Poland.

Jørgensen, C. R. (2006). Splitting i demokratiske samfund. *Psyke og Logos*, 27(1), 136–162.

Jung, C. G. (1913). Versuch einer Darstellung der Psychoanalytichen Theorie. *G.W. 4* (pp. 107–255). Olten: Walther Verlag.

Khaleelee, O. (2004). Not leading followers, not following leaders: The contemporary erosion of the traditional social contract. *Organisational and Social Dynamics*, 4(2), 268–284.

Kant, I. (2009). *Answering the question: What is enlightenment?* (H. B. Nisbet, Trans.). Penguin. (Original work published 1783)

Kellaway, L. (2012, 1 April) The female of the species is more scary than the male: Successful women are more frightening than men. *Financial Times.*

Kernberg, O. F. (1995a). Latency, group dynamics and conventionality. In *Love relations: Normality and pathology* (pp. 163–175). Yale University Press.

Kernberg, O. F. (1995b). The couple and the group. In *Love relations: Normality and pathology* (pp. 176–188). Yale University Press.

Kernberg, O. F. (1998). *Ideology, conflict and leadership in groups and organizations.* Yale University Press.

Kiselberg, S. (1979). *To og et halvt kapitel af mændenes historie. Et moralsk-sociologisk studie i den traditionelle manderolle* [Two-and-a-half chapters on the history of men. A moral-sociological study of the traditional male role]. Rhodos.

Klein, M. (1946). Notes on some schizoid mechanisms. *International Journal of Psychoanalysis*, 27, 99–110.

Klein, M. (1975a). Some theoretical conclusions regarding the emotional life of the infant. In *envy and gratitude and other works* (pp. 61–94). Simon & Schuster. (Original work published 1952).

Klein, M. (1975b) *Envy and gratitude*. Simon & Schuster. (Original work published 1957).

Krantz, J. (2006). *The fundamentalist state of mind in groups and organisations.* London: The Eric Miller Annual Memorial Lecture. 18 March 2006. [Unpublished]

Krarup, S. (2006, 6 April). *Sandhedens time* [The hour of truth]. Politiken.

Koefoed, P., & Visholm, S. (2011). Følelser i organisationer [Emotions in organizations]. In T. Heinskou & S. Visholm (Eds.), *Psykodynamisk organisationspsykologi* II. Hans Reitzels Forlag.

Lading, Å., & Jørgensen, B. (2010). *Grupper: Om kollektivets bevidste og ubevidste dynamikker* [Groups: On conscious and unconscious group dynamics]. Frydenlund.

Laing, R. D. (1967). *The politics of experience and the bird of paradise.* Penguin.

Lawrence, G. W. (1999). A mind for business. In R. French & R. Vince (Eds.), *Group relations, management and organization.* Oxford University Press.

Lawrence, G. W. (2005). Thinking of the unconscious, and the infinite, of society during dark times. *Organisational and Social Dynamics*, 5(1), 57–72.

Lawrence, G. W. (2006). Organizational role analysis: The birth and growth of ideas. In J. Newton, S. Long, & B. Sievers (Eds.), *Coaching in depth: The organizational role analysis approach* (pp. 29–42). Karnac.

Lawrence, G. W., & Armstrong, D. (1998). Destructiveness and creativity in organizational life: Experiencing the psychotic edge. In P. B. Talamo, F. Borgogno, & S. A. Merciai (Eds.), *Bion's legacy to groups* (pp. 53–68). Karnac.

Lawrence, G. W., Bain, A., & Gould, L. (1996). The fifth basic assumption. *Free Associations*, 6(1): 28–55.

Le Bon, G. (2016). *The crowd: A study of the popular mind.* Loki's Publishing. (Original work published 1895)

Lewin, K. (2000). Experiments in social space. In L. Kurt (Ed.), *Resolving social conflicts and field theory in social science.* American Psychological Association. (Original work published 1939)

Lewin, V., & Sharp, B. (Eds.) (2009). *Siblings in development: A psychoanalytical view.* Karnac.

Long, S. (2006). Drawing from role biography in organizational role analysis. In J. Newton, S. Long, & B. Sievers (Eds.), *Coaching in depth: The organizational role analysis approach* (pp. 127–144). Karnac.

Long, S. (2008). *The perverse organisation and its deadly sins.* Karnac.

Long, S., & Nossal, B. (2012). Beyond the family psychic template. In E. Aram, R. Baxter, & A. Nutkevitch (Eds.), *Group relations conferences: Tradition, creativity, and succession in the global group relations network.* Karnac.

Lorenzer, A. (1975). *Materialistisk socialisationsteori.* [Materialist socialization theory]. (P. Andreasen, Trans.). Rhodos. (Original work published 1972)

Lunøe, N. (1987). Frikendt efter den skrevne lov – dømt efter den hviskede: Om familier til skizofrene [Acquitted according to the written law – convicted according to the whispered law: On families of schizophrenics, I]. *Matrix*, 4(3), 52–72.

Lunøe, N. (1988). Frikendt efter den skrevne lov – dømt efter den hviskede. Om familier til skizofrene. II [Acquitted according to the written law – convicted according to the whispered law: On families of schizophrenics, II]. *Matrix*, 4(4), 15–54.

Lunøe, N., & Visholm, S. (1981). Bombemanden og 'Lille Danmark': Terror og rådvildhed [The bomber and 'Little Denmark': Terror and perplexity]. *Kontext*, 42, 97–111.

Lunøe, N., & Visholm, S. (1982). Bombemanden og 'Lille Danmark': Samfundet og dets forbrydere [The bomber and 'Little Denmark': Society and its criminals]. *Kontext*, 43, 88–99.

Manheim, K. (1993). The problem of generations. In K. H. Wolf (Eds.), *From Karl Manheim*. Transaction Publishers.

Mayo, E. (1997). Hawthorne and the Western Electric Company. In D. S. Pugh (Ed.), *Organization theory: Selected readings*. Penguin. (Original work published 1949)

Meltzer, D. (1992). *The claustrum: An investigation of claustrophobic phenomena*. The Roland Harris Trust Library No. 15. (Original work published 1990)

Meltzer, D., & Williams, M. H. (1988). *The apprehension of beauty: The role of aesthetic conflict in development, art and violence*. Clunie Press.

Meyrowitz, J. (1986). *No sense of place: The impact of electronic media on social behavior*. Oxford University Press.

Miller, E. (1993). *From dependency to autonomy: Studies in organization and change*. Free Association Books.

Miller, E. (1998). Are basic assumptions instinctive? In P. B. Talamo, F. Borgogno, & S. A. Merciai (Eds.), *Bion's legacy to groups* (pp. 39–52). Karnac.

Miller, E. J., & Rice, K. A. (1975). Selections from systems of organization. In A. D. Colman & H. Bexton (Eds.), *Group relations reader 1* (pp. 43–68). A. K. Rice Institute for the Study of Social Systems (Original work published 1967)

Mitchell, J. (2003). *Siblings: Sex and violence*. Polity.

Mnouchkine, A. (Director). (1978). *Molière* [Film].

Newton, J., Long, S., & Sievers, B. (Eds.) (2006). *Coaching in depth: The organizational role analysis approach*. Karnac.

Nicolson, P. (1996). *Gender, power and organization: A psychological perspective*. Routledge.

Nielsen, H. B., & Rudberg, M. (1994). *Historien om drenge og piger: Kønssocialisering i et udviklingspsykologisk perspektiv* [The story of boys and girls: Gender socialization in a developmental psychology perspective]. Gyldendal.

Nossal, B. (2010). Beyond the family-as-psychic-template in organisations revisited: Or authority relations in the leader/ follower dynamic [Conference paper]. ISPSO's Annual Meeting, Elsinore, Denmark.

Olsén, P., & Clausen, C. (2000). Tilpasning eller autonomi? Om magt og læreprocesser i det industrielle arbejdsliv. *Tidsskrift for arbejdsliv*, 4, 45–60.

Petriglieri, G., & Stein, M. (2012). *The unwanted self: Projective identification in leaders' identity work*. INSEAD Working Paper No. 2012/40/OB.

Rasmussen, A. H. (2005). *De gamle grækere* [The ancient Greeks]. Politikens Forlag.

Reed, B., & Bazalgette, J. (2006). Organizational role analysis at the Grubb Institute of Behavioural Studies: Origins and development. In J. Newton, S. Long, & B. Sievers (Eds.), *Coaching in depth: The organizational role analysis approach* (pp. 43–62). Karnac.

Rice, A. K. (2001). *The enterprise and its environment*. Routledge. (Original work published 1963)

Ritzer, G. (1993). *The McDonaldization of society*. Pine Forks Press.

Roethlisberger, F. J. (2001). The Hawthorne experiments. In J. M. Shafritz & J. S. Ott (Eds.), *Classics of organization theory* (5th ed., pp. 158–168). Harcourt Publ. (Original work published 1941)

Rose, N. (1998). *Inventing our selves. Psychology, power and personhood* (paperback edition). Cambridge University Press. (Original work published 1996)

Rosenfeld, H. (1988). A clinical approach to the psychoanalytic theory of the life and death instincts: An investigation into the aggressive aspects of narcissism. In E. B. Spillius (Ed.), *Melanie Klein Today* (Vol. 1, pp. 239–255). Routledge.

Rothstein, K., & Rothstein, M. (2006). *Bomben i turbanen* [The bomb in the turban]. Tiderne Skifter.

Ruszczynski, S. (1993). The theory and practice of the Tavistock Institute of Marital Studies. In S. Ruszczynski (Ed.), *Psychotherapy with couples: Theory and practice of the Tavistock Institute of Marital Studies*. Karnac.

Rösing, L. M. (2006). Manden Moses og den nomadiske universalisme. In O. Andkjær Olsen, C. B. Thomsen, & B. Petersen (Eds.), *Fokus på Freud*. Hans Reitzels Forlag.

Sanders, R. (2004). *Sibling relationships: Theory and issues for practice*. Palgrave

Scharmer, C. O. (2007). *Theory U: Leading from the future as it emerges: The social technology of presencing* (2nd ed.). Berrett-Koehler Publishers.

Shapiro, E. R. (1978). Research on family dynamics: Clinical implications for the family and borderline adolescent. *Adolescent Psychiatry*, 6, 360–376.

Shapiro, E. R. (2003). The maturation of American identity: A study of the elections of 1996 and 2000 and the war against terrorism. *Organizational and Social Dynamics*, 3(1), 121–133.

Scharff, D. E., & Scharff, J. S. (1991). *Object relations family therapy*. Jason Aronson. (Original work published 1987)

Scharff, J. S. (1989). The development of object relations family therapy ideas. In J. S. Scharff (Ed.), *Foundations of object relations family therapy* (pp. 3–10). Jason Aronson.

Schwartz, H. S. (2001). *The revolt of the primitive: An inquiry into the roots of political correctness*. Praeger.

Schwartz, H. S. (2010). *Society against itself: Political correctness and organizational self-destruction*. Karnac.

Schwartz, H. S., & Hirschhorn, L. (2010). Organization and meaning: A multi-level psychoanalytic treatment of the Jayson Blair scandal at the New York Times. In H. S. Schwartz (Ed.), *Society against itself: Political correctness and organizational self-destruction*. Karnac.

Senge, P. M. (1990). *The fifth discipline: The art and practice of the learning organization*. Doubleday.

Sennett, R. (1998). *The corrosion of character: The personal consequences of work in the new capitalism*. Norton.

Shakespeare, W. (2005). Macbeth. In *The Oxford Shakespeare* (pp. 969–994). Oxford University Press. (Original work published 1606)

Shapiro, E. R. (1978). Research on family dynamics: Clinical implications for the family and borderline adolescent. *Adolescent Psychiatry*, 6, 360–376.

Shapiro, E. R. (1988). *Seminar i Snekkerstenkollektivet* [Seminar in the Snekkersten commune].

Shapiro, E. R. (2003). The maturation of American identity: A study of the elections of 1996 and 2000 and the war against terrorism. *Organisational & Social Dynamics*, 3(1): 121–133.

Shapiro, E. R., & Carr, W. (1991). *Lost in familiar places. Creating new connections between the individual and society*. Yale University Press.

Shaipiro, E. R., & Zinner, J. (1971). Family organisation and adolescent development. In E. Miller (Ed.), *Task and organisation* (pp. 289–308). Wiley.

Sherif, M., & Sherif, C. W. (1969). *Social Psychology.* Harper & Row.

Sievers, B. (1994). *Work, death and life itself.* Walter de Gruyter & Co.

Sievers, B. (2007). 'It is new, and it has to be done!': Socio-analytic thoughts on betrayal and cynicism in organizational transformation. *Culture and Organization,* 13(1), 1–21.

Sigsgaard, K. (2001). Legen er børnenes arbejde (interview). In H. C. Lundgaard, O. Strand, & S. Visholm (Eds.), *Børnehaven Kongens Have 50 år: Jubilæumsskrift* [The Kongens Have Preschool 50 years. Anniversary publication]. Self-published.

Simmel, G. (1992). *Soziologie: Untersuchungen über die formen der Vergesellschaftung.* Suhrkamp. (Original work published 1908)

Shorter, E. (1979). *Kernefamiliens historie* [The history of the nuclear family]. Nyt Nordisk Forlag.

Smith, A. (1776). *An inquiry into the nature and causes of the wealth of nations.* W. Strahan and T. Cadell.

Stein, H. F. (2001). *Nothing personal, just business: A guided journey into organizational darkness.* Quorum Books.

Stein, M. (2011). A culture of mania: A psychoanalytic view of the incubation of the 2008 credit crisis. *Organization,* 18: 173.

Stein, M., & Pinto, J. (2011). The dark side of groups: A 'gang at work' in Enron. *Group & Organization Management,* 36: 692.

Stierlin, H. (1982). *Delegation und Familie* [Delegation and family]. Suhrkamp.

Sørlander, K. (2011). *Den politiske forpligtelse: Det filosofiske fundament for demokratisk stillingtagen* [The political obligation: The philosophical foundation of democratic decision-making]. Informations Forlag.

Tajfel, H. (Ed.) (1982). *Social identity and intergroup relations.* Cambridge University Press.

Taylor, F. W. (1997). Scientific management. In D. S. Pugh (Ed.), *Organization theory: Selected readings,* pp. 275–295. Penguin Books. (Original work published 1912)

Turner, J. C. (1982). Towards a cognitive redefinition of the social group. In H. Tajfel (Ed.), *Social identity and intergroup relations.* Cambridge University Press.

Turquet, P. (1985). Leadership: The individual and the group. In A. D. Colman & M. H. Geller (Eds.), *Group relations reader 2* (pp. 71–87). A. K. Rice Institute.

Visholm, S. (1993). Laing versus Laing: Om projektiv identifikation og psykodynamisk systemteori [Laing versus Laing: On projective identification and psychodynamic systems theory]. *Matrix,* 10(1), 5–28.

Visholm, S. (1993). *Overflade og dybde.* Om projektiv identifikation og det modernes psykologi. Copenhagen: Politisk revy.

Visholm, S. (2002). Diskursanalyse og psykologi – samfundskritisk reflek- sion eller krypterede beretninger fra livet i Claustrum.In B. Larsen & K. M. Munkgård (Eds.), *Diskursanalysen til debat. Kritiske perspektiver på en populær teoriretning* (pp. 229–265). Copenhagen: Nyt fra Samfundsvidenskaberne.

Visholm, S. (2004a). Organisationspsykologi og psykodynamisk systemteori [Organizational psychology and psychodynamic systems theory]. In T. Heinskou & S. Visholm (Eds.), *Psykodynamisk organisationspsykologi* (pp. 23–48). Hans Reitzels Forlag.

Visholm, S. (2004b). Autoritetsrelationen [The authory relation]. In T. Heinskou & S. Visholm (Eds.), *Psykodynamisk organisationspsykologi* (pp. 84–108). Hans Reitzels Forlag.

Visholm, S. (2004c). Intergruppedynamik [Intergroup dynamic]. In T. Heinskou & S. Visholm (Eds.), *Psykodynamisk organisationspsykologi* (pp. 127–158). Hans Reitzels Forlag.

Visholm, S. (2004d). Modstand mod forandring: Psykodynamiske perspektiver [Resistance to change: Psychodynamic perspectives]. In T. Heinskou & S. Visholm (Eds.), *Psykodynamisk organisationspsykologi* (pp. 174–201). Hans Reitzels Forlag.

Visholm, S. (2005a). Familiens psykologi [Family psychology]. In Hauge & Brørup (Eds.), *Gyldendals psykologihåndbog* (pp. 179–209). Gyldendal.

Visholm, S. (2005b). The promoted sibling: Sibling dynamics – a new dimension in the systems psychodynamics of organizations [PowerPoint presentation at ISPSO in Baltimore, 2005].

Visholm, S. (2005c). Uklare roller i postmoderne organisationer: Om ledelse og selvstyrende grupper [Role ambiguity in postmodern organizations: On leadership and self-managing teams]. *Arbejdsliv*, 7(1).

Visholm, S. (2005d). Uklare roller og medarbejderdeltagelse: Om ledelse og selvstyrende grupper [Role ambiguity and employee participation: On leadership and self-managing teams]. In P. Dragsbæk & N. Sejersen (Eds.), *Gør noget: Håndtering af psykisk arbejdsmiljo*. TekSam, CO-industri & Dansk Industri.

Visholm, S. (2006a). Demokratiets psykologi [The psychology of democracy]. *Psyke & Logos*, 27(1), 162–215.

Visholm, S. (2006b). They got the guns/But we got the numbers: Om familie og gruppedynamik [They got the guns/But we got the numbers: On family and group dynamics]. In O. Andkjær Olesen, C. Braad Thomsen, & B. Petersen (Eds.), *Fokus på Freud*. Hans Reitzels Forlag.

Visholm, S. (2007). Det udvalgte traume: Introduktion til Vamik Volkans gruppepsykologi [The chosen trauma: Introduction to Vamik Volkan's group psychology]. *Weekendavisen*, 16 February: 4–5.

Visholm, S. (2007). Leadership, gender and generativity: A research project on open and hidden family dynamics in organizations [Paper presented at the ISPSO symposium in Stockholm 2007].

Visholm, S. (2010). Familien som gruppe, familien i gruppen og familien og gruppen [The family as group, the family in the group and the group]. In I. B. Jørgensen & Å. Lading (Eds.), *Psykologiske processer i og omkring gruppen*. Frydenlund.

Visholm, S. (2011a). Ledelse af kreative og innovative medarbejdere i det offentlige [Managing creative and innovative employees in the public sector]. In P. N. Bukh & S. Hildebrandt (Eds.), *Børsens ledelseshåndbøger: Offentlig ledelse* (pp. 1–16). Børsen.

Visholm, S. (2011b). Psykodynamisk læringsteori og oplevelsesbaseret læring [Psychodynamic learning theory and experiential learning]. *Dansk Pædagogisk Tidsskrift*, 3, 49–59.

Visholm, S. (2011c). Uklare roller i postmoderne organisationer: Om ledelse og selvstyrende grupper [Role ambiguity in postmodern organizations: On leadership and self-managing teams]. In T. Heinskou & S. Visholm (Eds.), *Psykodynamisk organisationspsykologi II: På mere arbejde under overfladerne*. Hans Reitzels Forlag.

Visholm, S. (2012). Innovation og ledelse: Psykodynamiske perspektiver [Innovation and leadership: Psychodynamic perspectives]. *Erhvervspsykologi*, 10(2), 34–53.

Volkan, V. D. (1997). *Bloodlines. From ethnic pride to ethnic terrorism.* Farrar, Straus, and Giroux.

Volkan, V. D. (2004). *Blind trust. Large groups and their leaders in times of crisis and terror.* Pitchstone Publishing.

Volkan, V. D. (2006). *Killing in the name of identity.* Pitchstone Publishing.

Von Bertalanffy, L. (1968). *General system theory: Foundations, development, applications.* George Braziller.

Weber, M. (1930). *The Protestant ethic and the spirit of capitalism* (Talcott Parsons, Trans.). Unwin Hyman. (Original work published 1905)

Weber, M. (2003). Det bureaukratiske herredømmes væsen, forudsætninger og udvikling. [The nature, conditions and development of bureaucratic governance]. In H. Andersen, H. H. Bruun, & L. B. Kaspersen (Eds.), *Max Weber: Udvalgte skrifter* (Vol. 2, pp. 63–111). Hans Reitzels Forlag. (Original work published in 1922)

West, J. P. (2009). *What would Keith Richards do?* Bloomsbury.

Wilke, G. (1998). Oedipal and sibling dynamics in organizations. *Group Analysis*, 31 (3), 269–281. https://doi.org/10.1177/0533316498313003.

Williams, A. H. (1998). *Cruelty, violence, and murder: Understanding the criminal mind.* Karnac Books.

Winnicott, D. W. (1986). Some thoughts on the meaning of the word 'democracy'. In C. Winnicott, R. Shepherd, & M. Davis (Eds.), *Home is where we start from.* Penguin Books. (Original work published 1950)

Winnicott, D. W. (1997). *Deprivation and delinquency.* Routledge. (Original work published 1984)

Winnicott, D. W. (2005). *Playing and reality.* Routledge. (Original work published 1971)

Zinner, J., & Shapiro, R. L. (1972). Projective identification as a mode of perception and behaviour in families of adolescents. *International Journal of Psychoanalysis*, 53(4), 523–530.

Index

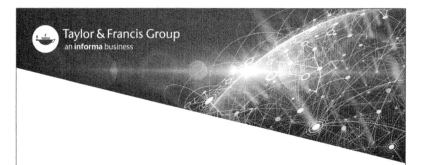

Printed in Great Britain
by Amazon

25734679R00117